A Guided Course in Zen Meditation

Venerable DaiJu Zenji

CONTENTS

ACKNOWLEDGEMENTS

For that one student meditator in each and every class I have taught who asked "Why haven't you written a book on this?" This is for you!

My deep thanks and appreciation go to all those who taught me, directly and indirectly with foremost being my master, the Rev. Shodo Harada Roshi. On four continents I have been blessed with the opportunity to engage with passionate teachers, students and beginners – diamonds polishing diamonds as we say.

A PERSONAL JOURNEY

For the practitioner of Zen speaking about oneself is not an easy thing to do. As you will discover in this book there is just so much more to us than the limited mind and distorted sensations we perceive. There are aspects of my own meditative journey that may be instantly identifiable by anyone who has experienced the highs and lows of life. Other aspects may not be.

Nearly 50 years ago a little boy named Simon Rowe sat down to read in one of his favourite sections of the library; the 'Religion: Other' section. Here he could find books on ancient Gods and myths; stories that were fanciful and yet somehow approachable.

Being brought up in a moderate Protestant household and receiving education in a Catholic school Simon had already heard more than enough of the Christian philosophy to know it did not resonate with what he needed.

On this fateful day little Simon grabbed a book on Eastern myths and opened the story of the Death of the Buddha. As the Buddha was dying he said:

> *"...be ye lamps unto yourselves. Rely on yourselves, and do*
> *not rely on external help. Hold fast to the truth as a lamp.*
> *Seek salvation alone in the truth. Look not for assistance to*
> *any one besides yourselves."* [1]

This hit me so powerfully that I felt I had been slapped. "Be a lamp unto yourself" has shaped so many aspects of my growth both spiritually and psychologically.

Unmon, one of the greats of Zen, once said of the Buddha and his message

"... I'd have beaten him to death and fed him to the dogs, in hopes that there might be peace on earth." [2]

Perhaps if I had not read the Buddha's words it would have been easy to go on with a life untroubled by thoughts of "who am I?" and "why am I here?" Perhaps not. All I knew is that very early on the Buddha had put a hook in my mouth and I could not shake it out. What did it mean to be that lamp?

As a young adult I faced a series of crises, some through my own actions, others through pure circumstance and it came to head one weekend. Always an avid reader I reached the conclusion of the most excellent 'Musashi' (Eji Yoshikawa, Kodansha International) just as these crises all climaxed at the same time. I felt like I was hanging over a whirlpool being held back from falling by a single thread. Those words, 'Be a lamp unto yourself' came back to me then… and as is often the case, I completely misinterpreted them.

Instead of sitting down in the room of mirrors and taking a long hard look at myself I instead decided to throw myself completely into the life expected of me. I purchased a house, got engaged, partied hard, wined and dined through dinner parties and an expanding circle of friends. My garden and bank account blossomed, but I still felt empty inside. No matter how much distraction I surrounded myself with the noise in my own head was still deafening. So I 'lived even harder'.

Within a matter of years I found myself back at square one. In the space of a few weeks my life crumbled down around me. My fiancé had found another, my job was soulless, the partying continued but the come-downs and hangovers intensified as well. Everywhere I went I was shadowed by my own lack of self-esteem and anxieties – and they were getting to the point where they were affecting my work and those few relationships I had maintained.

The turning point for me was on a spring afternoon.

I was in a dark place, one I would not see in another until I did some suicide counselling many, many years later. I was walking along the beautiful North Terrace in Adelaide visiting places that were precious to me as a way of saying goodbye to them. By chance I spotted a sign for free lunchtime concerts at the Music Conservatorium in Adelaide University. I went in, took my seat and watched as a young soprano took to the unadorned stage and began to sing from St. Matthew's Passion.

I fell to pieces.

Imagine holding a piece of glass in your hand and tapping it with a hammer, shattering it entirely in a single instant. This was my experience of a moment of beauty piercing the self-loathing.

How does one respond to such an experience? For me the feeling was that instead of living for myself, why not live for something greater than myself?

I still was not at ease with who I was as a person, the thoughts still swirled through my mind like a toxic avalanche. What would it mean to transcend that mess instead of fighting it or giving in to it?

Within a couple of days I had booked my tickets for Nepal and from there my Path started in earnest.

Some 5 years later, after encountering teachers from all traditions of Buddhism I was finally able to switch off that 'washing machine mind' for good. The methods I followed to achieve this are identical to those discussed in this book.

It is not necessary to experience an existential life crisis to make the decision to free yourself of the deluded self-limiting mind. Nor do you need to travel across South-East Asia searching for the doorway to peace. Everything you need is already yours.

Rabindranath Tagore wrote:

> *"I've travelled all around the world to see the rivers and the mountains, and I've spent a lot of money. I have gone to great lengths, I have seen everything, but I forgot to see just outside my house a dewdrop on a little blade of grass, a dewdrop which reflects in its convexity the whole universe around you."*

Freedom and peace are every human's birth right and my hope is that this book can help you claim what is rightfully yours. The Path has always stretched before you but you have not seen where it begins. You need something to pierce that darkness and give you the strength to take that first step.

Be a lamp unto yourself.

INTRODUCTION

For the past 20 years I have taught 4 or 10 session workshops on Zen Meditation (*zazen*). I have run them for married couples and families all the way through to corporate wellness programs. This book was born as a direct result of these classes.

These classes and this book are non-denominational. Zen Buddhism is not a proselyting religion. As a monk I wish to give you the knowledge to practice zazen whether you are religious or not. What is important is that you practice zazen with all the spirit you can put into it. I would rather you use this guide to be a dedicated Zen Christian or Zen Atheist for example than a lukewarm Buddhist.

There are 3 main traditions of Buddhism:
- **Theravāda** ('School of the Elders') is the oldest and most traditional branch of Buddhism. This is the school of Buddhism most practiced through south-east Asia. Its practices are closest to the original teachings of Siddhartha Gautama, the Buddha.
- **Vajrayāna** ('Diamond Vehicle') is also known as esoteric Buddhism. This is the core of Tibetan Buddhism.
- **Mahayāna** ('Great Vehicle') is the tradition that encompasses many of the Central and Eastern Asian nations. Zen (Chan – Chinese or Seon – Korean) is part of the Mahayāna Tradition.

Zazen itself is similar to aspects of the Theravāda Vipassanā (Mindfulness) practice. With this in mind I built the core of my workshops around a central tenant of the Theravāda which is the Noble Eightfold Path: Right Seeing, Right Thinking, Right Speech, Right Action, Right Living, Right Effort, Right Mindfulness and Right Concentration. You will find these as Chapters 3-10 in this book.

The Noble Eightfold Path is more of a moralistic teaching in the Theravāda teachings but when viewed through Zen eyes this Path becomes an exploration of the way that we can actualise the meditative mind into our inner and outer experience of the world.

As I introduce new terms, especially Buddhist, Zen or Japanese specific ones, they will be written in *italics* first along with a short explanation.

Buddha Mind deserves its own entry though, as it is mentioned frequently. It can refer to the actual enlightened mind of the Buddha himself, along with his compassionate nature for all beings. However, I use it to reference the clear pure mind which is our true nature, our birth right. It is that mind and Truth which we awaken to through enlightenment.

HOW TO USE THIS BOOK

This guide has been written to teach you the basics of how to sit and then lead you through how zazen can and will open your eyes to the world around you. It is written to be picked up and put down, to be explored as you sit and referred to as your awareness deepens.

It is essential that you take the time to read, understand and practice the posture and techniques of Chapter 1. Without learning how to sit zazen correctly the rest of the book will be wasted.

Each Chapter has two sections where you should sit zazen before continuing on with the chapter. Pace your sitting, it is not a race nor an endurance competition. When meditating, unless you are very experienced you should not sit for more than 25 minutes without at least stretching your legs. Even in the monastery, where we sit daily for hours at a time, we always change leg positions every 30 minutes and practice meditative walking once an hour.

In general my courses are run weekly or bi-weekly. Although I have taught the full 10 sessions in a single week this is hardly ideal. When run weekly we generally start off at 5 minutes for each sit and by the end of the 10 weeks are sitting 20 minutes with ease.

I recommend sticking with this basic schedule, working through an individual chapter over a week and sitting daily before moving on to the next chapter. Feel free to come back and explore the earlier chapters as your maturing meditation leads you.

HOW TO SIT ZAZEN

Zazen is a physical and mental posture that allows us to enter and experience certain states of mind; it is the act of Zen meditation. When we say "we are sitting zazen" we are not just referring to the cross-legged position, nor are we referring to the Zen techniques of quietening the mind, nor even the act of attempting to transcend the body/mind so we can enter the One which in Buddhism is called the Buddha Mind – we are all of these things in one action.

MOUNT FUJI AND THE CLOUDS

The image of sacred Mount Fuji is often used to describe a person sitting zazen. Like Mount Fuji they are a pyramidal shape with a firm base and strong centre. Also like Mount Fuji thoughts pass like clouds across the mountain top, flowing by, but never being held on to.

To a practitioner of Zen, Mount Fuji is the perfect image to describe the act of meditation.

- Mount Fuji is a sacred mountain to the Japanese and zazen should be performed in a place in our home and in our life that is sacred to us and our own Path.
- Mt Fuji is a perfect cone-shaped mountain with a strong base that supports it as it reaches for the heavens; this is the embodiment of our physical posture during meditation.
- The mountain sits with clouds flowing by, touched by them but not caught in them or clinging to them. This represents the mental attitude we adopt, allowing our mind to be free of thoughts and distractions as we dive into our meditation.

CREATING A SACRED SPACE

The Place of Sitting

Whilst meditation is as natural as walking, eating or sleeping it is also something which should be given a special place in our lives. The act of meditation is the act of honouring the divine in each of us and in the world. I cannot suggest highly enough the careful choosing of a place in which to sit. If you can, put aside even a small corner which is only used for personal meditation; if you cannot then find a spot that is roughly 1 metre square (3" by 3"). It can be in the garden or by the beach for example but choose a spot with cover where weather cannot cause you to miss a day's sitting. Make it secluded enough so unnecessary distractions cannot interrupt you.

When I was at our monastery in Seattle I stayed overnight at the house of friends. I noticed that their place was small and yet they meditated together every night. I asked them how they did this and they showed me how they would dim the living room lights, cover the TV with a thick cloth and then pull out their cushions from under chairs in the living room. They had sat together like this for years turning a simple patch of floor into shared sacred space.

Your sitting space does not have to be especially quiet; quietness is a function of the mind. Your sitting space does not have to be beautiful; if you are meditating correctly you are not going to be watching the scenery. Your sitting space should be devoted to just Meditation; just as your meditation is devoted entirely to your Self and your awareness.

Sitting with Others

When we practice zazen we practice to recognise that we are not an isolated island of Self floating through a much larger world. We practice to realise that ourselves and the world we experience are one and the same. With this in mind it is useful to sit with others. When we meditate with even one more we can encourage each other whether silently as we sit or verbally when we agree to sit for a length of time together. When we sit with others it is much more difficult to just write off the day and decide not to sit.

I am trained in the Rinzai Zen School and in this school we always face each other, our *ki* (spiritual energy) challenging, encouraging and nourishing each other in the silence of the *zendo* (Meditation Hall).

The Physical Posture

Cross-legged Sitting

When we sit we form a firm base, just like Mount Fuji. Our knees and our bottom are the base of the pyramid and our spine leads up to our head to form the mountain's peak. To make this base as firm as possible we have a number of different ways to sit, all of them cross-legged. For those of you who find sitting cross-legged to be physically impossible I shall introduce other options later.

When we sit we need to make a number of points very clear. As you learn to meditate you will discover that a lot of your initial experiences are about finding which position suits you best. Zazen is not an endurance contest and certainly not about grinning and bearing pain… it is about finding a balanced position that allows you to forget your body so that it might be transcended. In the monastery one's sitting location and cushions are sacrosanct, we spend so many hours sitting that even slight alterations can be quite unsettling. Find what is comfortable for you, find what works for you, and stick with it. You don't have to leave your cushions permanently set-up. Currently at home I use 3 old sofa cushions and a rug for under my knees, these get put away each time after I sit. I have used these same cushions for years though and know them like an extension of my own body.

Place one or more cushions under your bottom. These cushions should be high enough that you can feel comfortable but stable enough that you do not have to watch your balance. Place it right under the hip bones, any further forward than that and you run the risk of cutting off blood supply to the legs. Sitting like this will also impart a slight forward lean to your posture.

The knees should be touching the ground as much as possible. Ideally we want to form a pyramid with the 2 knees and our bottom on the cushion as the base. This is often the most difficult thing for beginners and until we make some effort we will find our hips to be quite stiff. Be patient, be gentle but also firm with yourself; I find that after 5 weeks of the meditation course most students' knees are touching the ground without any worries.

When it comes to crossing our legs we have these following options:

1.   The Burmese Position

This posture is for people with very limited leg flexibility. The knees are wide-spread and both feet rest on the floor; for this reason a comfortable and soft floor covering is essential. It is easy to feel stable with this posture though you might find that your ankles and then your thighs become painful after a length of time. In general this is a very relaxed and easy position to take.

2.   The Quarter Lotus

Here we go one step further. We lift one of our feet up to rest between the calf and the thigh of the other leg. This gives us greater stability whilst only needing a little more flexibility than the Burmese Posture. The biggest drawback with sitting like this is that we can cut off the blood supply to our legs leading to numbness in the calves and feet.

Burmese Posture   Quarter Lotus

3.   The Half-Lotus

This is the position that I sit in most of the time. We cross our legs even further and place one of our feet upon the thigh of the other leg. It is an excellent posture for balance and comfort (once you are used to it). As monastics we have to sit a minimum of 5 hours each and every day so we need a stable, safe and comfortable posture. This is the way that almost all the monks and nuns choose to use.

4.   The Full Lotus

I will admit that I only use this position when I am making a statement! Here we lift both our feet up to place them on the opposing thigh; it is the ultimate in stability and comfort. However, the level of flexibility required means that this position is out of reach for most people for anything more than short sits. My *Roshi* (Zen Master) sits like this and actually used to sleep like this for quite a number of years.

Half Lotus   Lotus Posture

When I first learned to meditate I was reading about the postures from a book not unlike this one. I remember sitting on my bed in a little hotel room in Kathmandu, confident that I had learned the posture correctly. As I settled into place I forced myself to take the Half-Lotus and started to meditate… the pain was so unexpected that I lasted just 36 seconds! However, I persevered and each day my sitting times grew longer and longer as I became more settled and flexible. 9 months later I was able to sit 4 hours a day.

Sitting requires a certain level of discipline and if you are constantly fidgeting and focusing on the discomfort of what is likely to be a new and unusual posture then you are never going to be able to settle into zazen. Find a way of crossing your legs and sit with it. Do not force yourself to sit through unbearable pain but also do not give up just because your body wants to move every few seconds.

If your body learns you can be distracted with a few feelings of discomfort then it will not stop trying to claim your attention.

In the monastery we would sit for 25 minutes at a time and then have a short break, this break was silent and we remained sitting but were allowed to move and stretch our legs. We would then sit for another 25 minutes. Following this was *kinhin* (walking meditation). For 5-10 minutes we would walk, sometimes briskly, around the *zendo* (meditation hall) in silence and with deep concentration before returning to our cushions. Try not to sit for too long before giving your body a chance to move and stretch.

Other Sitting Options

I am often asked if one can lie down or stand up to practice mediation. People usually ask this because of bodily pain. Certainly one can and eventually should be able to practice Zen in any of these postures, but if you are able sitting is by far the best way to practice zazen. For those who find the cross-legged postures impossible I shall examine some of the options available to you.

1. Kneeling

Seiza (Kneeling) is a common variant of the cross-legged posture. In the monastery we occasionally allow people to use it if they are having difficulties. It is such an accepted way of sitting in the United States of America that there are many excellent 'Seiza Stools' available so that you might plant your bottom comfortably on this stool and save your ankles from the pressure of having to hold your weight. During ceremonies we monks would have to sit in seiza on solid wood floors for an extended length of time, the Japanese manage it with ease but I found it very painful. If you are to sit with seiza get a comfortable soft floor covering, your knees, shins and ankles will thank you for it.

2. Using a chair or a stool

Injury or sickness is never an excuse to escape the hours upon hours of zazen that monastics sit. Even when we break a bone or hurt our back we still come to the zendo and sit in whichever way we can. Often a chair is used for those who cannot sit in any other way. In my own classes too I allow a chair or stool for special needs students. It is not as easy as it might seem; the body is not leaning forward like the previous positions which puts pressure on the back and chairs can be uncomfortable after a length of time. The seat can cut the legs' blood supply enough to be noticeable after a period of time. However, it is better to sit than to not sit! If this is the only way you can settle your body then experiment with chairs, stools and cushions until you find what works best for you.

3.   Standing

Standing is a technique which is more commonly met in the Taoist tradition through their Qi Gung practices. We use it in the monastery for students who fall asleep too often! We simply stand and place our hands over our mid-section in *shashu* (left hand over the right). This is also an excellent way to sneak a bit of meditation into time that would otherwise be wasted (when waiting for the bus or train etc.). Of all the non-sitting techniques standing is by far the best.

Seiza   Shashu

4.   Lying down

Lying down should really only be used when no other option is available. Not only is there the risk of falling asleep but it is also difficult to stop the mind wondering and to focus the meditation on the *Hara* (the centre of our being, more on this later). Like the standing posture we place our hands in shashu.

Keeping our Spine Erect

Now that we have our base we need to sit in such a way that we can rise out of that base. We do this by keeping our back and neck straight.

Through Traditional Chinese Medicine we understand that there is an energy channel that rises out of our pelvic region and through the spine up to the head and then down the face. This channel needs to be kept clear and straight if we want to be the picture of health. When we meditate this channel is also important as we draw the energy from our deepest and most primordial being and allow it to freely move though our body and mind without obstruction.

Many of us have bad postures from sitting poorly; we have hunched backs, tight hips & shoulders and sore cramped necks. Also, modern people have tight closed chests that don't allow us to breathe with our full potential. To avoid these things causing us discomfort in meditation we need to see the head as being the most important part of the back. When we hold our head high then our spine becomes naturally straight and we open up our chest and shoulders so that our breath becomes deeper and more vital.

Imagine that the head and shoulders are like a coat-hanger. Then imagine that the very top part of the head has a piece of string holding it upright. From this 'coat-hanger' the spine hangs down to the hips in a firm straight line.

We do not push up from the pelvis. This causes tight hips and hip/leg pain. We do not force our lower back and shoulders to hold up the head. This causes a sore lower back and tight painful shoulders. Instead we use the head as our focal point, the shoulders hang easily from the head and the spine extends naturally down to the hips from the shoulders. If you get this posture right you will notice your shoulders automatically relax from the hunched tense position that they usually take.

Placing the Hands

In Zen Meditation the hands are placed in the lap. We cross our hands over each other just as we cross our legs. This is to allow the top and bottom parts of our body to be linked so that our energy flows easily from top to bottom, left to right and front to back.

Our hands are either placed loosely with one palm cupping the other hand, or alternatively in the 'Concentration Mudra' where they cup each other but the tips of the thumbs lightly touch. In either case the left hand is at the bottom. The shoulders are relaxed and there is no tension in the arms.

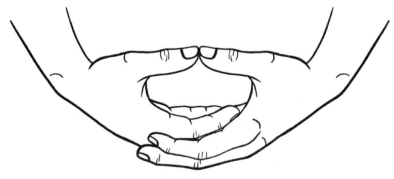

Concentration Mudra

Relieving the Eyes

So much of the world comes to us through our eyes. It might be said that the eyes are the door through which we are most easily tempted into distraction. For this reason we limit the ability of our vision to provide us with a constant flow of images whilst not completely denying it. Zen is not about denial, it is about Awareness. If our everyday mind and the eyes which feed it with information were able to provide us with that Awareness then we would already be enlightened!

The eyes are angled down at about 45° and then half-closed. Allow the eyes to drift out of focus. This way we accept the eyes even as we transcend what they show us. If our eyes are closed; this would make it too easy to day-dream at best and fall asleep at worst. This would be denying our eyes.

If possible set up your place of meditation where there are dull or natural colours and where the lighting is dim but not dark. Bright colours and bright light will lead to distraction. Darkness easily lends itself to sleepiness.

Advanced Points of Posture

There are other useful considerations for the physical posture but these are purely optional and should only be integrated them into your sitting when you are able to master the basic posture.

Touching the Tongue to the Roof of the Mouth

Just as there is an energy channel rising up from the pelvic region and through the spine, there is a partner channel which arises from the same place but runs up the centre of our body through our abdomen and chest. Both of these channels meet and unite in the mouth. To help this most important flow of energy we touch the tip of our tongue to the roof of our mouth – this is a technique which is used extensively in Taoist practices. At first it is quite forced but in time it will actually be quite natural. I am no longer aware of the fact that it automatically happens the moment I cross my leg to meditate; it is a reflex action for me now.

When we touch the tip of the tongue to the roof of the mouth we are literally 'closing the circuit' that circles our body's front and back.

Keeping the Lower Gates Closed

My Master would occasionally tell all the Monks and Nuns under his care to 'Keep your Lower Gates Closed'. The first time this happened I was quite new to the monastery and had no idea what he was talking about. I later asked some of my elder brother monks for an explanation, which gave everyone (except me) a laugh.

If we were to try to move a bucket of water from one side of the garden to the other we would carefully choose a bucket that did not have holes in the bottom of it. If we were careless in our choice then the water we had collected would drain away before we could put it to use. It is the same with meditation.

A large part of meditation is about the accumulation of energy and the free flow of that energy through our body and mind. But most people let that energy dissipate by letting it drain out of our lower orifices. As we age this becomes so bad that we end up with pelvic floor problems like incontinence, hernias and prolapse. The martial arts, Taoist spiritual practices and Zen meditation all agree that we should endeavour to keep our rectal, urethral and vaginal muscles gently (but not excessively) closed at all times. This is even more important in meditation where we cannot afford to have our efforts wasted by simple carelessness.

Exert gentle pressure on your genitals and rectum to ensure that your 'gates are closed' but like all things practice this in moderation. We are not using this as a chance to practice our Kegel Exercises and excessive force leads to other problems and blockages in the hips and urogenital region.

FIRM FOUNDATIONS: OUR FIRST SIT

Whether it is a house, skyscraper or mountain a strong physical foundation is essential - let's put ours to the test.

It is time for our first meditation. Take this chance to settle into the posture and feel how your body sits with it.

There is no need to sit any longer than 5 minutes at first, you just want to familiarise yourself with the posture and try out the various positions for your feet and hands.

Pay careful attention to the 4 steps of sitting.

1. Start off with the legs to build your base.
2. Keep your spine erect by drawing your head up straight.
3. Relax the shoulders and let the hands come together in your lap.
4. Finally release the consciousness from your eyes as they half-close and half look down.
5. Feel your body take this posture and come to a balanced place within it.

TROUBLESHOOTING THE FIRST SIT

Congratulations on the completion of your first sit! I am sure that all of a sudden you noticed many things; like how noisy it is in the environment and how difficult it can be to take this posture for even a short time.

Let us look at a few of the physical problems that might crop up as a part of this first exercise or even after years of experience.

- If you feel tension in your upper body then you are pulling your shoulders up instead of letting them 'hang' from your head. The shoulders cannot keep the back straight without causing pain and tightness.
- If your neck is sore make sure you are not 'craning' it forward. The head needs to be erect if you are to avoid pain and discomfort later.
- If your feet and legs go numb then you are compressing blood vessels in your legs. While it is almost certainly nothing to worry about, it is best if you can find a way to sit that doesn't cause this. Make sure you are sitting forwards enough on your cushion. Try to place your feet differently so that they are not cutting off any blood supply on the other leg.
- Your knees are not going to find it easy to settle on the ground at first. It helps if you have a slight forward tilt with your belly and slight backwards tilt with your hips.
- The stomach muscles and lower back muscles can help keep the back straight but if you use them too much you will end up with tightness and pain in the hips and lower back. Again, let the head gently and naturally pull the spine straight. Relax your hips and the rest will follow

Even experienced sitters will make sure that the first thing they do as they start to meditate is to settle their sitting posture. A solid foundation in the physical realm will allow us to let go of the body as we start on the next lesson in sitting.

THE MENTAL POSTURE

Obviously it is not enough to just settle the body down. We need to bring the mind into balance as well. For this we need something that links to the very core of our being, something that is a part of everything we do and represents life itself. It needs to be regular, continual and able to be consciously experienced whilst also being able to fade into the background. Are you aware of what this wonderful multipurpose meditation tool is?

The Breath

Our life starts from that first breath, our life ends at the last. It is regular and continual. It is also something which EVERYONE does in exactly the same way, no matter what age, sex and race they may be. The most evil person on the planet breathes as does the most pure. It is regular and it is life itself. For all these reasons it is the perfect base for linking the body and mind through meditation.

Once we settle the body we then start to practice the meditation technique known as *Susokukan* in Japanese. This is literally 'breath counting'.

When our body is settled we place our mind's attention onto the breath as it enters and leaves the body. We do not force the breath. We do not lengthen or shorten it. We just watch it with all of our mind's focus. Just as we have breathed every single moment of our existence in this life we keep it going, but this time we do it with awareness.

As we breathe in we do not watch the breath as it enters our nose, nor do we follow it down into the lungs, instead we watch the breath from our *tanden* or *hara* (energy centre of the body). This is a location about 2cm behind the belly button.

Hara & Tanden Location

Our Spiritual Centre

In Chinese Medicine, Taoism and Zen Buddhism we recognise that this tanden ("Cinnabar Field") is the location from which all our life energy springs forth. However, for us logically minded Westerners we can also see that it is place which is the centre of gravity for our body. When we place our 'being' in this location then we are naturally balanced in the same way that a plank of wood can be balanced on a finger if it is positioned correctly.

If you notice an animal which is scared you will see that it takes short shallow breaths from high in their chest. The same happens for us humans, when we are attacked we breathe quickly and shallowly, this is part of the 'fight or flight' mechanism which is designed to allow our bodies to gain a rush of oxygen to help us deal with danger. Now look at an animal or human who is relaxed and calm, they will be breathing slowly and deeply.

Breathing from deep in our core is our natural way of being, it is the way someone who feels safe and calm lives because it is centred and centring. If you work, as I often do, in the centre of a big city like Sydney then you will note that a lot of people going about their normal everyday lives are breathing high in their chest. They are breathing as though they are under attack because they cannot effectively deal with the stress that they are under. Because they are breathing high in their chest then their 'centre of gravity' (be that emotional, intellectual or spiritual gravity) is also high. The higher the centre of gravity the more unbalanced and stressed they feel. If it is in the chest then they are prone to emotional confusion. If it is in the head they are prone to intellectual confusion.

Breathing from the tanden is the quickest and the best way to calm and centre oneself and for this reason all our meditation will all be done from this place. In the monastery we learn to do everything; walking, talking, working and eventually even sleeping from our hara because as humans we can and should be calm and centred in each and every moment no matter what we do or which circumstances we meet.

Now I know that the lungs do not extend as far down into the body as the belly button but that is where you must perceive the breath as entering. This is to make sure that our breathing is as deep as possible and is in accord with this centred place in our body. Even though the breathing really doesn't physically extend down that far it is not too long before you will feel it there. Our mind is a powerful thing. Anyone who has had a dream know that even though we see the strangest things in those dreams, things that cannot be real, due to the power of the mind we believe them. We are harnessing this illusionary power of the mind to actually control the mind.

In Chinese Medicine and Zen we say that "where the mind flows the ki follows". *Ki* (or Qi in Chinese) is the life energy that is the difference between us being a living walking person and a lump of inanimate flesh. If we are stressed and constantly thinking then the ki goes to our head and we are 'lost in our heads'. If we are emotionally engaged and worried then the ki goes to our chest and we become depressed or sad, this is being 'lost in our emotions'. If we want to be balanced and calm then we need to focus our mind on the tanden, on our physical, emotional and spiritual centre, so that we can be balanced no matter what situations face us.

The Count

To keep our mind on our centre we add another part to this breath. As each and every breath leaves our body we count it. This technique is called *susokukan* (breath counting meditation)

When the breath transforms to an exhalation from an inhalation we start to count "One…" right until that breath is fully exhaled. The next breath enters and as it is exhaled we then start to count "Two…" until it is also fully exhaled. This goes on until we reach "Ten", then we start from "One" again. We count in silence, using our mind only and that counting also comes right from the tanden.

We do this to make sure that we have a way of keeping our focus on that breath. The mind does NOT like to be bored, it likes to wander off and notice new things and think about them. The mind wants to daydream, it does not want to be doing something as tedious as watching us breathe! If this wandering day-dreaming mind was the way to enlightenment then we would all be Buddhas by the time we finished kindergarten, there would be a fully-enlightened Buddha sitting behind the desk of every office in town.

The truth is that the mind is a wilful creature and it needs something to keep it focussed. This is what the counting is for. If we did not put our wholehearted attention into the counting then we would be telling ourselves we are watching the breath when in reality we would be thinking about everything and anything else.

So, this all sounds simple. Assume a physical posture and continue to breathe as we have done ever since we were born, just being careful to watch it from deep in our body. Count the breaths as they leave the tanden going from "one" to "ten". Easy! There has to be a catch, and indeed there is…

The Catch

Each and every time a thought arises in your mind, whether it is something as simple as thinking about a sound you heard or a sensation in your body, or something as complex as a day-dream, you have to return to the number 'One' and start the counting again.

Meditation, and indeed life itself, is about honesty. We use the counting to help keep us honest.

We have just 2 things to watch in susokukan:
1. The breath as it enters and leaves the tanden.
2. The number we are silently counting that matches the breath as it is exhaled.

You will be amazed to see how hard it is to do this for even a few seconds without some rubbish arising in your mind. Our mind has had it its own way for far too long and we are now going to take back the reins of this runaway beast. We have become addicted to our mind's need for amusement and the time has come to show it who is boss. Like any addict a part of that reform is the recognition of the depth of the problem.

When you start to count your breath your mind will be like a raging torrent, I have lost count of the number of students who, after their first sit, have expressed shock at the sheer volume of random thinking that is in the mind.

I lived in Japan for a decade and was a part of a culture where perfume was used very sparingly. Upon returning to Australia I went for a walk down Adelaide's Rundle Mall and I felt like I had been hit about the nose with a scented hammer! After so many years in a society where perfume was hardly used it was a real shock to the senses to be in a culture where it was apparently used so much that even in the open air it was overpowering to me. Now I hardly notice it any more. The same thing happens with our minds. We don't notice the never-ending chatter in our head because it has been so constant for so long that we have actually come to think it is normal. It is when we try to stop it and actually experience a bit of quiet that we suddenly notice how amazingly loud our mind is all the time.

There is another reason why we use the breath. A Buddhist teacher I had the chance to study with in India asked my class of novice meditators how vital our thoughts were. We said that they were vital, that they constituted 'us'. To this he asked for us to hold our breaths for as long as possible, so we did. As the seconds passed and our bodies strained more and more for oxygen the thoughts that made up this 'mind' dissipated. All we had left was the iron control needed to keep holding our breath. The thoughts were given up very early in this struggle because they are unnecessary for our life's energy; there is no need for our body to waste energy on them when it is struggling to get some fresh air.

When your life is on the line you will not be day-dreaming, you will be focussing 100% on staying alive. Meditation must be done with this state of mind. The breath counting helps us be aware of when we stray from being focussed on this one breath that is filling our lungs, when we lose our sharp awareness of our life right here and now.

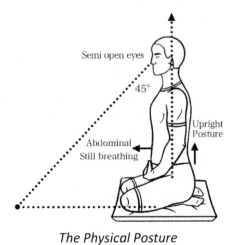

The Physical Posture

BODY AND MIND

Now it is time to bring it all together for our second sit.

This time we are going to incorporate the physical posture with the mental posture:
- Cross the legs with your knees and butt forming a firm base.
- Hold your head straight as though a piece of string is tied to the top of it.
- Relax your shoulders and bring your hands together in your lap.
- Half-close the eyes and direct them down at a 45° angle.

Allow the breath to naturally enter the body
- Watch that breath from your centre, the tanden.
- As the breaths are exhaled we silently count from "One" to "Ten" with each number stretching through the length of the breath.
- If any extraneous thought arises we start the count again from "One".

Sit for 5 minutes and learn to integrate the body and mind through the zazen. Keep with it until you feel you have been able to practice both comfortably before you move on the later sections of the book.

TROUBLESHOOTING THE BREATH TECHNIQUE

I ask my students how this practice went and the common questions they have are:

Do we count from "One" to "Ten" in a single breath or over 10 separate breaths?

Count it over 10 separate exhalations and do it silently with your attention on your tanden. We are trying to focus the mind here, not the voice.

Should we try to extend our breath to make it deeper?

Most certainly not - the breath is perfect just as it is, it suits us and our current needs. When we are relaxed then it will naturally deepen, when we are stressed it will reflect that. This meditation technique is not designed to 'control' anything, it is designed to allow us to let go of the things which are extraneous, such as our chattering mind and stressful states. Over time you will have a deeper breath as a result of this technique and that will be very useful for your physical health as well, but we are not trying to do anything except watch the breath and count it with our entire focussed awareness.

It is really hard to breathe like this, why?

You have breathed your whole life but done it unconsciously. Like someone who has a hole in their pocket and their money spilling out everywhere we waste most of our life because we don't pay attention to its passing. Now that you are trying to be aware of the breath your mind wants to play with it, it wants to control it and understand it; this is not the point of the meditation. The point is to just sit and watch it with every single bit of awareness you can muster. Just get your thinking mind out of the way and watch the breath.

Patience

Be patient. Understand that you have spent years and years with your body and mind being in control and doing exactly what they have wanted to do. It will take time to train it all to not be so wilful.

Every person who has learned meditation through our school of Zen learns susokukan and most of us stick with it for many, many years before moving on to another form of exercise. When you consider that a monastic meditates between 6 and 18 hours almost every single day of the year then the amount of effort put into this form of meditation becomes truly staggering.

In my own case I started susokukan before I entered the monastery and practiced it exclusively for 3 years in total. Even now when I sit I usually start off with susokukan because it is such an excellent way of focussing the mind and clearing away the detritus of the day. When something comes up during the day which causes me to lose my centre I return my focus to the tanden and count that breath. It is such a simple practice but if done honestly and sincerely it can and does lead one to Buddhahood.

INCENSE ASH

We burn incense when we meditate in the monastery because incense reminds us of the virtues of practice.

- A solid stick of incense burns down to only a small pile of ash. This ash is minuscule yet over time it will accumulate and become a great mass.
- When incense is burned the scent of it travels far and wide, but it cannot be captured, cannot be caught or contained, everyone and anyone can smell it and note its beautiful fragrance.

Incense is such a beautiful metaphor for zazen. We take this solid and unimpressive lump which has been shaped into a rigid form and then burn it all away. As it burns it releases a beautiful smell which manages to find its way through even the smallest spaces to spread its scent to places we cannot even see. As it burns it seems to disappear until there is only the tiniest residue left. However, over the years that tiny residue builds up.

I have never thrown away any of my incense ash. This might seem strange but even before I entered the monastery I had heard of a Zen teacher who used to lug a huge container with him wherever he went. He was going through customs at an airport once when the officers asked him to explain this big container and the grey powder that filled it. They must have thought he was a very brazen drug courier. The teacher explained that ever since he was a young boy and just starting his meditative practice he had kept his incense ash. Like virtue it was building up every time he sat to meditate.

Our practice can be seen to be like putting money in our spiritual bank account. With a normal bank account we only put a tiny amount in as we start off earning so little. Over the years we earn more for the same amount of work. Continual effort over the years also ensures that what we have managed to squirrel away starts to gain interest and our fortunes rise rapidly. Meditation is very similar.

At first we struggle just to fit our body into this strange shape. Then we struggle to control this 'bull in a china shop' which is our mind. Even whilst struggling with these basics though we are still developing our Path and gaining virtue for ourselves and those around us. Do not underestimate the power of just choosing to follow the Path of Meditation. Over time our body and mind settles and we find the meditation easier, we also find the benefits of the meditation start to return to us. Sleep comes easier, appetites stabilise, stress and emotional extremes dissipate. Even in the short 10-week classes I have heard students speak of the way their life has seemed to align itself with much more ease and direction.

If we want to fill a bowl with ash then we must burn a lot of incense. I have kept every single speck of incense ash burnt during 2 decades of Meditation classes and I am yet to fill the small bowl I use for burning it. But it is building up and every time people sit together as a group we add a bit more to it. We want to take our lifetime of ignorance and delusion and burn it all away with the bright light of the Buddha's Wisdom - this takes time and effort but it WILL happen, so long as you keep making efforts and accumulating that virtue.

WHY WE SIT ZAZEN

Now that we have our physical and mental posture settled we have to explore the question of purpose. Why do we sit? What can we hope to gain from it? In this chapter we examine the way that the mind works and why it needs to be focused. We also understand that meditation is about respect; respect for others and our world, but most importantly respect for ourselves.

AN UMBRELLA FOR THE WORLD

One day a man was walking down through his village. As he walked his bare feet were cut by the sharp stones that littered the way. He thought to himself, "These sharp stones cut my feet, but if I were to cover the whole world in rubber then no-one would ever be hurt again". He gathered resources and worked hard but eventually came to realise how much effort this was taking and how futile it was. The world was just too big. Thinking some more about the problem he instead took some small pieces of rubber and strapped them onto his feet, now wherever he walked his feet were covered. Other people saw this and started to copy him.

This same person was walking in his new shoes when it started to rain. Again he thought about the problem and resolved to cover the whole world in a massive roof, that way the rain would never wet him again and he would be dry. Again he allocated resources and tried to get others to follow his idea, but this too was unsuccessful. As he sat there pondering his failure he realised that if he took a small amount of what he had put aside he could make an umbrella with it, then he would be covered wherever he went! Other people saw this and started to copy him.

I remember my Master telling me this story and being struck by the simplicity of it. Zen and meditation are a lot like that, something profound being hidden within simplicity.

We all see problems with the world, with other people and the environment we live in. We want to resolve these problems and that is a noble aim. But the message you will hear me repeat is the one that those who practice medicine also need to be constantly reminded of; "Doctor, heal thyself".

In the West we like to start off big and work our way down to the small. We take the body and chop it up into smaller parts, and then we take those smaller parts and dissect them even further until eventually we have gone as far as we can. Sure we have reached an end point but have we understood anything at all, or have we just categorised and named bits of the whole? In the Eastern traditions it works the other way around; they start from the smallest place and work their way up... understanding begins with the self and then the way that self expands into everything it touches.

When we sit meditation, aligning our physical and mental posture to still the body and mind we are going back down to this starting point. Certainly there are important things to be resolved in our lives and in our world, but unless we can resolve the main question, "Who am I?", then anything we do will be based entirely on guesswork. Like using a flawed tool to fix something we know little about.

Self-Identification

One of the strongest indicators of someone who lives their life from a spiritual point of view is the way they identify with themselves. People who have no spiritual understanding identify 'negatively' i.e. based upon what they are not. People who have come to understand their self in relation to the universe identify themselves 'positively' i.e. based upon who they are.

Think about this in relation to your own life. The 'negative' state of mind is the one that says "I exist because I am not the person next door", "I am a teacher because I am not a plumber", "I am a good person because I don't rob banks". In Buddhism we called this 'Conditioned Existence'. We exist because all the other things around us provide a contrast; they give us a sense of separation and a sense of 'me'. When we think this way we define our life by the things around us and they provide us with a form of boundary between our idea of self and other. The negative side of this is that when those boundaries become fuzzy - when we lose our job, when we see parts of other people that mirror our own hopes and fears, when we are forced into an ethical/moral crisis that undermines our sense of right and wrong – then we also lose this sense of self. This is because it is not the true Self at all. It is just an illusion created by the need for separation with anything that is 'not us' and that we don't want to be 'us'.

The 'positive' state of mind is one that has realised its place in existence. It exists because it has tasted that existence for itself; in a way this is similar to the general understanding of the enlightenment experience. I do not exist because I am not my mother, an African, a chair, etc., I exist because I am here… right now… experiencing with these senses, moving with this body. I am not a builder but I do this job at some times, at other times I am a painter, a friend, asleep or dancing; these are just cloaks I wear to give form to my existence and to be of use to the world. I am not a 'good person' but I exist in harmony with the needs of those around me, thus I do the correct thing at the right moment.

One of these ideas of self is based upon what it is not; the other idea of self is based upon what it is.

For many people being comfortable with themselves is a horrible idea, for others it is a matter of being lost and not knowing how to find the way home; this is the same whether you are a sinner or a saint. Meditation is the way home, it is the way in which we honour and express ourselves. When you settle the body and mind to practice meditation there is no longer any self and other, no one else outside of you, there is just your body and mind harmonised through the awareness of the breath. If you practice the theistic religions, it is the way in which you and your prayer to God are one and the same. As you develop in meditation you find that it starts to be a part of you as you go about your daily activities; meditation is washing the dishes or walking to the train. Your whole being starts to become a centred place and a constant living prayer.

Honour Thyself

When we go to work we know that we are required to give all our attention to our job. When we come home we know that we need to spend quality time with our partner and children. We respect our family and community. But I would ask you, what part of your day to day life is spent respecting and honouring yourself?

You have this body and mind for the term of your life. It was given to you at the moment of your birth and will be gone when you die. You use it to meet all the obligations of daily living, but when do you take the time to be with it? We are all aware that we cannot take the material things with us when we die; our job title and even pages upon pages about us in Wikipedia or the history books are useless to us when we are dead. These things are all transient.

Our body and mind is transient too as it has a finite 'use-by' date but that place we come from, that place that unites us all is not. It is eternal and we exist in it for our lifespan in the same way that a wave spreads across the ocean – the wave passes and is gone, but the ocean continues on, giving birth to more waves and receiving them back when they too have come to their end. Separate waves but not separate to the ocean. The same water but different too.

Meditation at its highest level is not about possessing things and ideas of a finite nature, it is about identifying our connection with that deepest source that flows through us all. It is about the depth of the ocean not the short-lived waves that cross its surface. It is about spending our time to honour ourselves and honour the gift of this life. Crossing your legs and straightening your spine, letting the breath fill your hara to guide you deeper into that place your life originates from is time much better spent than TV or tennis. It is time spent with you, for you, and in respect of who you are, what you are and where you come from.

Ask not what you can do for meditation…

Before you go any deeper with your meditation it is important to understand what it is you want from it. There are 5 general aims for meditators:

1. To be calm
2. To become a better person
3. To develop extraordinary powers
4. To realise enlightenment in everything we do
5. To achieve nirvana and transcend existence

When you sit meditation it is useful to know WHY you are sitting and so I will explore these for a moment.

To be calm

When we sit to be calm this is really just like taking medicine for the symptoms of a disease. Certainly it is nice to not have to suffer, but if we want true healing then we need to go deeper than that. However, my students have often told me how in particularly stressful situations they have found themselves focussing their mind on their breath and their breath in their hara, and in doing so have become calm and relaxed. In this way this aim is important, if we are not calm and centred then we cannot live joyfully or completely, nor can we meditate at all.

To become a better person

We often wish we could concentrate more, sleep better or have a healthier body. Quite apart from the obvious benefit of teaching your mind to be more focussed and less distracted the body also gains quite some benefit from meditation. When we are less stressed then we are healthier and it is not uncommon for students to talk about the ease with which they are falling asleep and the depth and restfulness of that sleep. Scientists have done a large amount of research into the physical benefits of meditation too and shown its effectiveness in everything from sports through to recall. It is not uncommon to find oneself being more energetic and balanced as a result of even small amounts of meditation. We harmonise our body, mind and spirit through zazen and this can only lead to positive results, but why stop there?

To develop extraordinary powers

Martial Artists often use mediation to achieve this level. I have seen some pretty freaky things in my years following the Buddhist Path although I have no interest in distracting us from the reality of meditation with what can often be described as 'party tricks'. A sharp focussed mind and body can do some quite amazing things. My Roshi told a story about a man whose wife was trapped under their burning car after it had rolled. Due to the desperate situation he was able to summon up a strength otherwise not available to him and lifted the car high enough for his wife to escape – his love and the desperate need of the moment had focussed his mind to allow the body to go beyond its limits. Imagine what we can do if we make that focussed mind our daily reality rather than just a response to a life-threatening situation. However useful this focus can be to the martial arts in general this aim is looked down upon by true followers of meditation; why waste your time on tricks when you could dive into the heart of the Truth.

To realise enlightenment in everything we do

In my school of Zen, the Rinzai School, we believe that maintaining our meditation while in the act of walking, talking, sitting and sleeping is of prime importance. It is fine to be able to become one with the universe whilst sitting on the cushion, but if we cannot do it when driving a car or when we are sick then what is the point? Meditation is not an escape, it is an embracing of life and thus the mind of Zen should be with us in everything we do. Just as we focus our mind on our breath we focus our mind on washing the dishes, tucking the kids into bed and running to catch the bus. We act, think and move from the centred place in our hara and thus we are centred and balanced all day long no matter what circumstances we meet. The Buddha Mind never neglects us so if we feel alone or out of control it is because we have lost our way... take that peace, serenity and oneness from the meditation cushion and let it live through everything you do.

To achieve nirvana and transcend existence

The last stage is where we allow ourselves to completely disappear. Where we no longer exist but are just the pure experience of the Buddha Mind, of the universe or God. This is a truly beautiful place to be, an amazing experience and great joy... but we all have to stand up from the cushion sometime. We do have lives to live and aiming to be in this place can get in the way. If this is the stage you aspire to experience then certainly you need to find a monastery and a great Master.

HOW AND WHY – FIRST STEPS

Now that we have come to understand a little better why we meditate it is time to settle down and clear these thoughts from your mind.

Go to the place you have set aside for your zazen and cross your legs. Straighten your spine as though a piece of string was holding your head up and gently settle your hands together in your lap. Half-close your eyes and let them take a neutral 45° angle.

Watch your breath as it enters your hara; let it come in naturally and leave naturally. Allow the breath to enter into the deepest place in your lungs and belly and as you exhale keep your mind focussed on your belly as you count "Onnnneeeee….." right to the end of your exhalation. Move on to the next breath and the next number. As the breath arises and falls, as the numbers pass by, be honest enough with yourself to re-start from 'One' again at the slightest extraneous thought.

Try to sit for a little longer this time but don't push it and certainly don't cause yourself pain or discomfort. Be careful to not allow your mind and body to distract you from the breath and the breath counting.

1 *NEN*, 2 *NEN* 3, *NEN*

To the Japanese the 'Nen' (念) is the smallest unit of time. It literally means a "moment of awareness".

We are so used to processing vast amounts of information that we never really understand how the human mind works. We see, think and do so much all at the same time that we feel we can multitask almost anything. However, the mind does not work like this. The mind can really only do one thing at a time, it is just that it does it so fast that we have the illusion we are multitasking.

If you were to look at the streets in Sydney (especially if you were born in a less chaotic city or in the country) it seems to be that everyone is trying to shove as many cars as possible down roads that were not designed for this. When I used to drive to work in the morning I would find my main road of 3 lanes became a main road of 2 lanes and then finally a main road of 1 lane. As the roads became narrower drivers became more and more stressed since the number of cars had not changed, just the space to fit them! This is exactly how stress in the mind works too.

When we work and live at a rate we are accustomed to it is like a well-designed traffic system. Everything flows smoothly and things are resolved at a comfortable pace. When we are overwhelmed with demands of either an external or internal nature we are like those drivers who are trying to eat breakfast and navigate the car through hostile traffic whilst talking to the kids who are screaming the back seat. No wonder people (and drivers) snap… crying for it all to slow down for a moment – we are overwhelmed and just want a breather.

The question is: How do we become overwhelmed in the first place?

The Japanese word 'nen' illustrates the smallest unit of time available to us. It is a moment of thought or awareness. It is that instant where we see, hear, touch, taste or smell something. It is pure and unadulterated awareness before we can think about what we see, before we can conceptualise it. We cannot even describe it because it is pre-thought and thus pre-speech. We actually live like this all the time; this is the reality of the mind at work. 1 nen, a sound enters our awareness; next nen we smell something; next nen we see something.

However well pure awareness might serve the poet and artist it is no good if we cannot share it with another. To do this we have to name what we have experienced. Thus we hear a sound (1st nen) and then we name that "bird song" (2nd nen). We experience vision (1st nen) and then we name that which we see "tree" (2nd nen), and so on. To name the objects of our awareness we have had to make a sacrifice though, we sacrifice one nen of awareness to allow that time to be used for the naming of the first object, thus instead of two moments of raw experience we have one experience and one name for that experience.

Again, wandering through the world collecting experiences and naming them might be fascinating for some people but it is not going to be of much practical use for getting a report on your boss's desk by 9am. This is why we use at least another nen to conceptualise further. It goes something like this: I see an object (1st nen) which I recognise is a "dog" (2nd nen) then a thought, a memory or an idea is born from this: "I was bitten by a dog" (3rd nen). We have used up another moment of raw experience to categorise and intellectualise that first moment of awareness from the name we have given it. 1 nen, 2 nen, 3 nen. Instead of 3 experiences we have a single experience and a line of thought; though usually we will go on and on embellishing it further with ideas about the dog's pedigree and colour then our mind ambles off to think about the dog we wanted but could never have etc, etc… We are suddenly in a day-dream all starting from a single experience and time flows by as we become lost in our thoughts. Over the day these thoughts multiply. We take less and less in as our mind is overstocked and overfilled, our stress levels rise and we wonder why.

When we practice meditation we are paring our experiences back down towards the 1st nen by training the mind. We have the awareness of our breath entering our hara (1st nen) and then we give it a name "one" (2nd nen). There is nothing else to think about, there can be no 3rd nen possible because we catch our mind wandering and we bring it right back to the breath and "one". We keep this going for the length of our sit; experiencing the breath fully and then letting that experience go. There is no comparison of breaths ("wow, that one was almost as good as the one I had 10 breaths ago") and no holding onto the experience wanting it to be bigger and better. We experience fully, give it a name and do it over and over again.

When we stand up from our meditation we suddenly discover that we feel calm and centred again. Sure we might still have to write that report or drive through the mad streets but we have allowed the mind to go back to what it does best, just experiencing. We have 'done nothing' but are now clear, calm and centred. We are ready to do the work that seemed so daunting just 30 minutes before.

The 3 Challenges of Zen

Zen and Buddhism in general is unusual amongst the faiths. We do not seek nor encourage blind followers. Instead we emphasise the importance of each practitioner challenging Zen in exactly the same way that Zen challenges us. To this end we recognise that Zen has 3 great tests, each acting like the leg of a tripod; when all are developed in harmony nothing can cause us to topple.

The Three Challenges of Zen are:
- Great Faith
- Great Doubt
- Great Determination

Great Faith

Whenever we attempt something we need to believe that we can achieve it. There is no point jumping off of a building attempting to fly without having serious faith in your ability to achieve it through something like a hang-glider or parachute.

It is tantamount to any Spiritual Path that one has Faith in its reality, deep true and unshakable Faith. There is no point learning meditation if you are only doing it because your partner is, you will sit there and stare into space and dream along; you are sitting, sure, but that is all - just sitting is not meditating. You must truly believe in what you are doing and that people have done it before you. You must believe that this meditation leads to the answers to those deep questions which are at the heart of us all.

In the monastery one of the first chants we do in the morning is the Rinzai Zen Lineage, naming and honouring the masters extending all the way back to the Buddha. We do this to remind ourselves that just as these great masters have achieved the Truth so can we. The historical Buddha was a normal human being, you are a normal human being. If the person who became the Buddha understood reality then you can too. Without this Faith it will be hard to go far in your meditation.

Great Doubt

In Zen we are constantly prodded and poked by our Master and our Zen brothers and sisters. We are constantly challenged to search for the reality of each and every moment. Buddhism has over 5000 Sutras and yet even if I read them all twice over that would not come close to a moment of pure Experience. 5000 Sutras are just words, wise and inspiring certainly, but still just words. Without putting it to the test how are we to know if the Buddha spoke the truth or was peddling Snake Oil? Great Doubt is essential if we are to truly penetrate the Truth.

You MUST examine the teachings for yourself. How will you ever know that meditation leads to Enlightenment if you don't put it to the test? You can accept my word for it, you can accept the Buddha's word for it, but that is like telling a thirsty person that a glass of water will ease their dry throat. It is only if that person drinks the water for themselves that they gain the benefit and understand the truth of the words.

Great Determination

It is not easy to turn off the TV, put away your work or joggers and cross your legs to meditate. It is even more difficult to do this day after day. In the monastery we have our brothers and sisters with us when we meditate. We have set times and nothing, not even illness, allows us to escape our meditation. When we do sit, we have a mind that fights to keep us distracted and a body that can sit perfectly still when we are watching the idiot box but now has all sorts of aches and pains. This is the test that can only be conquered with Great Determination.

It takes a great act of will to constantly bring the mind back to the hara and the counting. It takes a great act of will to know that if I allow my body to move this time then I know I will feel that knee pain again and again. It takes a great act of will to set aside even 30 minutes each and every day to sit down, light a candle and some incense, and meditate. It is so difficult because we have lived as slaves to this noisy, self-centred and deluded mind for our whole lives because we never knew there was a better way.

- With Great Faith we know we have come across a better way to live and a better way to experience our Self.
- With Great Doubt we know we need to test the truth of it for ourselves and then test and test again the depths of our own understanding.
- With Great Determination we set it all in motion, maintain it and have the courage to see it through to the end.

The way the Three Challenges interact with each other can be explained by looking at how we learn to ride a bicycle.

- I can ride a bike in front of you and say, "Look, you can do it too!" You think to yourself, "Well, if he can do it, so can I." This is Great Faith.
- You then realise that just understanding it is possible is not enough, you have to do it for yourself and experience it for yourself. Your initial attempts failed, can you really ride that bike? This is Great Doubt.
- So you struggle on, first with trainer wheels and then all by yourself. You might scrape your knees and bump your head a few times but in the end, with perseverance, you are able to ride that bike and how good does it feel! This is Great Determination being seen through till the end.

THREE GREAT CHALLENGES

The path of meditation does not want blind followers.

It is best served by people who accept the responsibility of their actions and who desire to sit zazen because they know this is the best way to bring peace and harmony to themselves and their environment.

Over the next chapters we shall examine how that 'self' and the environment it lives in are actually one and the same. But for now it is time to sit down and unite the body and mind.

- As you settle yourself, reflect on what it is that you want from this meditation. What is it that drives your Great Faith?
- Once you know what you seek, use it to focus your mind and steel your resolve to actually get there; Great Doubt is not a depressing thing, it is the source of your energy for meditation.
- Lastly, as you are sitting, draw on all the reserves in your body and mind to keep going with single-minded honesty and focus. Use your Great Determination. Not to force your meditation but to ensure that you do not stray from it for even a single nen.

OLD MONK ON A TRAIN

At the turn of the last century a young working man and an old monk ended up sharing a carriage on a train. As they were travelling through the countryside the young man felt himself becoming more and more agitated by the monk until finally he spoke out.

"Old monk, I find myself looking at you and thinking that you are of no value. What do you do that helps society? What do you do achieve that is of value? Look at me, I have a number of children to enrich our community and I work hard to make sure I provide for my family and support our nation. Can you say that you are this useful?"

The old monk paused for a moment and then pulled an old style pocket-watch from his robes; he flipped its case and showed the young man its innards.

"Look at this, my young friend. Do you see all the gears and coils moving and working hard? This is like you. You do your work and help your family grow and I thank you for that. Just as the removal of any of these gears or coils would stop this watch from working so too are you essential to society.

"However, notice there is also a lot of emptiness in this watch, the gears all revolve around the emptiness in their centre and the coils need to expand and contract into that emptiness as well. Just as the parts which are 'there' are necessary, so too is the lack of such busyness. Fill even one of those empty spaces and the whole watch stops working too. This is my role, to be the empty centre around which all else revolves."

I find this story so fascinating. The wisdom and kindness of the old monk hits home as soon as you read it.

When we meditate we are not filling ourselves up with anything, not complicating our lives further. We honour ourselves but through 'less' not 'more'. It is easy to go out and buy a new pair of shoes or a video game but this is only transient. It is easy to lose ourselves in our work until we find the day is over. We come home and spend some 'quality time' with the partner and kids, then we party hard on the weekend. Before we know it we have aged 10 more years and wondered where the time has gone. The mind of meditation is about using every single second of our life to the fullest.

That old watch was as compact as possible. Every gear and every space is precisely integrated to make it beautiful and functional. In the same way those of us without the luxury of living in a monastery need to balance work, family, friends and Path.

- We DO need to work; society as we know it would fall catastrophically apart if we all suddenly become monks or nuns!
- We DO need to follow our Path; we cannot pass from birth to death in a state of apathetic ignorance about anything except sport and fashion as this is just a wasted life.

Empty your mind of its ceaseless and unnecessary thoughts. Empty your body of its tension. Allow the universe to rush in and fill those gaps. Until the monk exposed the innards of the watch all we could see was time ticking by. Until you immerse yourself in meditation you will also only see time flying by without knowing why you are here and what purpose you serve.

RIGHT SEEING

One of the most important teachings of all religions is the need for reflection – to see our actions in the light of reality and learn from them. But how can we be sure we perceive things correctly? Right Seeing is this essential first step as we begin the journey to integrate our mediation into our daily life.

BLIND MEN SEE AN ELEPHANT

An ancient king once had an elephant as a pet. Three blind men who were guests of the king asked to be allowed to 'see' it.

The first blind man walked up to the elephant. He grasped the trunk and running his hands along and around the end of it pronounced that "The Elephant is a massive creature like a snake. It is thicker and more muscular than the snake with course hair and 2 mouths."

The second blind man was feeling the belly and he pronounced, "No, my friend, you have got it wrong. The elephant is a huge round creature not unlike a whale and by virtue of the way it hangs in the air it must fly as well."

38

The final blind man who was feeling the leg of the elephant pityingly pointed out the errors of his friends. "Both of you must be more blind than me! Anyone can tell that the elephant is a huge creature not unlike a tree. It is so round that I can barely put my arms around it.It is so strong and heavy that the earth must shake when it hops."

Think of the things we see around us all day long. We see colours, shapes and forms, we see 'good' and 'bad' acts, we see things we want and things we don't want. Now ask yourself, do you really see these things as they are?

I remember being amazed some years back by a nature show which pointed out that birds see thousands more shades of green than the human eye can distinguish and that goldfish see deep into the infra-red spectrum. This made me think about those people with colour blindness; their view of things can be dramatically different to mine. Does a bird see 'red' the same way I do, does a goldfish or someone who is colour-blind? Cut yourself underwater at 10m depth and your familiar red blood is black; is it the blood that changed or just my perception? How about the person standing next to me, do they see the same 'reality' that I do or is my image of the things I experience based on my viewpoint alone?

We have to truly ask ourselves what is the nature of this world we perceive. If it is our own viewpoint which is the basis of our experience then are we 100% conscious and 100% aware? Are we seeing it all in its totality or are we like a blind person groping along, feeling only a part of it and thinking we know the whole story. When you consider that it is our perception which is directly responsible for the actions we undertake then the need to be sure we are seeing things clearly is even more important.

Seeing Things As They Are

Many years ago I taught myself to draw and paint. I learned from a most excellent book which pointed out that the act of drawing is really not as difficult as we think. It is a simple matter of copying down what we see onto a piece of paper. We perceive and then directly act from that perception. The book did note that the most difficult part of drawing was the act of 'seeing' itself. Through a series of exercises it forced me to realise that when I was trying to capture the image of someone's face I was often drawing an 'eye' from my idea of an eye's structure rather than just getting my mind out of the way and copying what I actually saw. Whilst I still am not a very inspired artist this lesson does bring us to one of the most important points about our senses...

The input we receive is limited by our perception and our consciousness.

We accept that one who is blind cannot see things clearly just as a deaf person cannot hear with clarity. We accept that a sleeping or unconscious person cannot understand the world around them properly. This is being limited by perception – it is purely a matter of physical circumstances.

In our own individual ways we are also blind, deaf and unconscious. Unless we can see this moment, right here and right now, with clarity and full awareness then we are only getting a shadow of the whole story based on our *idea* of what we have perceived – this is 3rd nen stuff rather than living in that 1st nen. The more we think about it and the more we need to compare it with other experiences in our past or the hopes and dreams we have for the future, the less we are actually right with it and fully experiencing it in the moment. This is perception being limited by our consciousness.

If we try to understand the world we perceive with our mind then we are forced to make comparisons with the past based on our limited life experience. In the story this is reflected by the blind men being unable to comprehend the elephant so their mind jumps to other objects that they do understand like the snake or tree. More importantly when we are looking 'back for causes' or 'forwards for meaning' we are divorcing ourselves from the present moment and the present moment is always about ourselves – who am 'I', right here, right now.

The blind men were not seeing the elephant correctly, but that is not the elephants fault. The elephant is what it is. They can look back into the past to try and understand what they experienced about the elephant, but that only led to erroneous conclusions. They can look forward to the future to imagine what their version of the elephant is capable of, but this is even more deluded as they cannot understand any more than a tiny part of its reality and thus any projection of its capabilities is skewed. It is only by understanding the moment and only by understanding their own blindness; by embracing their limited viewpoint and learning from it that they will truly come to appreciate what they face.

We look at an elephant and we see its form and that is enough for us able-bodied people. What about someone who understands the limitations of their blindness? In the monastery lived a nun who was almost completely blind. When we first met she placed her hands on my face to 'feel' how I looked. When I walked into a room just from my footsteps alone she could tell it was me and what mood I was in. From my scent she could tell where I had been. Do sighted people have this subtlety? By accepting the inability of one form of perception she was able to compensate by being so much more aware in other ways. By being conscious of the limitations imposed by her lack of sight she was not fooled into inventing something which was not there. This is a perfect analogy for meditation; the Buddhas and enlightened Masters live in the same world as we do, but they see it completely and in its totality. Accepting the limitations of perception they perceive fully. By being fully conscious in each and every moment they clearly understand what they experience.

Reflection

One of the central tenants of Buddhism is that of 'reflection'. We reflect on our actions, words and thoughts. This self-reflection is not some sort of guilt or ego trip nor is it about obsessively analysing everything we do; it is about being honest with ourselves and appreciating our grasp of the moment. It is precisely this which keeps us jumping back to the number 'One' in our meditation. An extraneous thought arises and we recognise it for what it is. Accepting it for what it is we start all over again – there is no good or bad, just an honest recognition of where we are and the need to try harder.

As we develop as a spiritual person we apply this same sort of logic to our life. When circumstances arise, be they good or bad, we deal with them with as much consciousness as we can. We turn that clear light of our meditative perception onto everything we meet and try to see it for what it really is and what it really means to us. This is why Right Seeing is the first step in our journey through the Eightfold Path, without Right Seeing we cannot hope to be clear because we will always be caught in an illusion.

When we look at a mirror we see an image there. If the mirror is dirty then the image is poorly formed. If we don't know what a mirror is then it appears that we are seeing another person through a pane of glass. It is only when we understand what the mirror is that we come to see the truth. We polish the mirror to see the image clearly, but it is still just that, an image. We understand with our mind that what we are seeing there is just a reflection of our self, but it is not flesh and blood. To find that true Self we must come at it from another direction. Eyes cannot view themselves. Ears cannot hear themselves. We cannot see ourselves by looking outwardly; all we will see is the reflection of that Self and that image depends on how clearly we see the reflection and whether we understand what we see.

We cannot see ourselves by looking inwardly either. If we look for a 'personality' we cannot find it. Take a photograph of your 'emotions' or describe their shape. We identify so much with our 'past' but when I ask you to describe its colour for me or put it in my hand you will look at me as though I am mad. We can see traces of all these things reflecting back to us through our interactions but if I ask you for evidence of their existence you will not be able to provide me with anything at all; even a mirror has more substance.

You might say, "But I know all these things, I have experienced them", yet at night when we sleep our dreams appear so real. We see it all so clearly at the time even though things can be so strange too. We see ourselves flying or being chased by monsters, in the grips of our dream it all appears to make sense. When we wake up we realise that it was all a dream and we can shake our head in wonder at how we could believe those crazy things that seemed so real.

Through meditative reflection you must align your body, mind and spirit to fully experience this one moment. You are who you are in this one moment, there is nothing inwards to grasp onto, there is nothing outwards that can show you the truth of your being. Right Seeing is the act of seeing with your entire being and not becoming caught on what you see. Do this with all that you are and you will one day stand up from your cushion and see the world as the Buddha and Great Masters do.

THE ULTIMATE ACT OF REFLECTION

It is now time to sit again.

Despite the nature of the discussion nothing has changed. We still sit in the same posture watching our breath with all our focus and all our determination. This meditation is an act of reflection, it is an act of total honesty with no witnesses and no one to reward or punish you. When sensations or thoughts arise let them go so you can experience the next moment fully.

As we half-close our eyes and take in that first breath it might be useful to ask ourselves once again; "Do I really see things as they are?"

A MATTER OF PERSPECTIVE

At one time in the monastery I was going through a rough patch. This was quite early on in my training when I was very easily moved around by my thoughts and feelings. I had become involved in a situation which brought a major crisis of self-identity and from this fear and doubt I went (against everyone else's advice) to see the Roshi.

"I am terribly sad and lost" I said, "I have no idea who I am or what I am." By this stage I was weeping uncontrollably. "How blind you are" replied my master with a neutral smile on his face. This was hardly the kind of emotional support or gentle advice I had expected.

He said; "Billions of people have existed on this planet before you. Billions of people exist on this planet right now. And in the future how many billions more will exist before the Earth is swallowed by the sun? You think your suffering is so important, but that is because you think you are alone and somehow special. It is special to you, because you see yourself as isolated."

Imagine that I have to measure a desk. I have an empty space in my room and I want to know if it will fit in there. To measure it I get a ruler and discover that it is 2 metres long, a finite and understandable amount which solves my present difficulty.

Now imagine that a virus living on that desk wants to measure it. This virus pulls out its ruler, which is based on the nanometre, and promptly discovers that for all intents and purposes this desk is infinitely large.

Finally a mad scientist wants to measure the desk but the only yardstick they have is the light-year. They whip out their light-year long ruler and promptly prove that the desk is so infinitely small that it essentially doesn't exist.

So… the question arises: Does the desk exist or not?

Each of these viewpoints is perfectly valid and each of them is based on their own experience of reality. In one case the desk is infinitely small, in another the desk is infinitely large and in my case it fits the room perfectly! It is all a matter of perspective. Neither the object nor the circumstances have changed, in each case the desk is exactly the same size in exactly the same room, it is only due to the limitations of each individual consciousness that things appear to be so different.

The same thing happens with us daily and it is exactly what my master was pointing to in the story. We can spend our time nit-picking the infinite number of things that will eventually make us feel powerless against their sheer volume. We can miss the importance of a situation by making it as small as possible through sweeping it under the carpet or by just being ignorant. On the other hand we can endeavour to see the true value of that which we meet and to put it in perspective. To do this we need an objective place from which to see phenomena. That objective place is the heart of our meditation.

As long as we focus on "me, me, me" we can never see any more than that. The best we can hope for is that psychologically we are mature enough to make the most of the opportunities we meet but we are always going to be limited by the fact that we are basing it all on a delusional idea of who or what we are. When we meditate we let go of everything including the idea of who 'I' am and the past from which 'I' came. Like a new-born with eyes freshly opened we allow experience to flood into us with no pre-conceived ideas – for the first time we actually 'see with our eyes' instead of our limiting mind.

A ROSE IS A ROSE?

> *"You can cut a rose flower. You can dissect it. You can put all the ingredients separately into bottles, methodically labelled. But one thing will be missing – there will be no beauty to be found. And no life to be found. No joy to be found. No dance of the rose flower in the wind, in the rain, in the sun."*

I have this on a piece of paper given to me in India many, many years ago. I think it is a quote from Osho. It is a really profound and succinct way of putting something that we in the West have forgotten through our fascination with science.

What is it that we see? How do we understand its being?

Is a rose a rose because of its structure? Obviously not, if I pull one of its petals off then it is still a rose, same if I remove the thorns and/or stem. If the petals are white instead of red then we might call it a 'white rose' but it is still a rose. Some people cannot see the colours of the rose at all; I might see it is red with a different tone of colour to you, does that mean it is a rose to me but not my colour blind friend? How about those with no sight at all? Does a rose cease to exist because one is blind?

Is a rose a rose because of its scent? No, there are some roses which are scent-free. How about if we define it by its chemical structure or its genetic marker; these are great for classifying the rose taxonomically but do they capture the essence of the rose's existence? As Osho points out, a spectrographic chart of the rose's chemical constituents is not what anyone would like to get for Valentine's Day. Dissecting it down to its component parts stops it from being able to blow in the wind; its cells or DNA might look different to a geranium's but those cells are dead - they lack life and they lack the essence of that life.

In truth it is the entirety of these things and more which is the essence of the rose. The rose certainly exists because of its form, scent, structure and DNA if you want to define it in such narrow ways. However, from the eye of Zen the rose exists because it is unique to those things which are 'not-rose'.

When you see a rose flower in the garden its life and its unique flavour of existence comes from the leaves and stem of the rose bush as much as from the grass and fence surrounding the garden. Everything from the fence surrounding the garden to the plane flying overhead provides a counter-point to the rose; they provide the rose with its 'life' as much as the structure of the flower itself. Even our friend the scientist can only see the genetic or biological differences inherent to the rose thanks to the existence of plants, animals and objects which are 'not-rose'.

The rose conceptually and physically exists because of its uniqueness which is only gifted through the uniqueness of every other thing we experience. Why is a rose a rose? Because a dog is a dog, because a breath is a breath. The rose 'dancing in the wind' can only do this because there is a wind to blow it, a stem from which it can balance and things which do not 'dance in the wind' against which we can compare it. Even more importantly it exists because we can experience it. Why is a rose a rose? Because my entire life experience gives it life.

Dwell on this for a minute, it is a quite an amazing thought. When we are lost in our head or listening to our earbuds we might blunder past the garden with that beautiful rose in it. No matter what the scientific name of the flower, no matter how beautiful it is, for us it doesn't exist. It might be a red blur amongst the green and easily mixed up with the other plants in the garden. This unique and fascinating experience of the rose is lost to us because we are ignorant of it and because we would rather give life to our music player than the world around us.

UNIQUE INSIGNIFICANCE

If we look at an existence from the point of view of the individual object or experience then it is unique precisely because everything else gives it life.

It is unique because it is one tiny insignificant part of this huge universe. However, just as the universe gives us our uniqueness so are we an indivisible part of the Universe.

When we settle ourselves down and align our body and mind we are at first striving for total objectivity, striving to be in that still-space from which we see things as they really are. In effect we are opening ourselves up past this tiny view of self and allowing the universe to flow through us just like it does anyway. As we let go of our thoughts and then let go of the effort of 'letting go' we become our zazen, we are no longer 'doing' it, we are it.

When you sit in meditation now, be aware that none of the experiences that arise have a life in and of themselves. Each of them requires you to notice them and experience them. Give life to your experience of your breath whilst you meditate and let the other things go. Give life to the numbers 'one' to 'ten' but allow your thoughts to subside. Keep coming back to THIS MOMENT, THIS EXPERIENCE until it eventually happens naturally.

THE SEE-R, THE SEEING AND THE SEEN

What is Vision?
Vision consists of three things: The See-r, the Seeing and the
Seen. They seem different but are not. What is their reality?

Over the next two chapters you will hear me repeat continually:

> True seeing is the seeing of no-seeing.
> True thinking is the thinking of no-thinking.
> True speaking is the speaking of no-speaking.

This does not mean one becomes like a rock sitting on the cushion; a rock cannot see, a rock cannot think, a rock cannot speak. We are sentient, we can see, think and speak with our body and consciousness but we often do them blindly. What this three-part saying means is that truth springs from the place where we see, think and speak as one with the universe and not separate to it.

In the previous story about the rose I mentioned how it is our experiencing of the rose which gives it its life. This is not a statement designed to give us delusions of grandeur because as much as we give that rose its life it does the same for us.

> The see-r can only exist because of the seen.
> The seen can only exist because of the see-r.

In my act of seeing the rose I give it a conditional existence – it is manifest as something 'separate' to me because I see that it is 'not me'. However, it is this very act which also provides the rose with that same power over me. Its existence as something separate to me is what gives ME life, what makes ME unique. Even the fact that I can 'see' it and it cannot see me gives my ability to 'see' meaning and value.

Understanding (even if only intellectually) that the see-r and the seen are essentially unable to exist without each other and thus are mutually dependent upon each other for their existence, what of the act of seeing itself?

One can say that 'love' exists but we now understand that it can only be 'love' if there is something that gives 'love' its special meaning, that thing is 'hate'.

Just as we can only know that the rose exists because of those things which are 'not rose' so too does 'love' only have its meaning if there is 'hate' to be its opposite. However, these things are useless without a way to manifest them. Love and hate can only manifest through our interaction with an object just as our viewing of the rose can only manifest through the act of seeing.

If we were shunted to another dimension where there was no visible light available to us then our ability to see would be useless. Even though we might still possess this ability, without any way to use it there is no meaning to it anymore. When we turn out the light in a room it is no longer my seeing the chair which gives it its meaning, it is the physical act of touching the chair (as I tumble over it) which brings it to our attention. In this case it is the Feeler, the Feeling and the Felt.

The See-r and the Seen only exist because of the Seeing - thus they are all mutually dependent upon each other. Take away any one of them and the others essentially cease to exist. Conceptually we know that the whole universe doesn't disappear when we turn out the light. I know that the rose is still in my garden even when I am blissing out to a great song and not being attentive to it. But reality is not based on concepts - concepts are 3rd nen. Experiencing is 1st nen and if we could have been enlightened from concepts then most of us would have been Buddhas long ago.

So if we understand that we exist because:
1. Everything else in the universe exists.
2. We are able to experience that existence.
What does it mean to 'not-see'?

Meditation is about directly experiencing reality not about forming lovely ideas about the nature of our limited view of reality. Right Seeing is the first step in our Eightfold Path because it is the first test we must face before we can penetrate any deeper into our meditation. Just as meditation is about putting ourselves aside as we try to experience each and every breath with all we are so it is with any other action we undertake during the day.

Do you have to consciously force yourself to 'see' a rose? As you are walking past the garden do you need to think "Eyes, turn to the left. Focus on the rose; make sure you experience the colour of it. Is it moving?" To take in that experience of the rose you have to see it, smell it or possibly even touch it, but these things happen automatically in that first nen. We don't need to consciously do it, it is just the union of the rose and ourselves united through the act of seeing. This is seeing with no-seeing. There is no conscious act, just the union of self and the wonderful universe that fills every nanometre of space and time.

We do not sit there in our meditation watching ourselves watching the breath! Separating from our meditation like that we might as well go and watch some TV instead. When we meditate we are 'in' our body and as we mature as meditators we also become more and more 'in' our breath. We start off watching that breath and naming it, but slowly we dissolve into it to the point where we are no longer 'watching'; it, we are being it.

This is not as unusual as it seems, it often happens to us many times each day. On our lunchbreak we are reading our book and it is such an engrossing story that we suddenly notice we have lost track of time. Other people like to watch TV or go to the cinema because they feel that they can lose themselves into the show. How about when we are walking along listening to music – we don't have to think about listening to it, we just do it and naturally fall into it.

Meditation is exactly like this. At first we start off trying to let go of our thoughts and trying to settle our body. Then we find that we are, slowly at first, able to drop off the 'act of meditating' and actually just become that union of breath, body, mind and spirit. We are not asleep, that is an unconscious act. Nor are we distracted by something external as this would just be deluding ourselves. We cannot even say that we are meditating because that would imply conscious effort and thus there would have to be a Do-er, a Do-ing and the Done. We are just there being our Self with our entire Self which we call 'meditating' for want of a better name. Eventually there will even be a time when the breath itself will disappear from your consciousness, and then your sense of that separate self will also disappear as you truly experience for the first time what you have really been all along.

Right Seeing is that place where for the first time we realise that we are not alone. We have never been alone; we just perceive it that way because we fail to understand the nature of things. Right Seeing alone will not bring an end to the confusion but it is the first step in the journey to true freedom. From now on, whenever we are lost we know that this first step of Right Seeing is the way back to the Path.

RIGHT THINKING

So much of our day is spent in useless repetitive thinking. The 'washing-machine mind' is how I describe the thoughts that constantly circle around inside our heads. Thought is a powerful tool, but just that, a tool. Like any useful implement we should be able to pull it out and use it at the right time, not carry it around with us all day and night. Even if we see things clearly we need to interpret them correctly as well and this is why Right Thinking is the next step on our Path.

HUI-NENG'S "MIND IS MOVING"

It happened that one day, when a pennant was blown
about by the wind, two monks entered into a dispute as to
what it was that was in motion, the wind or the pennant. As
they could not settle their difference I submitted to them
that it was neither, and that what actually moved was their
own mind. [1]

This was written by the 6th Patriarch of Zen in China, a great Master by the name of Hui-Neng. He had been forced, many years earlier, to go into hiding and this statement marks the moment when he revealed himself again and took up the role of teacher.

The pennant refers to the flag which was flown whenever a Buddhist teaching was to be given. It announced to one and all that they were welcome to come along to listen and even debate the Buddhist Truth. Because Zen had subsided to a large degree whilst the 6th Patriarch was in hiding the dominant form of Buddhism was doctrinal and thus concerned with discussing the meaning of the Buddha's words. Zen on the other hand is about actualising the Buddha's reality, the Buddha Mind.

As he walked to this debating hall Hui-Neng overheard two monks discussing this very flag. One of the monks said: "The pennant is moving" because to his understanding it was the flag that was flapping about, without the flag there would be nothing to manifest the movement. The other monk said: "The wind is moving" because he wanted to point out that without the wind to actually move the flag then there would be no movement at all.

This is not just a philosophical question, think of the ways this interprets the events and actions in our own life. One might say about their partner, "Oh they make me so angry. I work hard, put food on the table and they give me nothing in return. No thanks, not even kind words." The other partner likewise complains, "I see how stressed they are, they are constantly snappy and grumpy, but every time I offer to take some of the load off them they say they are fine and I feel less and less valued." This is the 'real-life' version of the chicken and the egg; what came first? We see this sort of dynamic played out in our own lives and the lives of others day in and day out.

To the mind of Zen there is no 'chicken and egg' game. What came first, the chicken or the egg? What moves, the flag or the wind? In both these cases the answer is: The Mind.

Without a mind to interpret what we perceive then there is nothing. Zen Buddhism is based on reality not concepts. People come up to me all the time and ask things like "Does a tree falling in the middle of a forest with no one to witness it make a sound?" The only answer I can have to this is "Why are you not completely alive and aware in THIS place and THIS moment?"

When that 1st nen hits us, even though our senses perceive it, without the awareness to appreciate that experience it is meaningless. Without a mind to appreciate the pennant in the wind there is literally nothing there, there are atoms/energy in the shape of a flag, atoms/energy in the form of wind but without us to see the difference between them in terms of form and function then essentially it is just a huge universal soup of atoms/energy. It is OUR experience of them which gives each phenomenon their special meaning.

Our mind flits along from experience to experience, taking in perceptions and then naming, conceptualising and storing them. This is a great tool, but it is also our greatest flaw.

A Flawed Tool

When I have a nail which I want to place in a wall I know that there is a special tool which can do this job like no other, it is called a hammer. I reach into my toolbox; whip out my hammer and after a few quick taps the job is done.

What if, after doing this for the first time, I thought to myself, "Man, this tool is so excellent; nothing can put nails into walls like it. There is no way that I can be without such a useful tool" and from that day on I take it with me wherever I go. Only at my death do I finally let go of this hammer.

Of course, because I am lugging this thing around with me everywhere I also try to make use of it as much as possible. It would be silly to be carrying it and not using it, right? Even though it may not be the best tool for the job I make do with it to get as much done as possible – I have used it before and I know it is great for putting nails in, so why not use it to open doors, clean the house or cook dinner!

This hammer, of course, represents our thinking.

Thought is a fantastic tool but it is ONLY that, a tool. It should be something we use when we need it and then we put it away again. Only a fool would carry a hammer in their pocket all-day every-day, but since we first learned to use this mind for thinking we have never let it go. Most of us are afflicted with what I refer to as the 'washing machine mind'. A mind that churns thoughts over and over and over, spinning them around until it all becomes a big sodden mess. When we do meet a situation which requires us to use this tool we can't because it is trying to do too much other stuff as well.

Meditation lets go of this endlessly moving mind. We have no thoughts to churn around because our universe exists in just the breath and the counting that goes along with it. When the mind does move and a thought rises to the surface we recognise it and let it go again so we can return to the breath which IS this moment, not a thought ABOUT this moment. We let go of our thoughts because there are no thoughts necessary – we are just breathing and counting, what thoughts do we need?

> True Seeing is the seeing of no-seeing.
> True Thinking is the thinking of no-thinking.
> True Speaking is the speech of no-speech.

True Seeing is that immediate moment when myself, my perception and the object I am viewing are One. I need to make no decisions about viewing, it happens because it is the nature of our perceptions to be immediate and instantaneous.

True Thought is likewise that moment when we use thought as the wonderful tool that it is, and then let go of it. There is no identifying with it, no need to hold onto it.

When I did my exams at university I used my ability to think so that I could complete the academic task in front of me. Then, once I finished the test, I returned to the breath so that I was in the moment, not back in the exam room. At work I might need to resolve someone's complaint but I don't carry that person around with me all day. When their situation is resolved then the thinking mind returns to the toolbox until I need it again. Even to speak of it as something separate is over-thinking.

The thinking mind arises when we need it the same way that hearing arises when our ears meet a sound; we don't need to put our 'hearing' away' when we are finished with it, it just subsides until next needed. The only difference is our obsessive need to pull out this thinking mind and use it for anything and everything we possibly can.

Lack and Suffering

We would openly laugh at someone who brags about the skilful way they just looked at a rose. This same person might tell us how they looked at a rose so excellently when they were 14 years old and how they have been trying to see roses like that ever since. If we heard someone talking like this we would think they were crazy. However, we see people doing this each and every day when it comes to their thoughts.

Everyone's thoughts are based on either looking back to the past or looking forward to the future. Thus they are based on suffering. We suffer because of what we lack or suffer because what we desire has yet to arrive. Even when we experience great pleasure we suffer as it is often not exactly what we wanted or it doesn't last long enough. Out of this suffering our pathological attraction to thinking arises.

From an early age we recognise the ability of our thinking mind to solve problems and to get what we want. There is nothing wrong with this. We recognise that vision is a better tool for navigating the car than closing our eyes and driving by smell or touch! The problem comes from not letting go of this tool when the job is done.

We are conditioned from such an early age to believe that we can solve any situation that comes to us if we use our mind well enough and as a result we are afraid to let go of this thinking mind. Like the person who brags about how well she saw a flower 15 years ago we are focussing on those times when the thinking mind did the job it was supposed to do with great efficiency. We compare our present experiences with ones that happened a long time ago. This is suffering because we think we lack something. We are living in the past wanting to do something as well as we did in our memory or we are wishing that we could think/act/do as well as we assume other people do.

This is not living in the here and now, this is living in a dream or nightmare and refusing to wake up.

Desire is a cause of suffering that arises from a lack of Right Thinking. When we idealise something we put our energy into it. We kick-start our mind, which is quiet, calm and centred from the origin, and put in front of it the object of our desire. Our mind grabs hold of it and starts to rip it apart; "How can we (not) be like this?" or "How can we (not) have this?" There is no chance to freshly experience it anymore. No chance for it to unfold for us naturally because we have it in our mind now and are working it over like a puppy with a rag-doll. Our mind is running a million miles an hour as we struggle with a CONCEPT of what we desire, rather than dealing with this moment and what we actually have right here and now.

CLOUDS PASS THE MOUNTAIN

With so many new and exciting thoughts about our thoughts I am sure you are ready to put it all aside and just let the reality of it all manifest through your zazen.

Right Thinking is the Thinking of No-Thinking.

Do not mistake this for becoming a rock! Our mind is a great tool and worthy of our respect, but we overuse it and it ends up running our life rather than enhancing our experience of it.

Just as we allow our eyes, ears and other senses to fade into the background as we experience each and every breath, so too do we allow the mind to settle to its place of natural stillness until we need it again.

There is no past to go back to, so thoughts about that past are purely for reflection or about moments lost. There is no future for us to live in so any thoughts about the future are purely based upon desire and guesswork. There is only this moment and this moment is about crossing your legs, straightening your spine and allowing each and every breath to be your whole world.

BUDDHA'S RAIN

"Imagine a huge tract of land, each piece of land equally
fertile. Over this land falls a constant and gentle rain so
that no part gets more or less than any other part... Out of
this combination of heaven and earth come the plants.
Some of these plants are tiny; some of them are the biggest
of the big trees in the forest.
All of them are nourished equally but according to their
natures they grow differently." [2]

This is a much condensed version of the initial chapters of "The Parable of the Herbs" from The Sutra of the Lotus Flower of the Wonderful Law. When we read a sutra from a Zen point of view we do not try to 'understand' it, we meditate until our mind is back to its true stillness and then let the sutra flow straight into our awareness without any obstructions. Trying to understand a sutra is like describing a glass of water to a thirsty person – they might be able to understand what it is and how it can help them, but it still won't quench their thirst unless they drink it down for themselves.

This parable presents sentient existence as though all of us were a living part of a massive forest. This forest has come about through the interaction of Heaven and Earth.

Heaven represents the spiritual core of our existence (i.e. the Buddha Mind, God(s), the Spirit, etc). One might not be a follower of a theistic religion and still recognise that there is an innate purity and harmony which flows through the things which even our own limited consciousness can perceive.

Earth represents the physical manifestation of this spiritual energy (i.e. the physical realm, karma). Just as electricity cannot light our homes or cook our meal without a physical way to manifest its energy so too does the Buddha Mind need a physical shell to be revealed. This takes us back to the previous story of the pennant in the wind where the young monks were using the analogy of the flag and the wind. To their mind the wind represented heaven giving the flag (earth) life.

In this parable the forest represents our existence coming about through the combination of the spiritual and the material. In the world we have so many types of people, each passing through their life with as much consciousness as they are able to muster. All these different levels of awareness are represented by the various types of plants in the forest. Some plants are only small whilst others are the biggest of the big trees in the forest. This is in accordance with their natures and their circumstances just as an oak seed will naturally have a better chance of growing to be a firm steady tree than a dandelion seed.

Over the whole forest falls a gentle and equal amount of rain. This rain represents the Buddha Mind; another word for it might be Grace or even Total Consciousness. This rain hits every part of the forest equally and is used by the various plants in accordance with their needs. The biggest trees have the widest area covered with their leaves and branches, thus they can take in so much more of this rain than the smallest weeds whose needs are only tiny. Although the rain is the same, the amount each plant is able to receive depends on how much they have grown.

We all make every effort to live our lives with as much meaning as possible. For some people this might be just as a small plant, their aims might be small; they want a happy enough life, to be well thought of at their job and to have a comfortable slide into old-age – consciousness isn't important to this type of person. Another type of person might spend their entire life searching for the answers to "life, the universe and everything" they might have the aim to achieve full consciousness and know that they have to do it in this lifetime; this sort of person is one of the trees. The aims are identical; to live with as much meaning as possible, but the manifestation is different depending on the level of their understanding.

Whilst this is easy to recognise it is also important to understand that to each and every one of these various types of plants comes the same amount of rain. Whether a plant is the smallest weed or the biggest tree the rain it receives is identical. Big trees take in a lot of the rain, just as a person whose awareness is highly developed will live a bigger and fuller life. The smallest plants take in a tiny amount of rain, but that too is enough for them and their limited needs. A Buddhist does not believe that only those who follow Buddhism are to be granted any special privileges in this world – they get the same portion of Grace as a mass-murderer or saint. The difference is in how that is manifest. A short-sighted person who forgot their glasses sees the beautiful rose in the garden as a coloured blur, the person standing next to them with clear eyes can see even the dew drops on the rose's petals and is validated and nourished by them. It is not the roses' fault it cannot be seen clearly, it is manifesting its 'rose-ness' completely, the fault lies with the viewer.

Right Thought is to be like the trees in this forest. Right Thought is to be aware that despite the circumstances we are experiencing we are getting all the nourishment we need to grow right here and right now. We are only bound by our consciousness and circumstances - it is only these things which stop us from being any more expansive. Even though the circumstances in which we exist act to aid or hinder the amount we can grow it is the consciousness we manifest which allows us to use each and every moment as it comes along. No excess thought is needed for this, we just act in accord with the moment.

The universe truly provides - it is only our own lack of awareness which stops us from feeling content with that. Thus one plant will use that rain to grow bigger and stronger; another will use it to maintain the status quo; still other plants will complain that they are getting less than everyone else and will stunt their own growth through Ignorance, Anger or Desire.

Consciousness and Circumstance

When we lose sight of the role that consciousness and circumstance play in our life we start to think that it is all 'out there'. We start looking back to the past or forward to the future to try to understand why we are not getting 'what we deserve'. This is the pathway to the Three Poisons: Desire, Ignorance and Anger. The naturally still and quiet mind becomes agitated (by Desire) for what it wants or feels it lacks (through Ignorance) and we become unsettled and lost (manifesting as Anger). This is the path of the stunted plants.

Circumstances cannot be ignored. Some of us have karma that allows us to have our material needs met or to have the opportunity to be exposed to wisdom. Other people might have a large amount of material adversity to overcome or be surrounded by dull or deluded people. Each of us has our own history and upbringing to overcome and thus a large part of Buddhist teaching is about the need to resolve one's karma to provide the best opportunities for our own development. For example: It is harder to devote oneself to a life of meditation if you work 9-5 and have a busy active household. It is easier to do when you live in a monastery. Some of us have the good fortune to be able to leave their job to enter a monastery, others do not – this is due to karma. It is neither good nor bad, it is just circumstance.

Consciousness is where we actually put the potential of our circumstances into action. An oak seed might have the POTENTIAL to be the biggest tree in the forest, but only if it uses the nourishment it receives to grow and manifest itself to the fullest. A monk in a monastery might have the better opportunity to develop their meditation, but only if they devote their whole being to this.

To wish for something different in our circumstances is to raise this moving mind and to thus lose sight of Right Thinking. If there was something more to this moment that we could see then we would be able to see it. This is the simple rule of awareness.

Buddhism believes in innate purity. The whole universe is perfect and complete just as it is – however it is our human nature to not see it this way or to want more of what each of us already has. All of us feel that we are missing out on something, we feel that something is there waiting for us to understand it but tantalisingly just out of reach. That thing is Truth (Buddha Nature) and it is waiting for us to open our senses and our mind fully so that we are no longer blind to it. The problem we all have is that when we attempt to experience it we try to understand with our narrow thinking minds and our limited consciousness which puts up walls and barriers of our own making. Like the blind men feeling an elephant we are ignorant to our own limitations. Like the two monks arguing over the wind or the flag and missing something far greater.

I remember once talking with a group of young Christians. They were a very determined group who were full of faith and I admired the way they were trying to actualise their love of Christ through their day-to-day lives. One of them in particular stood out though. This man talked non-stop about what God wanted from him and how God was manifesting in his life. In fact it quickly became obvious he was so stuck on his own idea of what God wanted from him that he really was making himself deaf to the Word of God all around him. It was no surprise that in this bright group his energy was the darkest. He had the fortunate circumstance to be with a group of similar minded people all working towards a common wisdom but his own thoughts were stopping him from using this chance to the fullest.

All of us struggle to rationalise our understanding of our Path with our understanding of the circumstances we exist in and we constantly bash up against the brick wall of our own ignorance. This is like trying to use our eyes to see a rose on the other side of a brick wall. It is only when we become conscious of the fact that our circumstances do not meet our needs that we are able to walk around that wall and see what is on the other side.

LET GO OF YOUR THINKING

Right Thought is the Thought of No-Thought.

Stop trying to understand Universal Truths with the mind that has trouble deciding what to watch on TV tonight or often fails at simple maths! Go to that objective place where you are at one with your surroundings and have cut away the thoughts which are blocking you from evolving any higher awareness.

When you want something other than what you have right here and now then you call forth suffering. That suffering acts like a seed for even more pain.

In your meditative breath there is no past or future, only right here and now. There is no suffering because each and every breath sustains us and gives us life.

When we face difficulties in life we keep going with all the integrity and strength we can muster so that we can be ready for things to turn around for the better. Every breath is fresh and new, every moment is fresh and new, there is no need to pollute it with a mind whose basis is ignorance.

Clear your senses and quieten your mind to open up to the Great Truth of the Buddha Mind.

THE KANSEI-SAN'S COMPASSION

I had the honour of being the attendant to the Kansei-san (the retired Abbot of Sogenji Monastery) for a period of time. He was an old man and his health was such that we had a constant live-in attendant with him at almost all times.

He enjoyed his peace and quiet so it surprised me one day when he invited a pair of guests in for a chat. They were hospice workers from the United States of America who were visiting the monastery as guests of the Roshi to speak with us about the work they did. The guests were suitably awed by the invite and once they were settled the Kansei-san asked (through me), "What is it you want to ask me?"

This again took us all by surprise but immediately one of them spoke up. As a hospice worker his job was to ease the pain and suffering of the dying process yet he was amazed that so many of his patients were angry with him or treated him poorly. He couldn't understand how people who were dying could be upset at him as he tried to make things easier for them. This was obviously a very heart-felt question for him and we were all moved by it.

The Kansei-san said, "Look at me, I am old, I am sick, I am suffering." He then patted me on the head as I knelt by his chair, "Look at this young monk, he is also suffering, even though he is not sick in the body he has doubts and fears and pain – this is the source of his suffering. Both of you before me are suffering too; emotionally, physically or because you understand that you too will die one day without fulfilling all your dreams.

"When you go before a person who is dying how do you

approach them? Do you meet them as a fellow traveller on the path of life who is suffering just as they are? Or do you meet with them as someone who is better off than them and can offer to take away their pain from this 'better' place. They are angry with you because you stand apart from them and that makes them feel sicker, sadder and makes their suffering even more intense.

"When you meet with someone who is suffering reach into your own being and find that place of your own suffering. Compassion is not about pity, it is about putting yourself in another's shoes."

Even though I have a shaved head this story still makes the few remaining hairs on my neck stand each and every time I tell it.

The pure and quiet mind starts to move and grab onto things when it fails to see the whole story. Why do we obsess about someone talking behind our back? Because we don't know what they are saying. Because we don't feel secure in ourselves or our position. The thinking mind arises when we meet our own ignorance head on and we (ignorantly) believe we only have this one tool available to solve the problem. From a position of ignorance we try to solve the problems we face, this is similar to one blind person asking another for directions.

- **Ignorance** is the lack of awareness.
- **Desire** is the feeling of wanting more than we have.
- **Anger** is the manifestation of our frustration at not being able to understand or possess.

These are the Three Poisons which lead to Suffering. Suffering is the condition which causes the quiet mind to become noisy. The bigger our distress the more we struggle to understand it and solve it with this faulty tool of thought.

There is nothing more distressing than our own mortality and thus when we do finally turn our awareness onto it all sorts of fears and pain arises. A Master once said:

Ordinary people live with two denials: Denial of their own
mortality and denial of that denial.

Even in hospice work you see people who might only have hours to live clinging on to false hope in the face of their impending death. This is not some deep faith in the ability of medicine to come up with a miracle cure, it is nothing more than the mind going into overdrive as it tries to find a way to not have to face the fear which has haunted each and every one of us since we first appreciated our own limited lifespan. To a larger or smaller degree we face this problem of death in each and every thing we do, even if it is something as minor as the 'death' of our job or relationship.

We all suffer from this and it haunts us all, but it can also unite us.

The mind stirs and starts to worry over all sorts of things that it meets due to the suffering they cause but what if those things were also born from another's suffering? The person who speaks badly of us is suffering too. The person who stole our car is likewise suffering. We all suffer, it is just that some people act with a sense of personal responsibility while others want to blame the rest of the world and pass off some of their pain and fear onto others.

In 2007 while walking home from a meditation class I was randomly attacked in the street. My assailant hit me over the head from behind and attempted to make off with my bag which was full of clothing. My injuries left me in hospital for the night and took a few months to fully resolve. I was incredibly lucky not to have died from the nature of the blow. An event like this is sure to cause some suffering in the victim (in this case me!) but the way we deal with it is going to differ from person to person. Some might rail against the police and society insisting that we need more laws, cameras and restrictions to 'make us safe', though in essence this is making everyone pay for one person's crime. Another might raise the mind of a vigilante to go out and hunt down their assailants to give them a taste of their own medicine. Personally I just wanted to rest and reflect; what kind of life has a person lived that they would consider the possibility of accidentally killing someone justifiable for some insignificant material reward? All of us are suffering and surely it is not in accord with the Buddha Mind and Right Thinking to cause more suffering because of one's own pain.

I do not pity my assailants because pity is not a sign of compassion; it is a sign of contempt. When we pity we are saying that we are morally or physically better off than our target. If I had suffered to the point where the potential of a small amount of money was more important than another's life maybe I would act in the same way too, who knows? Pity also makes it seem like another is powerless to change but they are not. My assailant had a choice and the choice they made was one of the worst possible. We all have the chance to transform, to turn away from our selfish and narrow-minded behaviour. All of us are born out of the innate purity of the Buddha's Mind, thus all of us have the ability to gift the world with light and joy. Some of us choose to work for the betterment of ourselves and others, some of us choose not to.

The Kansei-san was close to death and with as much consciousness as he could muster he had accepted that death. He didn't need to pretend that he was not suffering to make another feel better or to feel superior in himself but his own suffering had eased to the degree that he had accepted his own doubts and fears. Using his years of spiritual practice and Right Thinking he understood that we are all united through our suffering and from that place he was able to say "It's OK, we are all in this together and we will resolve it together too."

RIGHT SPEECH

We do not live in isolation. We need to share our experiences with other people and for this speech is essential. Right Speech is not only about learning how to speak clearly and openly but it is also where our path of zazen starts to alter the focus from reflection on ourselves to reflection on our interaction with the world at large. Right Seeing and Right Thinking are purely individual processes. With Right Speech we turn that awareness outwards to how we interact with the world.

There is a saying that 'the eyes are the window to the soul' but in this Chapter we discover that it is actually our voice. What we say and how we express our nature clearly illustrates how far we have travelled on the Path.

4 MONKS IN SILENCE

Four monks agreed to meditate together for the whole night and to not speak a single word. As the hours went by they all maintained silence but early in the morning the flame of their singular candle began to flicker.
"Oh, the flame is going out", said one monk.
"We should not speak a single word!" admonished the second monk.
"Why are you two breaking our vows?" asked the third monk.
"Ha! I am the only one who did not talk!" gloated the fourth monk.

There is bit of a tradition of 'dim-witted monk' stories in Zen teaching techniques, and why not? Sometimes it is easier to learn about our own failings by laughing at situations like this especially since they are not too hard to imagine.

How often do we see this sort of scene played out, where one criticises another for actions they both do? Buddhist philosophy calls this falling into 'the Realm of the Asuras'.

In Buddhist Cosmology there are 6 'levels of existence' one can be reborn into. Being born into any of these realms is a direct result of the karma of your previous life. You will note that the first 3 are based around the 3 Poisons (Greed, Anger & Ignorance).

The realms and their causes are:
> **Hell Realm** – Anger
> **Hungry Ghost Realm** – Desire
> **Animal Realm** – Ignorance
> **Human Realm**
> **Asura Realm** – Judgement
> **God Realm** - Bliss

Like any religion some interpret these realms literally but I think it is useful to view it figuratively. Although most people know about the Buddhist concept of reincarnation it is usually viewed as an alternative to the monotheistic view of Heaven & Hell. That is to say that the soul somehow continues after our physical death to be reborn again depending on the way we acted during our life. Does this happen? I cannot say, I certainly have no knowledge or experience of it. I am certainly in no rush to find out.

Where I do have certainty is that in each and every moment we can be 'reborn' into one of these realms.

The Hell Realm is self-explanatory. It is being consumed by anger, hate and division. To enter the realm of the Hells is be guided by anger. Lashing out at the ones we love because we have lost our centre and are stressed and overwhelmed. Angry at a stranger because they don't think, look or love the same way we do. The place of Hell is a hard one to navigate and much easier to enter than it is to leave.

When we give into Desire we become a Hungry Ghost. The Hungry Ghosts feed and are never satiated. They take but never give back. Whether it is drugs, money, sex or even the last chocolate in the box, to be reborn in the

Realm of the Hungry Ghost it is make a decision based on your own desire with no thought of any other except perhaps in terms of what they can do for you.

Ignorance is the home of the Animal Realm. Animals live from moment to moment but not in an enlightened way, they experience a need and seek to fulfil it. Whether it is mating or defending territory it is acted upon by instinct but with no aim in mind, with no higher purpose. From Ignorance we as people only focus on what is right in front of our face without being able to see the consequences or opportunities. It is the doorway into Greed and Anger.

Seeing it this way we can pass through a whole series of realms in a short period of time. From the Animal Realm we can decide that an object we see is of utmost importance to us, we pass into the Hungry Ghost Realm as our desire for that object consumes us. Finally we enter the Hell Realm as we lash out at someone else because they have what we want. All of this can literally take minutes.

The Human Realm is the realm of the person of the Way, so we will look at this later.

From the point of view of Right Speech though the 'Realm of the Asura' is most interesting. Asura are 'fighting demons' who were conquered and tamed by the wisdom of the Buddha and now act to defend Buddhism by any means necessary. These represent the people who have understood to a large degree. They have a strongly formed sense of right and wrong but they cannot help but impose this on the world around them. We call this Judgement. Judgement is being intelligent or wise enough to understand a situation but unable to see its full depth and breadth. When we live in this realm we feel nothing can be accepted at face value because we trust only our own understanding of the situation. Because of this, opportunities to evolve and understand further are often cut short. For the meditator this is someone who sits down convinced they are as deep as they can be and not making effort to explore further.

It is also the realm of those consumed with fear. Fear arises because we understand a situation enough to know that it might be a threat, but not enough to find a way through it. Through our concerns we make a judgement and then shut down any further options past that point. Judgement is the closing of doors, it can only open a door to those who feel the same as us. Through this judgement we limit ourselves, and demand that others be limited as well, even if they do not share our fear.

Personally I find this type of person easy to spot because it is the lack of Right Speech that gives them away. This is the state of mind that constantly looks for loop-holes, twisting and turning any sort of discussion in an attempt to make their viewpoint come out on top. If circumstances do not match their opinions then they just push their point harder. From a logical point of view it can be frustrating as one watches the mental gymnastics but from a Buddhist point of view it is such a waste. What if a tenth of that mental energy was harnessed to just let go? What if the mind which actively searches for argument and counter-argument were to have the strength of will to shut off and listen, to realise that the universe stretches in an infinite direction through both Past and Future. Being so sure of themselves cuts them off from experiencing that further.

Now one would look at this list and think that the last, the God Realm would be a great place to be born but unfortunately this is not the case. The God Realm is a wonderful blissful state which lacks for nothing. But as the old saying goes 'the higher one climbs, the further one falls'. Although one can exist in this blissful state for a very long time, when it comes to an end, and it always comes to an end, then the differences become stark. Suffering, once something that happened to other people now affects this person harder as they have never suffered before and they do not know how to handle it. Once those first cracks show then the whole facade can crumble quickly. Before then though there is no impetus for change; every need is met, every desire satisfied, what space is there for growth?

We do not often see those in the 'lesser realms' in the meditation hall though we are all challenged by these feelings regularly. The Angry person is too self-consumed to be able to seek a quiet place to sit and a centre to live from. Desire leads us to look outside ourselves for our own centre, it weakens our strength to look only at ourselves even if we do come to the cushion. The state of mind that Ignorance brings hardly leads itself to sitting zazen, why sit and worry about something when there is a football match on or a reality TV show to watch? The Asura generally gravitate towards other paths and towards people and teachings that validate their fears and judgement. Those living in the God Realm rarely come to the cushion either, what need do they have when all their needs are met?

To a Buddhist it is the Human Realm that is of most importance as not only is the chance of being born in it exceedingly rare but it is only in the Human Realm that one can seek for and achieve enlightenment.

The Buddha says that the chance of being born as a Human is the same as finding a single particular grain of sand on a beach.

Before we go on I want to reflect upon this for a moment.

Does this seem far-fetched? Arthropods (insects, spiders, scorpions) make up 80% of the animal biomass on the planet, ants alone are estimated to be equivalent in biomass to 20% of humanity. Consider all the Animals, Plants, Fungi and Bacteria. Lastly the planet holds roughly 8 billion of us. What are the chances that you are born here and now as a Human? How lucky is it that your consciousness is in this body instead of a cow's or that of a mosquito? Many readers will be blessed with the chance to live in a developed nation with clean water, abundant food and a comfortable home thus making this existence rarer still.

What is it about the Human Realm that makes it so special? As a human we have the ability to learn, we have the ability to know our mind and the urge to know more than what we can currently conceive in our mind. A human suffers and instead of lashing out (Anger), ignoring it or wishing it would go away (Ignorance) or looking for a distraction (Desire) humans look for a solution. Being unable to feel suffering (God Realm) or pushing up against the current to force the situation to the shape to one's own limited understanding (Asura) is not going to lead to a resolution. A human has the ability to accept that sometimes things are out of our control & understanding and through this realisation discovers an urge to evolve, to want to know more. A human has the humility to accept the need to change and the determination to follow through with that change.

Each of these states is revealed when we open our mouths.

WORDS FROM SILENCE

The eyes may be the window to the soul, but it is our words that are the first to expose the Truth we live.

It takes immense determination and faith to trust our voice. To know that every single time we open our mouth we reveal just how much further we have to go to be truly Awakened.

We have a way to practice this though, through our susokukan, through our honesty watching the breath. If we cannot be honest with ourselves about the random thoughts that arise as we count our breaths what hope do we have for being honest with the words that roll off our tongue.

Like the breath our words can be a clear indication of how truly we are living in the moment. When we are honest we can see how quickly thought follows word as we assess and reassess what we said, getting ourselves tongue-tied overthinking each and every syllable.

We sit in silence on the cushion because centred silence is our birth right. It is crystal clear, true and waiting for us to find it. Once we find it each and every word is likewise crystal clear and true.

WHAT HAPPENS AFTER DEATH?

In Zen it is said that the teacher doesn't find the student, it is the student who finds the teacher. This is a function of the pure mind of the student understanding there is an awareness they lack but is theirs by right. Suddenly they experience that awakened mind in another. More often than not it is through Right Speech, the right thing said, to the right person, at the right time. Being centred is like a perfectly tuned radio; we might not see the wavelength it is picking up but nothing is lost and everything is transmitted with perfect clarity.

The Buddha's own teachings are filled with examples of his Right Speech guiding students back to the core questions that keep us on the mediation cushion.

> In the *Cula-Malunkyovada Sutta* (MN 63), the Buddha is asked by a monk about the end of the universe and where buddhas [sic] go after they die. In that case too, the student is reprimanded for his curiosity. "Did I ever promise you the answer to those questions if you follow me?" the Buddha demands. "Did I ever tell you that this was the point of my teaching?" The point is to reach Awakening. Don't waste your time on anything else. [1]

When we have not mastered Right Thinking it is very easy to fall into the trap of the 'grey zone'. This is that place where we split hairs instead of clearly seeing the situation in front of us. Right Speech illuminates this state of mind like a car light on a dark road. In reality almost every choice we have is a binary one: Do we make this choice because it is the best thing to do or do we make it because the outcome suits our own limited and personal needs. This is the core dilemma of any problem you face – do I want the outcome to suit me or suit what is best for everyone?

Like the student in the example above, our thinking mind likes to distract us by looking elsewhere rather than accepting what is right in front of us. This question of death is such a core one that some religions are entirely built around providing some sort of answer about what happens when we die. Promises and bargains are made in the name of religion all in the hope of something that comes 'next'. The fear of death is so prevalent that throughout history there are voluminous examples of people giving up their 'now' to ensure the promised 'what comes next' occurs.

Of course people fear death but the Buddha knew a truth that is even more frightening; the fear of surrendering to the moment and living in the NOW.

Without Right Seeing to guide us we do not see this one precious life we have and this equally precious moment that we exist in, we do not see how even our struggles and suffering validate us and give us a chance to awaken to something bigger than ourselves.

Without Right Thinking we are constantly looking elsewhere, looking for something external to change or be changed so that we can finally feel some peace and belonging.

Right Speech immediately exposes this confused position with words like 'if' and 'but' or with arguments entirely centred on something in the past/ future and coloured in shades of grey. Like asking a lawyer or politician a yes/no question and getting a 1000 word answer that deals with anything but the question asked.

The Buddha is kind enough to rip all that away: What happens after we die?

Are you fully alive right now?

Your zazen, if sat with honesty, can likewise provide you with that kindness. Who cares about the breath you took last week or may take in a year from now! Have you truly experienced this breath right here, right now?

It is so easy to find something to complain about, even when we are fit and well and have a roof over our head and food to eat. The words spill out from our mouth one after the other. Complaints, sports results, the latest celebrity news, each word showing how far away from our own centre and our own breath we are. But like the humans we are we can learn from this.

THE UNFETTERED MIND

True Seeing is the Seeing of No-Seeing. We do not have to force our eyes to take in all that is around us. Seeing is their nature, they do it spontaneously.

True Thinking is the Thinking of No-Thinking. When our mind is free of distraction and perfectly meets the moment then our thoughts flow along with that moment, neither more nor less than necessary.

74

True Speaking is the Speaking of No-Speaking. When we exist from the truth at our core then we naturally express ourselves in perfect harmony with the moment. This is a part of the reason that the Enlightened Masters test their students with words.

When Ippen Shōnin met Hottō Kokushi, the founder of Kōkokuji in the village of Yura in Kii Province, he said, "I have composed a poem."
Kokushi said, "Let's hear it"
Shōnin recited:

When I chant,
Both Buddha and Self
Cease to exist
There is only the voice that says
Namu Amida Buttsu

Kokushi said "Something's wrong with the last couple of lines don't you think?"

Shōnin then confined himself in Kumano and meditated for twenty-one days. When he passed by Yura again, he said, "This is how I've written it":

When I chant,
Both Buddha and Self
Cease to exist
Namu Amida Buttsu
Namu Amida Buttsu

Kokushi nodded his enthusiastic approval and said, "There, you've got it!" [2]

Ippen Shōnin went on to become one of the greats of the Pure Land School of Buddhism. This form of Buddhism is perhaps the closest to the monotheistic religions in that it teaches that all one need do is chant The Buddha of Light's name with absolute faith to be reborn in that Buddha's Pure Land (Heaven). This chanting "*Namu Amida Buttsu*" is called the *nenbutsu* and translates as "Hail to Amida Buddha" (Hail to the Buddha of Light). In many ways it is similar to our susokukan, instead of focussing on the breath counting it instead focusses entirely on the chant.

As in almost all Japanese traditions the student will present to their Master, or even another Master of their school, a phrase or poem that expresses the depth of their understanding. Masters do not exactly grow on trees, especially in the old days a student might wait years for a teacher to visit or travel for many weeks for the chance to present their state of mind.

Here we see Shōnin grabbing that chance with both hands as he presents his poem. He expresses his state of mind honed through years of meditation on the nenbutsu only to have the master Kokushi point out that there is something missing. Kokushi did not explain where to look. A part of the trust inherent in meditation is that anyone and everyone can find the answer if they are willing to make the effort. Like any good student of the Way Shōnin accepts his teacher's wisdom and makes every effort to go that little bit deeper.

Like describing food to someone who is starving, Right Speaking is not about explanations, it is about the real essence of our existence manifest through words at the right time and place. Both Shōnin and Kokushi understood this.

After weeks of meditation Shōnin is finally able to express that truth for himself. True Speaking is the Speaking of No-Speaking, Shōnin got out the way and allowed himself to be real.

A WORD FOR LIFE

No matter what our state of mind - Anger, Greed, Ignorance - we have a choice in how we wish to exist.

How we exist is how we express ourselves.

The honesty in our being is reflected in the honesty of our words just as the sense of beauty or desperation in our existence is expressed in our words. Through these words we draw in like-minded people.

The truth in our expression and being allows us to shape our world.

Zen is not about flowery words and pithy catchphrases. A breath is a breath, no matter how much you try to dress it up or make it feel special - it is just one of the many hundreds you will breathe today.

We sit on this cushion to experience each moment with absolute honesty. In time our words match this.

If this was the very last breath you were ever to take, what words would you use to sum up your life-time of existence?

ARIGATO

The story is told about a woman Zen master named Sono who taught one very simple method of enlightenment. She advised everyone who came to her to adopt an affirmation to be said many times a day, under all conditions. The affirmation was, "Thank you for everything. I have no complaint whatsoever." [3]

Have you ever heard of something so horrifyingly profound and simple? An attitude like this should be classed a superpower.

> I am caught out in the rain – thank you.
> I lost my job – thank you.
> I have been diagnosed with cancer – thank you.

Every situation we meet is a binary one and Sono's thank you is a guarantee that she will choose the right path. Moreover her "thank you" smooths the way forward. She is not living in denial, the rain is dripping down her neck, she has lost her job, been diagnosed with cancer; all real and immediate things. She accepts the situation and can allow a solution to present itself. Be it finding shelter, looking for a better opportunity (or accepting underperformance) or seeking a cure and accepting that I will live out my time to the fullest.

Even more importantly she is using this Right Speech to train herself in Right Thinking, Right Seeing and living in the moment. Just as our words can lead us further and further into Anger, Greed and Ignorance they can motivate us to humility, acceptance and greater awareness.

Our knees hurt when we sit. We have an important meeting this afternoon or are just not feeling the mood to sit. All these distractions work to pull us off the cushion. Use that Right Speech to refocus your effort to come back to the cushion, the pain, demands and feelings can all melt away through your zazen. Just as Right Speech illustrates the truth of our Seeing and Thought it also is the starting point for the next part of your journey – Right Action.

RIGHT ACTION

Speech alone is not enough. Right Action is necessary because actions do speak louder than words. Likewise with meditation it is not enough to see our own place in the world, we also need to take that clarity of Mind out and share it with others. This is not about performing 'good deeds' – these are useful but transient. It is about being in harmony with our Self and our environment.

TAO TE CHING #38

> *A truly good man is not aware of his goodness,*
> *And is therefore good.*
> *A foolish man tries to be good,*
> *And is therefore not good.*
>
> *A truly good man does nothing,*
> *Yet leaves nothing undone.*
> *A foolish man is always doing,*
> *Yet leaves much to be done.* [1]

The Tao Te Ching is not only one of the core texts of Taoism it is also the 4th most translated text in the world. I have two copies of the Giu-Fu Feng, Jane English translation and have carried at least one of them with me for the last 35 years. My Advanced Meditation Classes are based on the Tao Te Ching and we go over a chapter of the book in each session.

Following on from our exploration of Sight, Thought and Speech we can see how Right Action is about drawing from that centred wellspring of calm that we achieve through our meditation. From this place we act in perfect coordination with our world because we are fully part of it and fully attuned to it. The world flows through us and we through it, like each breath nourishes and centres us. A glass might be knocked from a shelf and in an instant we are there catching it, there is no need for thought, just action.

On the other hand when we are not in-tune with our world then we speak and act in a way that is discordant, not only to others but to ourselves. Rather than acting in tune with the moment we instead think about what we should be doing, but the moment to act is past. Feeling like we are not a part of all that is going on around us we then start to try harder, attempting to force a connection that we do not really feel. This makes seeing and thinking clearly even harder and so the cycle feeds itself.

With Right Speech we saw that even just saying we can accept our circumstance, even if we are not fully able to accept them, can start the maturity of wisdom. By accepting our situation, even if only verbally, we can begin to align ourselves with accepting these changes. The same goes for Action, perhaps even more so because words may hurt but it is action guided by Anger, Greed and Ignorance that can cause truly catastrophic problems for ourselves and others.

John Wooden once said:

> *"The true test of a man's character is what he does when no one is watching"*

When we sit on the cushion the first, the VERY first thing we do is start to watch ourselves. At first we do sit alone with our washing machine mind. Initially we only have our innate drive to be more and to understand more to keep us honest. To be fair the majority of people who may see you meditate cannot tell whether you are dreaming on your cushion or honestly watching that breath to not let a single extraneous thought through. With time though, and with honest effort, we realise that even in solitary meditation not only are we not alone but we never have been alone. At all times the earth has been under our feet supporting us, the world around us is full of life, noise and action that validates us and the universe itself passes into, through and out of ourselves with each and every breath.

Likewise we have never acted in isolation. Karma is nothing more than a metaphysical study of cause-and-effect. It is said:

Even the touching of sleeves in the street is due to karma
from former lives

Each selfish act we commit, each time we are motived by the 3 Poisons we affect the world around us. Perhaps not with witnesses, perhaps not directly, but the action lingers. In Buddhism we do not kill, steal, lie, assault or pollute our minds because we are told it is wrong. We avoid these things because we understand that all they can cause is suffering, suffering for ourselves but most often for others. Buddhism, at its core, is the Path that leads to the cessation of suffering. How can we be honest with ourselves on the cushion if we cannot be honest with our fellow human beings?

We can train ourselves to return to this pure mind that is ours from birth. Acting with integrity in our zazen it naturally starts to shape the rest of our actions. Just like the breath counting at first it is forced. We must constantly watch the breath and watch the mind to be sure it is not dreaming or chatting along happily. Yet slowly we start to experience flows of awareness where we are not <u>watching</u> our awareness but actually <u>being</u> our awareness.

The first time this happens it is so exciting, but also fleeting. Recognising that moment of crystal clarity we start to hunt for it, desperately trying to recreate that moment of clear mind. This is not Right Action though and instead of revisiting that clarity we instead force ourselves further away from it again. Like the foolish man in Tao Te Ching #38 the harder we try the deeper our despair. The more we are 'do'-ing the more needs to be done.

Eventually we give up trying & doing and instead submit to that which brought us to this clear place. We humbly return to the susokukan, no longer hunting for that clarity but trusting that it is there and waiting for us to stop flailing around looking for it.

PATIENCE AND TRUST

Patience & Trust come with the understanding that we are playing the long game.

Sitting on the cushion we half-close our eyes because we trust that Right Seeing comes from within. Our eyes are always there, always open and yet for most of our life we have been blind.

We sit in silence because a lifetime of words has left us confused and also confused those around us. Sometimes it can be hard to know if it is lies or truth that we speak and hear. Right Speech is borne out of being silent and centred within so that every word matches the circumstances.

Our time on the cushion is one of complete stillness because this is the Path to Right Action. Instead of being a stranger in our own body it is through the meditation that we fully become that body. No longer a distant distracted mind trapped in an uncoordinated shell we instead allow them to merge so that each movement is an extension of the complete awareness gifted to us through our breath.

THE STUPID SAMURAI

A Samurai was once crossing a river when his sword fell from his belt and into the water. Although initially upset at this loss the Samurai pulled out his dagger and carved a notch in the side of the boat, telling himself that the notch would show him where the sword fell.
Thinking he now knew where it was he continued paddling to the other shore confident he could come back to retrieve it later.

My Master told this story once of a Samurai crossing a river. Samurai were the elite soldiers of Japanese history and a mark of their office was the right to wear 2 swords in their belt. For a Samurai these swords, especially the longer of the two, represented their honour and their life. To be without it or even worse to lose one's sword would be an incredibly tragic event.

The fact that this Samurai was able to lose his sword overboard in the first place might show us something about his state of mind. Sometimes we can get caught up in circumstances, sometimes events conspire to put us in a tragic situation, so let us give him some leeway here. It is when we see him cutting the notch in the side of the boat that we realise he has truly lost his way. What kind of crazy person would do such a thing?

Unfortunately we all do. That Samurai is us. The sword falling in the water is the tragic events we collect through our life time. The notches on the boat are the memories and fears we hold on to due to past events and the efforts we make through the rest of our life to go back to that place and 'make it right'.

Walking from Point A to Point B in a straight line will get me there without fail. But constantly looking backwards to the events that happened long ago is what causes us to step off our straight path without even recognising it. To make it worse we also lug that boat along with us, its weight making each step harder. So there we travel along our straight path, looking back to a river that has long flowed on and carrying a heavy boat which tires us out and slows us down because we want to keep the notches that no longer correspond to our current reality.

STANDING ON A BRIDGE

If we were to stand on a bridge with the water flowing downstream this would perfectly illustrate our life and the urgency of Right Action.

The water flowing downstream is the Past. We can see it but very quickly it is too far away from us to reach. Even though we can still see it, eventually it also fades in to the distance and we have to rely on our memory to tell us what it was like. In time all the water starts to look the same after staring for so long.

On the other hand the water coming towards us, from behind us, is the Future. We cannot see it, we can make assumptions on what and how it might be but even that is a guess. If we are realistic we might recognise that it could hold opportunity, perhaps a fish swimming down towards us. If we are less realistic we might be hoping for pirate treasure to wash down to us and solve all our problems.

Where we stand is the Now. It is that Right Here and Right Now that we use our zazen to come home to. Even if that pirate treasure washed down the river it is useless to us if we are not present enough to grab it as it washes by. The fish is useless to feed our belly with its meat or our soul with its beauty unless we can experience it in that moment that it appears.

Without Right Action we are constantly hoping to experience a future that we will never be able to fully grasp or pining for a past that that is eternally out of our reach. With Right Action we recognise that fish, those gold doubloons are in our grasp because we are in the here and now.

STEP BY STEP

No matter where you seek to go, what you seek to do, it all requires patience and Right Action

To the meditator sitting on our cushion the world spins by like the gears of a clock. Our action is to be the calm centre around which all the movement occurs. We are part of it and yet free of it.

We hear a bird call and it fills our consciousness then is immediately replaced by the next experience - be it our breath, the pain in our knee or wind ruffling our hair. Releasing these too we just keep going.

Each time we meditate we train ourselves to walk in a straight line towards our goal trusting each step to bring us that little bit closer to it.

Discarding the luggage of the past and recognising that the wounds of past hurts no longer serve us each step becomes easier, each breath brings us closer to home.

Every step is a good step.
Every breath is a good breath.
Every day is a good day.

EVERY DAY IS A GOOD DAY

I don't ask you about before the fifteenth of the month, try to say something about after the fifteenth.
[Master] Yunmen himself answered for everyone, Every day is a good day. [2]

If I could time travel and meet any of the great old masters Master Yunmen (~862-949 CE) would be close to the top of the list. Like a laser shining into darkness he illuminates exactly that which needs to be seen and forces us to face that wisdom.

Like Master Sono in Right Speech Yunmen brings us back to the core point here. Our life, your life, is a precious gift of untold rarity. Among all the forms of life in existence you have been fortunate enough to be born in a human body and thus able to take responsibility for your own path. Your circumstances do not matter, your choices and actions do.

If I were to choose to walk to Melbourne from Adelaide it would be around 800km. If I started now and kept walking without deviating then, without fail, I would get there. Each footstep, one after the other, takes me closer. On the other hand each footstep to the left or right takes me further away. One after the other in a straight line towards my goal, each footstep is a good footstep.

When Layman Pang took leave of Yao Mountain, Shan ordered ten Chan travellers (Zen Monks) to escort him to the gate. The Layman pointed to the snow in the air and said, "Good snow -- flake by flake doesn't fall in any other place." At the time one of the Chan travellers named Chuan said, "Where do they fall?" The Layman slapped him once. Chuan said, "Even a layman shouldn't be so coarse." The Layman said, "Though you call yourself a Chan traveller this way, the King of Death still won't let you go." Chuan said, "How about you, Layman?" Again the Layman slapped him and said, "Your eyes see like a blind man, your mouth speaks like a mute." [3]

Layman Pang was an extraordinary fellow. He is highly regarded in Zen (the Chinese Chan in the story above) lore because he was no monk, he was a lay practitioner who scaled the kinds of peaks of understanding that most monks can only dream of. He practiced his Zen as he made and sold kitchen utensils. To put him in modern terms he was like the person who goes to worship weekly, who lives a normal life and yet still manages to penetrate the deepest levels of his faith and inspire those around them with their humble wisdom.

It is important to note that his daughter, Ling Zhou, was also deeply realised. Buddhism like many religions tended to be quite strongly patriarchal as it developed and spread. Initially the thought developed that females could not even realise Enlightenment unless they were fortunate enough to be reborn in a male body. Chinese Buddhists gradually corrected this obvious error and Ling Zhou is a perfect example of why that correction was necessary.

In the story here Layman Pang is being escorted by 10 monks to the gate of the monastery, a huge honour and a sign of the esteem in which the Master of the monastery held Pang's understanding. As is right the Layman seeks to test the monks and points out the snow, challenging the monks to show that they too live in the here and now. One of the monks falls for this bait and pushes back: you talk big Pang so where does it fall? For this effort he gets slapped.

The slap here is not violence, it is not aggressive, it is designed to be a wakeup call. You might experience something like it during your meditation when a bird call or similar sensation shakes your awareness like a hammer hitting a gong. Where does that snow fall? Slap! Right here, right now. Do you feel it?

Unfortunately the monk does not understand this kindness and his words expose him further. Pang attempts once more to shock him into seeing, truly seeing that snow for the very first time in his life but it is in vain. The Layman's words and actions are true, this is the Zen equivalent of staging an intervention for a wayward friend.

How do we react when life slaps us to show us the way? Like Master Sono do we say 'thank you' and open ourselves to something bigger than ourselves. Like Master Yunmen, do we recognise that 'every day is a good day' and put down one foot after the other to make sure we never lose sight of our goal? Perhaps we are like the monk in the story, complaining about how badly he is being treated when he cannot even see what is right in front of his face.

RIGHT LIVING

Through Right Seeing and Right Thinking we have learned to take responsibility for our own experience and understanding of the world around us. Through Right Speech and Right Action we have learned to express ourselves clearly in harmony and clarity with all that we meet. These are immediate concerns and personal responsibilities. Now it is time to evolve these lessons into a way of life, Right Living.

Zen does not believe in judgement, there are no 'sins'. Karma exists to expose the meaning of our actions, but this is not 'punishment' or 'reward' it is just a natural consequence, like an apple falling due to gravity. Morality and ethics exist for those who have lost their way; laws are created for those who cannot understand the basics of living in harmony with our Self and others.

Right Living is the path of maturity where we take responsibility for our own actions.

FRIENDS OF THE WAY

When I first started intensely practicing Buddhism I was living at Bodhgaya in India. It was a truly wonderful place and the foundation of all that followed afterwards. At that time I came across this writing in a copy of the Dhammapada (a collection of the Buddha's sayings) but I have not been able to find a version of it with this quote since so I assume it was part of a commentary on the Dhammapada. Much of Right Living can be summed up in this one statement.

There are three types of people that one should associate with:

- *One who understands more than you and is willing to teach,*
- *One who understands less than you and is willing to learn,*
- *One who understands the same as you and is willing to be a Friend on the Way.*

There are three types of people that one should not associate with:

- *One who understands more than you and is not willing to teach,*
- *One who understands less than you and is not willing to learn,*
- *One who understands the same as you and is not willing to be a Friend on the Way.*

Even without following a Path we grow at a different rate to those around us. We had BFFs in Child Care, then Junior, Middle and Senior school. There are workmates that we spend all our time with and friends we might see every weekend. But responsibilities, circumstance and maturity can shift these deep friendships. Some of us fight to hold on to them, to try and keep them as they were. Some of us are lucky enough to grow at the same rate as our friends. However, even with friendships, we occasionally have to be honest and look at the relationship and ask if we are giving all we can or getting all we need.

This is even more the case when we start to follow the Path of Zen. As we have seen fully half of the Eightfold Path is about internal honesty and effort, it can be hard to achieve this level of honesty if we are around those who do not see the need for spiritual growth. The Monastic system in many ways grew around the idea of it being a safe haven for a meditator to be able to devote themselves 100% to their zazen without having to be distracted by the necessary influences that the rest of the world brings.

More than any other step Right Living is about accepting that, like in the Monk's pocket watch from Chapter 1, we now choose to be the empty space around which everything else can continue on its way. Some of our friends, lovers and family will accept this, some will not.

If we sit meditation daily we will soon recognise that there are many who are not willing to be Friends of the Way. Most people are happy enough to live without the honesty needed to sit and breathe with one's entire heart and soul – and there is nothing wrong with that. Like seeing the rose in the garden we accept this, breathe and move on. There is no right or wrong in this, they choose not to meditate, and that is right for them at this point in time. We choose to sit and meditate, and that is right for us at this point in time.

Likewise most of the people we meet will not understand why we sit. They may even go so far as ridiculing us and trying to convince us that we are wasting our time. Like clouds passing by the mountain peak, we use this as a chance to be sure that our foundation is rock-solid and nothing sticks to us as we let it pass by. We do not sit to force others to change, we sit to take responsibility for our own evolution. We do not practice zazen to convert others to Zen or Buddhism, for their admiration or social media likes. Only we can experience our breath, only we can be honest enough to know if we truly let go of our thoughts or whether we are just posing.

As a Buddhist Monk I have met some outstanding Buddhists of all sects but also met very many non-Buddhists that inspire me. I have read Christian, Hindu, Muslim and Jewish works that have spoken directly to the heart of my zazen and the Taoist Tao Te Ching is never far from my side.

I do not teach you to sit Zen Mediation to become a Buddhist but to show you how to travel the Path to becoming a True Person. Right Living does not just apply to those who follow a particular religion or football team. Right Living is a choice and a consequence of being connected to the deep Truth that lies at the calm centre of every human.

If you can imagine a steep mountain then the very peak of that mountain is Truth. Like any mountain there are many paths we can travel to get to that peak. Some meander, some lead to dead ends or only partially up that peak. The Path of Zen is a steep straight line from the bottom to the top; it can be challenging but each step along that path takes you closer, each breath brings you that little bit nearer.

At the core of Right Living is the understanding that we are now, with our greater awareness, part of a greater whole. Some of that greater whole cannot even see the mountain we climb, though these people usually have the strongest opinions about it. Others are already on the mountain or are looking at it wondering if it is worth the journey.

No mountain excludes a traveller because of their religion, race, sexuality or gender, these are entirely constructs of human delusion. Likewise we can encourage and celebrate anyone who walks with us, even for the briefest of times because we know that the same ground that lifts the mountain at its very peak also supports the rest of the world no matter how distant.

Friends of the Way are of vital importance. In the Rinzai Zen School of Buddhism we sit with eyes half open to not shut out the world. Likewise we always sit facing each other to encourage each other to take that next step. The most and least experienced of us all sit together, each and every day. Guiding and being guided by example.

If you can, sit together with other Friends of the Way and approach your sitting with them as honestly as you do your breath. Zazen is not a competitive sport, it is honest awareness. Encourage your Friends of the Way if they tire. Let them lift you up if you feel you are losing your way but most of all walk with them.

Recognise that not all Friends of the Way are walking the Path. The boss that allows you meditation time in the office. The Partner who does not sit zazen but respects your Sacred Space & time, who supports it and you.

Unfortunately we must likewise be honest enough to recognise when friends, families and partners are not supporting us and are trying to distract us. This is why Right Living comes after the previous steps because without the honesty and strength that comes from observing each and every breath on the cushion it can be very hard indeed to accept that someone we love or care for is not supporting our Path.

Wisdom is a two-edged sword. One side gives life and the other side kills. Honesty is knowing when to give life and when to cut free. We do not hold on to a breath in the hope we can keep it forever; we let it in, experience it fully and let it go. Right Living is applying this to each and every circumstance. Letting go of work when the day is done. Letting go of our concerns and worries when it is time to sleep and even letting go of friends who seek to distract us from our Path.

THE MOUNTAIN

As you cross your legs to sit do not look at the huge mountain that appear to tower over you, nor the ones beyond it that appear to climb even higher.

Recognise that your feet are on firm ground, ground that has always supported you even though you have always taken it for granted.

Look to the True Friends around you.
- Some are ahead, showing you the path is true and urging you on.
- Others are behind you, gaining strength from your steady actions.
- At your side are yet more friends; helping to shoulder your load, giving you encouragement or travelling with you as far as they are able.

The view is stunning on this mountain, the air more crisp, clear and vital than you have ever experienced before or could ever have imagined. There is so much further to go and that too is fine.

Like the clouds that flow past the peak none of this is held on to. All that matters is to give your all and let the rest float away.

BURNING THE BUDDHA STATUE

It was a freezing night in the monastery and there was not enough firewood to boil water let alone warm the monks. The Master was so worried that he took one of the Buddha Statues and placed it in the fire place. The monks were shocked and alarmed, "Master!" they cried, "That is the Buddha, what are you doing?"

Seeing their confusion the Zen Master whipped the statue out of the fire and placed it on the High Seat. Putting on his ceremonial robes he lit incense and bowed to it as though the Buddha himself was about to give a discourse.

The other monks were again alarmed, "Master, have you gone mad with the cold? Why are you treating this statue as though it is a living person about to speak the Dharma?" "Isn't it the real Buddha?" the Master asked of his congregation.

"You silly old fool!" replied the Head Monk, "How can it be the real Buddha when it is made of wood!"

"Ah" the wise Zen Master replied as he whipped it off of the High Seat and threw it back onto the fire, "Then you would have no problem with me burning this piece of wood so we can have some tea."

There are very many versions of this story attributed to a few different Zen Masters but the essence remains the same.

Zen is the most pragmatic of faiths. The incense we burn as we meditate is just incense, nothing more, nothing less. The ash we collect to remind ourselves of efforts made and of how much further we have to go is just ash, nothing holy or special. Our cushion might be hand-made and luxurious but is just a cushion, nothing more. Even our own being, the conduit through which the universe can experience itself is, in the context of human existence, as fleeting as a wave rising and falling in the ocean – individual for the briefest of times but never separate from something far deeper and more vast than it can understand.

We call the Buddha the Buddha because he exemplifies complete awakening. The Buddha is a historical being named Siddhartha Gautama as well as an ideal. Siddhartha Gautama was a person, not a God nor special being, and lived and died just like we all do. Unlike us though Siddhartha Gautama awoke completely to that place we fight hard to find on the cushion. Although just a human he achieved perfect understanding and showed us the way to replicate that. Siddhartha Gautama is the Buddha because this human being sat and opened himself to the Universe, asking the question "who am I?" and "why am I here?" with everything he had until all else dropped away and only the Truth remained. We call him The Buddha out of respect but also to remind ourselves that we too can understand and become one with this Buddha Mind if we truly want to and are willing to make the effort. We place statues of the Buddha not because the person was something divine or special but as a reminder that the Truth is there and to inspire us to make the effort required to experience it.

From the point of view of Zen, from the point of view of Right Living the statue is both a hunk of wood and an item worthy of respect. I picked up my main statue of the Buddha on transit through Bali. It was one of perhaps 20 sitting in the small shop and I was immediately drawn to it. It was cheap and compared to the ones we had in the monastery quite plain but it just felt right to me. I always face it when I meditate at home and make every effort to keep the area clean. For me it is the focus of my meditative life at home. But it is just a statue, a piece of carved wood. If it was stolen my meditation would not change one bit. If I teach a meditation class I do not need to bring it with me before I can sit. It is the centre of my Zen life at home, but it is just a piece of wood.

We often make excuses for not living our life to its fullest potential: "I am too busy", "I don't have enough money" or "It is not the right time just yet". But these are just excuses for not understanding that Right Living does not need circumstances, it just needs us to be awake. My Buddha statue at home does not give me the power to meditate – that comes from my choice. The historical Buddha, Siddhartha Gautama, died but his message was to live, live, live. We surround ourselves with so many things and become conditioned to them being in our lives and being available to us, but if we lost them through war or misfortune could we still find a way to live to the fullest?

The Master in the story respects the statue of the Buddha, but without being alive to experience it the statue itself is meaningless. The Statue reminds him and his students to make every effort to awaken but if all it is doing is propping them up then it would be better off as just a piece of wood. Those of us who follow the spiritual path of Zen Buddhism are not required to give up our possessions to do so but generally this occurs voluntarily. Right Living needs just one thing, that we be fully alive. To be fully alive all we need is total honesty with ourselves.

SIMPLICITY

Do not get hung up on the concept of meditating.
- What we do is nothing special
- Who we are is nothing special.

What is special is that we have this unique life for an unknown period of time and even that will pass.

The act of counting our breath is simplicity incarnate. If you are alive then you hold the key to the universe in this simple act.

The act of honest awareness is a personal choice, one that comes down to simple effort.

When we sit, it is honest awareness that matters more than the fanciest statue of the Buddha or the most expensive hand-made incense.

What matters is that which YOU bring to the cushion and the effort you make. The where, when and how of it are irrelevant.

THE THIEVING MONK

In ancient times Monasteries were huge communities full of many monks and supported by near-by towns. In one of these communities there was a problem as it appeared that one of the monks was a thief!

Eventually the monk was caught and brought to the Zen Master by his Head Monk. The thieving Monk was ashamed to be finally exposed but to the surprise of all the Zen Master let him go.

The next time the monk was caught stealing it was from the town and the local mayor brought him to the Zen Master. Again to everyone's surprise the thief was let go without any punishment.

It was the third time he was caught that the Head Monk had decided something needed to be done. He again took the culprit to the Master and said, "This is the third time this monk has been caught and you have done nothing to make him change, what kind of Zen Master are you? If you don't do something about this monk then I, and my brother monks, will leave."

To this the Master replied, "You know the mind of right and wrong so well, I am sure that wherever you go in the physical world you will be accepted, of course you are free to leave. This poor monk on the other hand cannot understand even the basics. If he leaves here he will sink further and further into his own hell and be beyond salvation. You and the rest of the monks may leave if that is what you wish, but I will stay here with this poor man until he can see for himself why thieving is a poor way to use his life."

Our world is becoming more and more polarised. We are so desperate these days to find people who think, look, or have the same morality as us that we are willing to cast off as enemies any who do not meet our personal high standards. The Internet is a wonderful tool that can bring us knowledge and connection, yet it has been weaponised as a source of constant delusion, distraction and division. Wars, crimes and scandals constantly titillate us and we respond to this by thinking that 'only I have the answers' or feeling under constant stress from a world that seems to be out of control.

Let me tell you one truism.
The only thing that does not change is change itself.

The world is in constant flux. We are in constant flux. Our breath comes in, changes us and is exhaled, changing the world 17000-30000 times a day. Without understanding this what hope have we on the meditation cushion?

Why would we bother sitting and aligning ourselves to our breath if we do not accept that we can change and let go of the deluded washing machine of conflicting thoughts spiralling through our heads? If we can accept that we can change, that Right Living is something we can achieve through our own efforts, then how can we fail to understand that others can achieve this too?

This is what the Zen Master is pointing to in the story of the Thieving Monk. The monk has lost his way to the point that even theft seems normal to him. Zen does not teach moralism because it understands that if we cannot be honest about our actions then we have no hope of being honest on the cushion. However if we can sit and develop that honesty then without fail we will start to experience Right Living.

Putting the monk in jail, kicking them out of the monastery or killing him as some cultures have done will not solve the problem. All these sweep the thief under a rug and say "all gone" whilst leaving a monk-shaped lump under the carpet.

On the other hand the Head Monk, so quick to judge and condemn has exposed through his speech his own lack of understanding. If judgement could cure the world of its problems we would already be living in a glorious Utopia and last I checked it was not the case. Remember that state of being, the Realm of the Asura, where even though we have some wisdom we use this for judgement instead of humility. It is from here that the Head Monk speaks. He is like someone accusing another of being dirty whilst standing knee-deep in the mud themselves.

Mud can nourish as well as despoil and the Master understands this. The thief is not welcome in the world outside of the monastery in this story, and rightfully so, but his life is precious nonetheless and all it would take is an act of will to turn that life around completely. The Head Monk cannot accept this, his mind is of judgement and right and wrong — essential tools to survive in the mundane world but huge impediments on the cushion — his judgement blinds him to the fact that he too needs to be honest about how lost he is.

An act of effort is all it takes to return to, or depart from the Path of Right Living. Because the vast majority of us go our entire life without honesty in our own experience of the universe that flows around us, through us and within us we are constantly pulled, like the Thieving Monk, towards selfish desires. We might even be like the Head Monk; angry at how unfair everyone and everything else is. All it takes is an act of effort though, of strength and determination to say "the buck stops here. Right here, right now. On this cushion, with this breath."

RIGHT EFFORT

Each and everything we do is an opportunity to turn sitting zazen into zazen in motion. Mowing the lawn, driving the car, even talking or tapping away on our keyboard provide us with unique opportunities to live from that deep centre we learn to find so easily on the cushion. Right Living is where we take our own awareness into our day to day life but Right Effort is where we engage with the clutter and noise that is society. Right Effort is about recognising that meditation cushion is not the only place we should remain deep in our centre.

THE PHILOSOPHER AND THE CUP OF TEA

Nan-in, a Japanese Master during the Meiji era (1868–1912), received a university professor who came to talk about Western Philosophy's ideas on Zen.

Nan-in served tea. He poured his visitor's cup full and kept on pouring.

The professor watched the cup overflow until he no longer could restrain himself. "It is overfull. No more will go in!"
"Like this cup," Nan-in said, "you are full of your own opinions and speculations. How can I show you Zen unless you first empty your cup?"

The Meiji Era was a time when Japan finally opened itself up. It was a time of huge upheaval as its isolated feudal system was suddenly exposed to the rest of the world. The birthing pains were long and still linger in places but some Japanese embraced the new and travelled to explore ideas, places and technologies that had been unavailable to them for so long. In this example the university professor had returned to Japan after studying western philosophy. He called in to visit his local temple and speak with the Priest there about his new understandings.

Unfortunately as is often the case to those who have not sat on the meditation cushion it seems we deal in many philosophical topics. These people do not realise that Right Seeing and Right Thought are at the root of Right Speech and Right Action. You will notice that in the noble Eightfold Path there is no 'Right Concepts' or 'Right Philosophy'. Zen is not interested in *ideas* about life but in fully and actually being alive right here and now. This is why we use breath counting as our meditation. No matter what we are dealing with we always return to the simple count. Right Thinking is the Thinking of No Thinking. No philosophy, no concepts, are as vital or as real as the breath you are taking right now.

This is not to say there is no place for concepts. Law, philosophy and ethics are all vital aspects of society. They shape our cultures and enable harmony no matter what level of understanding the individual has but they can quickly lead to distraction. Existentialism or Decartes' "Cogito Ergo Sum" (I think therefore I am) are fascinating lines of enquiry but they quickly turn into 'thinking about thinking'. Like someone pointing out the moon to us, do we look at the moon or do we mistake the finger pointing at it for the moon itself?

Nan-In brought this all into crystalline focus for the visiting professor. With that simple cup of tea spilling over he showed that when we are full of our own ideas we have neither the willingness nor space for any growth.

Right Effort is just this sort of challenge. We take in the breath on the cushion and use it to centre our entire existence in its clarity. As we explore Right Living we then realise that Zen is not just for the cushion but for filling each and every moment with that Truth. Right Effort is the constant checking that our own cup is empty and that there is space for the 'new' to pour in. Each sight and sound is a gift, each experience 'good' or 'bad' is a signpost pointing directly to that truth that was born at the moment we took our very first breath. Every action is a chance to live from the clear pure centre at the very core of our being.

When we first started our susokukan we would count, watching the breath and starting again whenever a stray thought arose. At first we might have felt how easy it all was, breezing our way to '3' or '5'. With a little more experience and effort we came to understand that even at our clearest moments there was an undercurrent of thought bubbling away. Breathing, counting, watching but with a cup we did not realise was still close to full how could we see what we were missing out on? What helps us realise this is Right Effort.

If we sat on the cushion a few times, felt we were clear enough and declared ourselves fully awakened then we would have been lost. It is only through constantly being willing to test ourselves, by being willing to open ourselves more and more that we come to the realisation that this quiet mind we found on the cushion is not really that quiet. It is just not yelling as loudly as we were used to.

If we do not truly believe that we can awaken then we will never really start to see if it is possible. If we do not truly believe that there is more there for us to experience then we quickly become stagnant. If we do not challenge ourselves to go further and understand deeper then we become trapped in concepts. Thoughts about thoughts, a dreamer dreaming.

From the day I entered the monastery my Master used to repeat to me 'Great Efforts bring Great Results'. Even if you sit on the cushion just once before having a social media influencer-worthy enlightenment experience, if that effort is not maintained then it will all be wasted.

GREAT EFFORTS BRING GREAT RESULTS

There is nothing more vital than the breath, it keeps us alive. Through our meditation it can also bring us closer to being fully alive. This tool has been with us since birth and we have mostly wasted it, now we see it for what it really is.

Seeing it is not the same as using it fully.

Great Effort reminds us to continually return to this most simple of practices, susokukan, counting the breath. Each breath fresh and new, each moment of our life fresh and new.

If our body is a vessel then from our core, the hara, each breath fills this cup to the very brim leaving no space for greed, anger or ignorance. Then as the breath releases it empties this vessel completely apart from the count.

Completely full with his moment or completely empty and ready to be filled anew.

CHÖKYI NYIMA RINPOCHE'S GENEROSITY

In Bodhgaya I heard a story from an attendant to Chökyi Nyima Rinpoche (Rinpoche - Tibetan Buddhist Master). The attendant said that during a trip to Rajasthan in Western India he was woken in the middle of the night and decided to check on his Master. There he found the Rinpoche sitting meditation on his bed, not an uncommon occurrence. What was unusual was that instead of his maroon shirt he was wearing something in black. To his amazement upon looking more attentively he noticed it wasn't a shirt, Chökyi Nyima has taken off his shirt and opened up his mosquito net. The teacher was covered in feeding mosquitoes! When the attendant asked about this in the morning he said the Rinpoche could not bear the thought of the mosquitoes suffering when all they needed was food. He had it to give, so why not give it.

I lived for a time in Boddhgaya, India. It is the town where the Buddha achieved his enlightenment under the Bodhi tree. I found it to be one of the most inspiring places I have been in my many years of travel. It was there that I had the chance to meet and learn from teachers of other schools. Through naïve enthusiasm rather than any great design my cup was well and truly empty and the town was full of teachers who could pour wisdom into it. I learned Vipassana (Mindfulness) from the Burmese teacher S.N. Goenka. Chanted and practiced walking meditation with the Dalai Lama underneath the Bodhi Tree. I was taught the basics of zazen by a Japanese Theravada monk who had devoted his life to meditation to atone for his actions in WW2. Just sitting down for a meal in Bodhgaya was a chance to discuss aspects of the Buddha's teachings with followers from a wide range of schools.

For me it was Chökyi Nyima Rinpoche whose teaching made the strongest impression at this time even though I knew my Path was to be Zen. His school, the Tibetan Dzogchen School, like Zen, is focussed on being fully alive through meditation, not analysing the Buddha's words or memorising them but actually living them. Meeting a teacher like this is an immense wakeup call if one is ready. We say that it is not the teacher who finds the student, it is the student who finds the teacher because without some level of understanding, how could we possibly notice a teacher even if they were speaking directly at us.

I do not condone offering oneself as an all-you-can-eat buffet for mosquitoes, especially in India where there are some truly scary mosquito-borne diseases, but like much to do with Buddhism let us look at the Effort rather than the Action.

Do you have the ability to bring a Mosquito back from the dead?
If not what right do you have to kill it?

The mosquito is one of the smallest animals but it is also the most lethal. They kill more humans each year than any creature. On the other hand they are a life giver being one of the most important sources of food for a wide range of creatures. Nothing, not even a mosquito, is inherently 'good' or 'bad'.

If I were to give you a coin and asked you to put money on it landing in a certain way when I flip it then you will quickly feel that the 'good' side is the one that wins you money, the 'bad' side is the one that loses you money. The coin has not changed in the slightest but because of the potential gain or loss what it does next is suddenly very important. 10 minutes ago this coin and what side it rested upon meant less than nothing to us; we did not even know this coin existed. Now it has a 'good' and 'bad' side and personal consequences for us.

Replace the coin with a person and that binary choice can switch to love/hate. A person we have never seen before enters our consciousness and already opinions form – the person themselves has not changed but we have assigned them one side of the coin.

In reality these feelings, these expectations are binary choices. We cannot have 'good' without 'bad', there is no 'love' without 'hate'. Completely remove the existence of one and the other cannot exist either. The fact that they are binary immediately shows us that they are 2nd nen experiences.

Right Effort is to move through the world free of these judgements.

To the Subjective mind everything around us is composed of good or bad. This type of mind is constantly searching for the path of least challenge and most superficial benefit, yet never realising they are fooling themselves with every object, experience and person they encounter. To the Objective mind they are likewise challenged by every object, experience and person they encounter but this challenge is towards more objectivity and more freedom.

Although I would not voluntarily follow Chökyi Nyima Rinpoche's example in the story above we were often faced by similar choices in the monastery. Whether it was summer or deep winter the windows and front doors were kept open. In winter I would regularly end up with chilblains from the cold air and in summer, well, living next to bamboo forests meant an endless supply of mosquitoes and creepy crawlies.

Deep in meditation, as your body and mind start to become one, a mosquito landing on your skin is an amazing experience. Hearing it choose you, then being totally aware of it landing on incredibly sensitive skin. Feeling it move around searching for the place to puncture in search of food. All of these experiences could be horrifying if your centre is not strong. Aligned with Right Effort though we stay on the cushion, experiencing the mosquito fully but not adding 2nd & 3rd nen judgement to it. The mosquito from this state of mind is no more important than the smell of incense or the knee pain; a distraction if we allow it, just another experience if we don't.

As we go out into the world away from the cushion it is likewise Right Effort that keeps this state of mind centred no matter what our circumstance. Mowing the lawn, we are centred. Driving the car, we are centred. Ironing our clothes, talking to strangers or standing in the rain watching a missed bus drive off – these are just experiences, through the lens of Right Effort none of them are inherently 'good' or 'bad' unless we make it so.

THIS ONE THING

No matter what we do, experience or relate to, unless we are completely objective then we are engaging with our own delusion.

To meditate is to at first find and then eventually live from that source of pure honest objectivity.

It is true that this would be easiest if we were to close the doors, lock out distractions and just sit day & night but is this what it means to be human?

Right Effort is not just the strength to continuously return to the breath, our core, but also the determination to maintain this throughout the day.

Right Effort is the determination to challenge ourselves to be more with our understanding, not to squirrel it away.

Right Effort is what encourages us to try new things; painting, dance or speaking perhaps, being born anew through the freedom to express and experience.

Right Effort allows us to wholeheartedly throw ourselves into our family, friendships and even work because these too are expressions of our true state of mind.

BUDDHA'S POISON ARROW

It's just as if a man were wounded with an arrow thickly smeared with poison. His friends & companions, kinsmen & relatives would provide him with a surgeon, and the man would say, 'I won't have this arrow removed until I know whether the man who wounded me was a noble warrior, a priest, a merchant, or a worker. 'He would say, 'I won't have this arrow removed until I know the given name & clan name of the man who wounded me... until I know whether he was tall, medium, or short... until I know whether he was dark, ruddy-brown, or golden-coloured... until I know his home village, town, or city... until I know whether the bow with which I was wounded was a long bow or a crossbow... until I know whether the bowstring with which I was wounded was fibre, bamboo threads, sinew, hemp, or bark... until I know whether the shaft with which I was wounded was wild or cultivated... until I know whether the feathers of the shaft with which I was wounded were those of a vulture, a stork, a hawk, a peacock, or another bird... until I know whether the shaft with which I was wounded was bound with the sinew of an ox, a water buffalo, a langur, or a monkey.' He would say, 'I won't have this arrow removed until I know whether the shaft with which I was wounded was that of a common arrow, a curved arrow, a barbed, a calf-toothed, or an oleander arrow.' The man would die and those things would still remain unknown to him. [1]

The ability of the Historical Buddha to cut through the noise and strike right at the heart of the matter is inspiring even to this day. From over 2500 years ago this still resonates with clarity.

Who would be crazy enough to look for insignificant details when what is clearly needed is immediate life-saving intervention? Struck by an arrow would we really want to sit there and ask these questions? We have the doctor standing right by our side, every tool she needs to fix us is available to her but instead we ask her to wait: "Doctor, before you treat me I have a few questions about this so-called arrow first".

Every single nen, every thought or action wasted on hypotheticals is your own life energy wasted; a moment of time gone, never to return.

Zen is awareness and awareness springs from the deep centre that flows through the least and greatest of us; this returns us to the story of the rain falling over the forest nourishing each plant equally. The only difference is that some of us live with awareness and some of us are ignorant to its existence. Some of us make an effort to accept the nourishment that comes to us in each and every nen and make the most of it. Others let those nen slip by, never to be experienced again, as though they were to live forever.

Right Effort brings us back to the cushion each and every day, it allows us to make excuses as to why we should put aside time each and every day for our sitting, gives us motivation to 'just sit for another 5 minutes' instead of pretending we are far too busy and important. Right Effort is the doorway through which we realise that washing the dishes or the car, vacuuming the carpet or sitting on the bus are all spaces that we can make sacred through our breath counting.

Meditation shows us a way to live our life with full awareness. Without Right Effort all we are doing is putting a band aid over the arrow that has pierced us and pretending it is cured.

RIGHT MINDFULNESS

Continuing on from Right Effort, which seeks to make the whole world our meditation cushion, we start to turn inwards again as we understand that it is our responsibility how we feel and our responsibility how we act. How we interpret the world and react to it is an indication of our own state of Mind.

TAO TE CHING #42

The Tao begot one.
One begot two.
Two begot three.
And three begot the ten thousand things. [1]

All the way through this book we have constantly talked about the mind; we watch the mind for random thoughts, we allow the mind to experience the world fully etc. However this brings us to an essential paradox:

Who is it watching the mind?

We quite happily sit on the cushion watching ourselves chatter away with ourselves. Through our meditation we have learned that this is just noise, thoughts trying to justify their existence by creating more thoughts. But what is the source of these thoughts?

The Tao, from the quote above, can be seen as the natural way of the universe. This is the concept around which Taoism was born. Taoism is the practice of harmony with self, others and the universe. It is a powerful practice and the source of many spiritual techniques like Tai Chi and Qigong.

Even the meditation we practice in Zen is heavily influenced by Taoism. Zen itself is deeply rooted in Taoist spiritual practices.

This natural way of the universe, this Tao, is what gives rise to us. The 'me' which is able to hear a bird's call or feel pain when stubbing our toe. However it gives rise to us in the same way that the ocean gives rise to a wave or the sky gives rise to a breeze. From a certain point of view, yes, we are an individual, there is no other like us, just as no two waves or winds are the same. Yet no matter how high we rise as a wave we always return to the source, because we were never apart from it. As strong as this breeze, or even tornado, might be never once do we ever leave the sky that 'birthed' us. The Tao is not conscious, just as the ocean or sky is not conscious, it is a flow of energy and life energy.

The Tao begot one refers to that wave rising above the sea, individual and yet an integral part of its source.

Let us return to the concept of nen.
- The first nen is the immediate raw experience experienced by any of the senses.
- The second nen is where we name or assign a meaning to this experience: 'tree', 'dog bark', 'pain'
- The third nen is the associations we make because of this

These nen correspond to the next parts of the stanza.

The One (us) is able to recognise that there are things seemingly separate to us (not-us). This separation might be as obvious as a mountain compared to a dog or as subtle as waking up in a bad mood but not sure why. This is "One begot two". It is a moment of pure awareness, the first nen, where we notice we are not just swimming in a planet and atmospheric sized soup of atoms but are actually influenced by a horde of stimuli outside our control.

"Two begot three" is that second nen act of naming and giving life to these external stimuli. Being 'one with all things' is not so useful if we are unable to recognise a car driving towards us is not only separate but also a potential threat. A huge part of a baby's first years is made up of this stage as the initial shock of separation which happens not too long after birth gets turned into something useful. Parents provide comfort and food, hitting one's head brings pain etc. These are all second nen, they are pure lessons in navigating external interactions in a way that brings the most benefit.

Through the personal nature of these lessons we come to "three begot the ten thousand things". In Eastern thought "the ten thousand things' is a way of saying 'everything', not just material things but all emotions, experiences and delusions. It is through the act of differentiation that we come to recognise that some of the things we experience can help us, harm us or do not affect us. However this is where that washing machine mind starts to be born too as we actively try to hunt down the things we like, avoid the things we dislike, and allow our awareness to ignore those things we decide are irrelevant.

From essentially nothing, all our personal thoughts, feelings and prejudices are born and when we die all of those personal thoughts, feelings and prejudices immediately cease to be. The universe continues as the wave returns to the ocean. The ten thousand things we clung to so dearly leave no trace, not even a ripple.

The awareness that is born with us is able to experience this great Tao, this natural way of the universe but only through discarding ten thousand things and experiencing the world free of distraction and personal distortion. An analogy for this might be viewing the moon by walking upon it as opposed to viewing it with the naked eye from earth. Getting as close as we can to the nature of reality nothing can stop us from experiencing it in its entirety.

Existence gives rise to the recognition that there are things that act independently of us. The act of naming, categorising and reacting to them also causes us to create something to interact with them, this is the conditioned mind. This is that mask we use to watch ourselves meditate and live through. Most of us add even more layers on top of this, as T.S. Eliot put it:

To prepare a face to meet the faces that you meet [2]

It is no more real than calling a cloud the moon because it happens to obscure our view for the moment.

THE TRUE PERSON

The founder of our school Zen Master Rinzai (Linji Yixuan) once said:

> *Here in this lump of red flesh there is a True Man of no rank. Constantly he goes in and out of the gates of your face. If there are any of you who do not know this for a fact, then look! Look!* [2]

Does the meditation you are to sit today have the courage to strip away the layers and find that True Person?

Right Mindfulness is the reward that comes from this courage. It is when we notice that we are not living through Right Mindfulness that we know it is time to return to this cushion and time to return to the basics.

If we are watching ourselves doing something then we know we have lost our way because there is no 'other you' to watch.

Any time we are not experiencing directly, acting directly or even analysing/thinking directly then we know we are divorced from that source.

THE PAPER FOLDING MONK

When I was new to Sogenji monastery one rarely had the chance to spend time with the Roshi except for formal meetings in the Sanzen Room. However, one day, as we were approaching the New Year, a few of us were roped in to join the Master and the Head Monk in folding 'Protection Papers'. These were gifted to families who supported our monastery & training as a way of offering our blessings for their health, happiness and prosperity over the next year.

As I was folding these papers in silence and with as much concentration as I could muster (I was under the eyes of the Zen Master after all) the Roshi turned to the Head Monk and said something in Japanese, he also mentioned my name. The Head Monk replied and all went silent again. I was quite confused by this... I could not yet understand much Japanese and I wondered what they were talking about. My mind was all over the place as I tried to work out what I might have done to attract the Master's attention. After only a short while the Master again spoke, and again mentioned my name... then he, the Head Monk and the others who could understand Japanese cracked up in laughter.

The Head Monk translated for the Roshi who explained that the first time he spoke was to say how rare it was to see such beautifully folded papers in such an immature monk. He said that he was impressed with my concentration and dedication to such a simple task. The second time he spoke was to point out that since I had heard my name mentioned all that concentration had left... my mind was so fixed on attempting to understand what had been said that I had neglected my task.

*The Roshi held up the papers I had folded first, they were
perfect. Then he held up the papers I had folded later, they
were so poorly done that they had to be thrown away.
Ever since that day I have tried to be as Mindful of the task
at hand as possible and it is something which has served me
well as a Monk, in business and as a human being.*

Losing our way can happen at any time. Even waking up in the morning we can sometimes just wake up feeling 'off' and distracted. Our responsibility to ourselves and others is to recognise that and bring our mind back to its source.

We go through every day with a healthy body and never think twice about it. Then one day we wake up with a flu or worse and we feel like we have been hit by a truck. Days perhaps weeks pass and every day we are painfully aware of how sick we are but through this time we slowly notice that things are on the improve. Eventually we wake up and go through our day, perhaps once or twice remembering how sick we were and marvelling at how much better we feel, but otherwise back to normal. Others may point out how much better we look now that we are well.

When we live through Right Mindfulness then we do not notice that we are in tune with the world, we just are. Like that sick person, it is only when we lose our way that we start to notice 'our self', the rest of the time we are living in the moment.

If a healthy person starts paying too much attention to their healthy body then they can quickly find things 'wrong' with it. A pain they had never noticed before or lumps that suddenly seem significant. This is why Right Mindfulness cannot be forced. As soon as we are looking for something then we have set it up as something we are not - it is separate to us.

This is why zazen does not ask you to sit on the cushion and search for some True Person. Even if we knew what we were looking for how can a True Person find a True Person? Zazen asks us to focus our entire being on our breath and the counting because the act of doing this clears away the façades and constructs. Susokukan reveals to us the delusion bubbling away even in our sub-conscious mind. Instead of using the wrong True Person to somehow find the right True Person it clears the rest away so that the True Person can just be.

In the monastery, especially in the first few years, we are always doing some task, perhaps some of the endless cleaning that makes up a monastic's life! When sweeping the floor or dusting a table the Roshi would appear next to us; "CUT!" he would say and then walk off. There was no explanation, no one practices at a Zen monastery if they need explanations, just "Cut!"
Days might go by when suddenly he would reappear: "Cut!"
Day in day out: cut, cut, cut!

The kindness the Roshi was doing was to remind us to cut away those extraneous thoughts. Were we really sweeping the floor with our whole being or was some day-dreaming involved too? Cut! Cut away anything extra to that which is right in front of you.

It should be noted that this is not at all the same as repressing or denying what we are experiencing or feeling. We cut away the thoughts and attachments to what we are experiencing, but not the actual feelings or perceptions themselves.

Even to this day I rely on this technique. Like Pavlov's Dog we are training ourselves to respond instinctively. The breath count or even the simple act of stating 'cut' immediately brings me home and causes anything unnecessary to be let go of. This is Right Mindfulness.

CUT!

CUT!

Cut it all away

The future is a dream – CUT
The past is gone - CUT
Your thoughts about the moment - CUT

Anger and strong emotions rise - CUT - let them go and re-join the moment with clarity.

Desires push and pull you - CUT - Any fleeting pleasure or escape will pass in no time, there is nothing to grab on to here.

Do you think you understand? - CUT - What is there to understand? How can a human mind comprehend the forces in the centre of a black hole or the reality of quantum physics let alone the Buddha Mind or Tao.

Cut it all away and in time, with honest effort, even the breath counting itself will be cut away by pure open awareness.

HEAD SHAVING

When a Zen monk shaves their head it is called Teihatsu.
Teihatsu happens on any day with a 4 in it (4ᵗʰ, 14ᵗʰ & 24ᵗʰ
of the month) or a 9 (9ᵗʰ, 19ᵗʰ & 29ᵗʰ of the month).

The number 4 in Japanese is written 四 and pronounced
'shi'. However, shi can also mean 'death' if written as 死.
The number 9 in Japanese is written 九 and pronounced
'ku'. However, ku can also mean 'suffering' if written as 苦.

When we shave our head on any day with a 4 in it we
remember that we will die.
When we shave our head on a day with 9 in it we remember
that life is suffering.

There is no shame in using day-to-day activities to attain Right Mindfulness. We sit in the same place, at the same time, because it allows us to know when we are going astray. Saying we will sit meditation for 30 minutes a day and then getting to bedtime with the realisation that we have still not put that time aside for ourselves is an easy trap to fall in to. The thinking mind, which has been calling the shots for most of our lives will do anything to keep in control. Filling our day with mental junk it leaves us no space left. Instead of sitting for that 30 minutes we promise ourselves we will do it tomorrow and jump into bed, sleep escaping us as the thoughts continue to swirl around.

Even 30 years after first entering Buddhist monastic practice I use Teihatsu as a reminder.
- I was born, I will die – am I using my time to the fullest?
- Every day is a good day – Suffering or no suffering, just being alive is a gift of infinite value and I might not be this lucky tomorrow.

Right Mindfulness is born of the willingness to start each day fresh and new. Once this is achieved then each hour starts to becoming fresh and new, then each minute, each breath. Work or family commitments stop becoming an excuse to be less and instead become a pathway to becoming so much more because we recognise that these too are moments of infinite value.

RIGHT CONCENTRATION

Having sat through this book together we have come to see the world in a different way and come to realise that meditation is not another hobby or way to fill time. Zazen is the solid core around which we can build our whole life. How do we maintain it? What gives us the strength to return to the cushion day after day, year after year?

CARRYING A BOWL OF OIL

A King once commanded a criminal to face trial by ordeal. He was handed a small terracotta bowl with the oil filled to the brim, directly behind him stood the King's executioner with his razor sharp sword. The prisoner's task was to carry this bowl of oil from the King's throne down the palace steps and across the bustling market. Should he spill even a single drop then he would be executed on the spot.

It is said that the samurai of ancient Japan would ensure that each day they wore clean clothing just in case this was the day they died. Mentally they prepared themselves for this day to be their last. Theirs was the Way of the Warrior, their whole purpose in life was to fight and if necessary to die for their Lord and their personal honour.

What is it that motivates and drives you? Do you have this same passion? Can you say that you want to live with the same honest integrity of a Samurai's willingness to die?

In reality we are all like the condemned man in the story above, each day we wake up carrying this precious bowl that contains our life and every day there is the razor sharp sword waiting a hair's width behind our neck.

Is today the day your only life comes to an end? How would you use this time if you knew it was your last?

To call the Monks, Nuns and lay-people to meditation at Sogenji the *han* is sounded. The han is a wooden board that is struck with a solid wooden mallet. It has a discordant sound that resonates throughout the monastery and across the neighbourhood. On the han is written:

Time flies like an arrow.
The One Great Matter of Life and Death waits for no one.
If you have not seen it, see it now, see it now!

It is so easy to be waylaid on this essential journey, to find paths that distract us, delight us or offer us a sense of safety from our fears. But ever since birth we have been on a single road and that is the road that leads from Birth to Death. In this time we have available to us, do we just want to just 'get by'?

Having worked in the health sector for many years I was constantly amazed by the amount of healthy people I see who lived each day as though they have 1000 years more guaranteed to them. On the other hand there would be those with chronic or even terminal conditions who lived each and every day to the fullest, squeezing every second of life they can from what time they have left. As my wife & children would be able to tell you, there is nothing that makes me grumpier than having to waste time. Time is precious, time is vital, time is life!

What is Right Concentration? It is the realisation that we have something unique here and that it is not worth wasting for a moment.

If I gave you a gold bar worth $10000 would you just leave it lying around? As a monk I regularly see people put more attention into their car or a video game than they do into their own life.

This is not to say that the only place we can ever be alive is on the cushion. Think back to the chapter on why we sit zazen. The aim of Rinzai Zen is be fully aware and alive in all that we do, not just to hoard it or maintain it only on the cushion.

> *Someone asked a Zen Master, "How do you practice Zen?"*
> *The master said, "When you are hungry, eat; when you are tired, sleep."*
> *"Isn't that what everyone does anyway?"*
> *The master replied, "No, No. Most people entertain a thousand desires when they eat and scheme over a thousand plans when they sleep."* [1]

It is not the WHAT we are doing that is sending us astray, it is the HOW. We have breathed every couple of seconds since we were born and yet for the majority of that time we have only breathed ourselves further away from the Source. In our weeks of meditation with this book we have seen that these same breaths can bring us closer to it instead, it just depends on how we use them. It is the same act from the same source with only the intensity and purpose with which we breathe making the difference.

Right Concentration allows us to spend time with our loved ones with full awareness instead of just filling in the time. Right Concentration allows even our work to be the conduit to a deeper awareness rather than a sacrifice of time in the pursuit of money. Right Concentration allows us to sleep deeply at night with a clear mind because we are not living in the past or mulling over the future.

RIGHT CONCENTRATION

For this sit let nothing else in.

For the next 20 minutes of your life, sit as though this is it... this is the end of all things and if you cannot see the Truth of your existence now then you never will.

Each breath is your last.

Each distraction is nothing but an attempt to have your entire life's energy wasted for nothing.

ITTEKISUI'S ONE DROP

Giboku had been at Sogenji for only a short time when it became his turn to make the bath for the Roshi (Gisan Zenrai). The bathwater was a little too hot, so he brought buckets of water from the well and cooled the bath down. When it was sufficiently cool he set down the last bucket, in which a few drops of unused water remained. Then, before going to bring more water, he dumped those last few drops out onto the ground. Since he was going to get more water, he probably thought those last few drops weren't necessary.

Gisan Zenrai Zenji saw that and said to him, "What did you just do?"
"I went to draw some water."
"Before you drew the water, what did you do?"
"I threw away some old water,"

The Roshi answered simply. "If you do training with a mind like that, no matter how much training you do or how long you train, you will not awaken. That bit of remaining water, if you dump it out there--how can it be used? If you take it outside and put it on some plants, then the plants will be given life, and the water will also be given life. If you give it to the cucumbers in the garden, the cucumbers will be helped and the water will be satisfied too!" [2]

After being admonished by his master for wasting the water Giboku secluded himself and devoted himself to his meditation with intense purpose leading to an enlightenment experience. In one of the rooms at Sogenji is a dedication paper marking the spot where this occurred.

Upon his awakening Giboku took the name 'Tekisui' which means One Drop (of Water).

Just before his death, Tekisui Giboku Zenji said:
The one drop of water of Sogen,
For seventy-four years
It was used, never exhausted,
Throughout the heavens and the earth.

One drop of water to sustain a whole life. Some would say it is impossible. I think it depends on your point of view.

I grew up in Adelaide where, ever since I was a child, we were told that we lived in the driest State on the driest continent. From childhood I was already aware of how much life required of water and rarely wasted it. My experience in Tekisui's Sogenji only honed my awareness. When I came to live in New South Wales I lived with a people who rarely lacked water, they had so much of the stuff! We were still on the driest continent but there appeared to be no lack here. However when water restrictions came in due to an extended drought I was able to adapt quickly, whilst many of those around me struggled to understand why they should or how they could make the most of the limited supply they were allowed.

To one stranded in the desert each drop of water is life itself. Each drop is carefully used to make it last as long as possible, nothing is wasted. Does your zazen nourish your life like this?

THE OCEAN

We cannot deny that there is something larger than us, something which is 'total' and from which we all derive our awareness and consciousness. I like to imagine it as being like the ocean.

The ocean is made up of a countless number of water molecules, each of them individual and perfect in and of themselves. The ocean cannot exist without being manifest through this infinite number of water molecules. The water molecules are given 'meaning' through their being part of the ocean as opposed to just drifting alone and pointlessly through the ether. This meaning might express itself (through the interaction of ocean and wind) as a wave. The wave rises and falls, just as we are born and die, but it is never separate to or alienated from the ocean. It is 'born from' the ocean, 'exists' as it travels along the ocean and then 'dies' back into the ocean – it was never separate during this entire time. The wave has the appearance of moving but actually the individual water molecules have essentially stayed in their place their whole time. So it is with our own existence.

- We have the feeling that we are moving. That is just our mind moving.
- We have the feeling that we exist separately. That is just like a water molecule experiencing the other water molecules around it and not the entirety of the ocean.
- We think we are born, live and die. This is just karma (the wind) animating us to a higher energy (the wave) for a limited length of time. It is not a permanent phenomenon, nor does it take into account the true depth of the ocean as our wave skims across the very surface.
- We search for the source of our existence never realising that at all times it is eternally there because it cannot possibly be anywhere or anything else.

There is no final sit. Although this book ends here the sitting and the Truth which gives us life in each and every moment does not.

Right Concentration leads us directly back to Right Seeing just as the Noble Eightfold Path brings us to Right Concentration.

You were born from the truth that is the Buddha Mind.
Your life is a precious gift beyond comprehension.
Each breath is the Path leading home.
Every day is a good day.

BIBILIOGRAPHY

A Personal Journey
1. The Buddha's Farewell, https://sacred-texts.com/bud/btg/btg94.htm, accessed 4/03/2024
2. Zen Marrow, Treasury of the Eye of True Teaching #150, https://zenmarrow.com/single?id=150&index=sho, accessed 28/12/2023

Right Thinking
1. Price, A., Wong, M-L., 1990. The Diamond Sutra & The Sutra of Hui-Neng. Shambhala Dragon Editions, pp76
2. Kato, B., Tamura, Y., Miyasaka, K., 1997. "The Parable of the Herbs", The Sutra of the lotus Flower of the Wonderful Law. Kosei Publishing Co, pp126

Right Speech
1. Takuan S, translated by W. S. Wilson, The Unfettered Mind, Kodansha International, pp62
2. Sasson V., Where Do Buddhas Go After they Die? A Lesson on How to Waste One's Time, https://www.buddhistdoor.net/features/where-do-buddhas-go-after-they-die-a-lesson-on-how-to-waste-ones-time/, accessed 21/11/2023
3. Japanese Zen, THANK YOU FOR EVERYTHING. I HAVE NO COMPLAINTS WHATSOEVER!, https://japanesezen.net/appreciation-arigatou/, accessed 21/11/2023

Right Action
1. F. Gia-Fu, J. English, 1989, Tao Te Ching, Vintage Books, pp 40
2. Cleary T., Cleary J. C., Blue Cliff Record, Shambala, pp 37
3. Cleary T., Cleary J. C., Blue Cliff Record, Shambala, pp 253

Right Effort
1. The Shorter Exhortation to Māluṅkya Cūḷa Māluṅkyovāda Sutta (MN 63)

Right Mindfulness
1. F. Gia-Fu, J. English, 1989, Tao Te Ching, Vintage Books, pp 42
2. B. Watson, 1993, The Zen Teachings of Master Lin-Chi, Shambala Dragon Editions, pp13.
3. T.S. Eliot, 1988, Selected Poems, Faber and Faber Ltd., pp 12.

Right Concentration
1. Tibetan Buddhist Encyclopaedia, Buddhist Story: Eat When You're Hungry, http://tibetanbuddhistencyclopedia.com/en/index.php/Buddhist_Story:_Eat_When_You're_Hungry, Accessed: 21/11/ 2023
2. Shodo Harada Roshi, Sogen's One Drop of Water, https://usercontent.flodesk.com/256506d1-cdd7-4f93-912f-1cdf5dd80f9d/upload/fb62c291-8f06-45fd-8774-81cf9582e32e.pdf, accessed 21/11/2023

ABOUT THE AUTHOR

The Venerable Daiju Zenji (Simon Rowe) is an Australian-born Japanese Monastically-trained ordained monk of the Rinzai Zen Buddhist lineage. He has practiced and taught meditation in Buddhist monasteries and communities in India, Japan, the USA and Europe. For the last 20 years Ven. Daiju has been based in Sydney, Australia.

Whilst he has had the opportunity to learn from teachers of many different schools of Buddhism, including the Dalai Lama, it was not until he found his way to Japan that he met his true teacher. Under the Reverend Shodo Harada Roshi, he experienced many years of continual training in the harshest of conditions and it was this Master and this Teaching which continues to guide his choices in life now.

For more information on Daiju or to look at opportunities for Meditation workshops and public speaking engagements (including at schools for Religious Study purposes) please visit www.daiju.com.au

Printed in Great Britain
by Amazon

57647400R00079

Full of Life

Discover the path to success
in your life, career and business

To Carol:

Enjoy your Journey!
The best is yet to come

Hans

Hans Horlings & Ashirvad Lobo

Use this book as your guide towards living a full and fulfilling life

"Fulfilling"
Feeling satisfied or happy because of fully developing one's abilities or character."

"Synonyms"
Satisfied, Content, Happy, Pleased, Gratified, Comfortable, Serene, Placid, Untroubled, at Ease, Accomplished, Matured, Realised, Joyous, at Peace.

"Life is a Journey"

*"The biggest adventure you can take
is to live the life of your dreams."*

~Oprah Winfrey

Table Of Contents

Prologue

People are unique, yet their stories are all the same. We all go through many ups and downs, and experience both happy and unhappy times. This book is the start of a new and exciting personal journey to get more out of life. The stories and exercises in this book will make you aware of who you are, what you want to do, and how to live the life of your dreams.

Let's start by telling you who we are and why we created a system to help you find your path and start living the life of your dreams.

HANS HORLINGS

I was not motivated to study and got through my teenage years without a real focus to the point of being considered 'difficult' in class. I moved through quite a few different primary and high schools being bored and disinterested until I started a technical study. I finally completed an internship as a mechanical engineer and began working full-time. I was shocked, treated as cheap labour, and given unpleasant hard physical work. I almost believed the people around me when they told me I was not university material.

My environment wanted me to keep working, get married and have children. I decided to go against the tide, got out of my comfort zone and created my path.

Three years later, I graduated with a business degree. Fifteen years later, literally on the other side of the world, I completed my Masters.

I lived and worked in the Netherlands, the USA, New Zealand, and the Middle East. I changed jobs many times and eventually found the job of my dreams: public speaking, training and facilitating. It took a while, and some strange turns to go from engineer, software developer, business owner, manager and teacher to corporate trainer and facilitator, but I got there.

I enjoyed most of my jobs, but I love my current job so much that I do not want to retire from it, even though I could. I love what I do, not because of the recognition I get, the colleagues I have or what participants say. Doing my job makes me happy from the inside out. I genuinely love my work, and this makes me fulfilled. This feeling of internally driven satisfaction is what I wish for everyone to discover.

It has not always been this way. I made many mistakes, lost a lot of money, and experienced sadness when bad things happened to me. As a student, intern, young manager, senior manager, university lecturer, business owner, consultant, executive coach, management trainer and speaker, I touched and influenced the lives of many individuals. Such as a royal family member, chief executive officers, general managers, middle managers, supervisors, team leaders, and university graduates. I found that people all seem to struggle with the same fundamental question: "How to become happy and successful?"

Few people realise that understanding who you are, why you exist, and ultimately doing what you love drives effectiveness, success and fulfilment in life.

Someone who realises how this works is my co-author Ashirvad Lobo whom I met at a conference in Dubai a long time ago. His presence, confidence and drive were contagious. We stayed in touch, and embarked on an adventure of co-authoring this book. We share a passion for helping people understand what they can do to discover their path to fulfilment and success.

ASHIRVAD LOBO

My background and path are very different from Hans. I am 33 while he is 59, I am Asian while he is European, I am quite ambitious and disciplined, while Hans is now much more relaxed. My dad, who is a retired journalist, inspired me to dream about travelling the world and writing articles to inform, inspire and move people.

My dream took a different turn when I took a summer job at a Call Center in Mumbai. The new industry provided a well-paid and exciting lifestyle with many young people and a fun environment. The entire first month involved induction training. The charisma of the trainer inspired me to become a corporate trainer and impact the lives of thousands of people.

Ten years later, I had trained across many industries and travelled extensively within India and to the United States, China, Greece and Sri-Lanka. The wide variety of cultures I interacted with and my love for travelling, inspired me to leave Mumbai. I moved to Dubai to use my coaching, facilitation, and HR competence in a multi-cultural environment. I am now living my dream, having travelled to over 16 countries for various work assignments. Two years ago, I went through 165 hours of Innermost Shift Coaching from Alphastars Academy. I did this to get my Professional Certified Coach (PCC) qualification from the International Coaching Federation (ICF). This training and the recently completed MBA from Quantic inspired me to write a book.

During our time together in Dubai, Hans and I bonded over a common aim - to impact individuals and organisations all around the world by helping them become aware of their path to fulfilment and success. We realised that while we have already touched and influenced the lives of over 25,000 people as corporate trainers, through this book, accompanying workbook and an online course we can help many more. To us, "Full of Life" means doing something meaningful, something you love to do. It involves a never-ending adventure of personal development and having a positive impact on the people and the world around you.

FINDING YOUR PATH

Becoming "Full of Life" is a journey and not a destination. It is a way of living or as the French would say - "Joie de Vivre" (zhwädə-ˈvēvrə) – the joy of living, the delight of being alive. Even the richest, most successful people continue to desire and seek out "Joie de Vivre" - pure enjoyment of life and all that it has to offer.

It means acknowledging your life's ups and downs and appreciating all the small things which often go unnoticed. It also means being grateful for everything you have, instead of wanting the next best thing. It means making choices which bring you joy and allow your soul to expand. Allowing yourself to explore, discover and experience new things and meet new people. Embracing all of life, knowing why you exist and creating a better world. It is all about the passion behind your human existence.

When you begin to acquire that "Joie de Vivre" feeling, you start to truly feel good about your life, feeling full of life and being positive about life in general.

FEELING TRAPPED AT A DEAD-END

It sounds wonderful you might say, and you want "Joie de Vivre". But the reality might be quite different when you have a very demanding job or a business that keeps you busy six days a week. You might struggle to pay your loans and feel trapped in a dead-end day job without much free time. Your first reaction might be Joie the what? Seriously!?

Feeling good about yourself and finding that "Joie de Vivre" is possible for everyone, it is a personal choice and has nothing to do with your situation or anyone else. Most people don't know what drives them because they tend to live a life from the outside-in, driven by external situations and demands rather than living a life from the inside-out.

Attainment of "Joie de Vivre" is not dependent upon your socio-economic status. It is all about your awareness, attitude and perception of life. It is about understanding your purpose, getting comfortable with it and working towards it, taking the first steps on your journey.

first

love what you do

then

do what you love

to get the most out of life

What Do You Want?

A 45 metre tall marble Buddha sits on one of the highest peaks in Phuket, visible from most places in the south of the island. Arriving at the top, you have an amazing 360-degree view of Phuket. Amongst this beauty and serenity, I observed tourists being invited to write a wish on a small metal leaf, which is hung by the entrance of the temple. Intrigued, I started glancing at the many years of wishes made by people from around the world. I spend an hour reading their heartfelt desires; it was like a wishing well or shooting stars with personal messages attached.

Health and Happiness worded in different ways were by far the most common wishes. Only a few wished for a promotion, a new car, a big house or success in business. *Fame or fortune was missing. It could be because of the spiritual context of those who visited a Buddha temple, but looking around, I was surrounded by tourists like myself!*

It is clear that most people see health and happiness as a priority – When we ask participants in our workshops: "What are you looking for in life?" - the most common answers are "Health, Happiness and Success" – but what does that mean?

HEALTH, HAPPINESS AND SUCCESS

This book introduces a step by step process to make you feel good about yourself and what you do. We wrote it to counter the current negativity around us. Too many people feel miserable, unhappy, neutral and empty inside, even when others see them as "successful". This book will show you how to recognise, savour and enjoy the small things and the great times we all have. It will also explain how to deal with life's struggles and challenges.

The book will provide you with all the tools to start living from the inside-out. The tools will help you to understand who you are, what you want and what actions to take. When these actions become habits, they ensure that you start living a life full of purpose, making the most of new opportunities.

How to use this book

This book consists of an introduction and four parts. It is supplemented by a workbook and other web-based material that you can access at fulloflifebooks.com. The introduction explains what we mean by "Full of Life", it gives an overview of the key steps to living a full, successful and satisfying life.

Part 1: "Reboot Yourself" will help you to start the process with a positive mind. It also explains the difference between being happy or positive and being "Full of Life". A positive mindset is an excellent launchpad for beginning your "Full of Life" journey. However, the primary focus of this book is to help you discover your personal path to a fulfilled life.

This is done in Part 2, 3 and 4 by exploring three key questions:

1. **Who are you?**
2. **What do you want?**
3. **How do you get there?**

The book concludes by revealing the "Full of Life" model. It will help you assess your level of fulfilment in life and understand how to bridge the gaps. A bonus chapter looks at the application of "Full of Life" at work and what it could mean for managers and organisations.

After each part, you will find summary questions and suggested actions to check your understanding and build your awareness. We recommend you spend some time to reflect and write down new insights in the workbook and apply the learning. Do this before continuing with the next part. This way, the book will become a journey of personal discovery and transformation.

On the fulloflifebooks.com site, you will find support material like assessments, exercises and learning options to make the book come alive. You can also join the "Full of Life" community on LinkedIn and Facebook to meet and learn from like-minded individuals and be inspired by their success.

Just reading is not enough,
only actions will help you start living
a full and fulfilling life.

READER BEWARE!

A final disclaimer, this book can be dangerous. Success might be different than what you expect. Awareness about who you are, what you want and actions on how to get there, might change you and your life in unexpected ways!

Our Promise:
To Guide You Towards Living
A Full And Fulfilling Life.

Introducing
"Full of Life"

"The tragedy of a life that is never fully lived is not simply the loss of that one life. The tragedy is the endless number of lives that would have been forever changed if we had chosen to live differently."

~Erwin Raphael McManus

WHAT IS A FULL LIFE?

"Enjoy the little things in life, for one day you may look back and realise they were the big things." ~Robert Breault

We would like your permission to challenge you, as you begin this journey with us. Are you ready to review your current situation and make appropriate changes? How happy are you with what you do today? Do you work mainly for the weekend or your annual holiday-break? According to a 142-country study on the state of the global workplace, only 13% of employees worldwide are engaged at work (Gallup 2015). That means 87% of employees worldwide are either neutral or not engaged. Based on our own experience and such research reports, we feel that most people see work as a form of punishment. Why do so many approach work so negatively?

How do you approach your work and life? Are there some areas where you would like to feel more fulfilled? Then you have picked the right book. This book will provoke you to evaluate your current mindset. The stories and exercises in this book will make you more aware of your current mindset towards work, your business and life. This awareness will start to transform you into a healthier and happier person.

Next, you will be asked to define your path, by understanding and describing your personality, your preferences, your purpose and your favourite activities.

Finally, you will start to recognise new opportunities and take positive actions towards living a life with purpose and meaning. Your commitment and belief will deliver a powerful presence which will get you noticed and on the path to success – as you define it.

We truly believe that each person has unlimited potential and just needs to find out how to access it. So we wrote this book based on the coaching principles that we live and follow. Instead of telling you what to do, the book will take you on a journey of self-discovery to unlock your potential. Awareness is a key aspect of becoming "Full of Life". Awareness about who you are, what you want and what actions you need to take to set you on your path towards your chosen future.

A Self-Awareness Journey

A happy go lucky 39-year-old university lecturer moved from New Zealand to the Middle East. He had the opportunity to inspire young lives and develop future leaders. The university was filled with impressionable students and delivered a varied curriculum. For the first four years of his new teaching career, his life was on autopilot like most other colleagues. He just did his job, day in - day out, semester in - semester out, year in - year out – delivering the same classes and dealing with the same student issues.

Lunch, and coffee breaks were spent with a small group of colleagues. Harold was the life of this group, slowly sucking life away with his complaints! Harold complained about everything – the weather, the cafeteria food, the management, the students, the facilities, the lack of organisation and, the decision making. The entire group joined in as usual and became master complainers. Complaining was fun!

They lived for the weekends, the holidays and dreamed about getting out of the rat race – retirement! A lot of time was spent discussing how many contracts they still had to do and counting the days. Their daily sessions always ended with the phrase: "just keep counting", counting the number of days and the money in the bank at the end of the month.

This teacher was me! I think it was an illness in the family which made me re-evaluate my life. I realised that while complaining can be good, it was making me negative about work. I suddenly became aware of how much this useless negativity affected me. So, I quit the common coffee breaks and started to actively look for things to keep myself interested and bring variety in my work. I took on new tasks, started teaching new subjects, volunteered for the development of new programs, organised student trips and student conferences, supported work-placement initiatives, assisted with career counselling, delivered commercial training and introduced initiatives like "Toastmasters".

My colleagues thought I was mad and gave me the

nickname "Initiative Hans".

Yes, my life was much busier than my "Coaster" colleagues. Many of my former colleagues might still be sitting there, doing the same thing every day. For me, life was much more satisfying, more enjoyable, and more interesting than coasting and moaning. I met many new people, had great new experiences and enjoyed my job. It became my longest ever employer-job experience; I managed to do this for eight years and quit to start an exciting new venture – sailing with a mix of able and special needs students on a large dhow delivering life-changing experiences.

Now almost 15 years later, I still have students from that time reaching out and telling me how I positively impacted their lives, which still makes me feel proud.

Self-awareness helped me to reinvent my life. I had to go against the generally accepted norms and make my own choices. It started with small changes, learning new things and accepting new challenges like becoming a Personality Dimension accredited facilitator.

It made me aware that doing something for others is fulfilling, that busy days are better and more satisfying than coasting and moaning. Learning new things keeps me interested and taking the initiative to do something I believe in, makes me live a much more satisfying life.

DREAMS, HOPES AND CURRENT REALITY

How self-aware are you about your current level of fulfilment? What was the level of self-awareness when you began your career or business?

The dream at the start of your career, profession or business and the reality you experience today is often quite different. You might still be doing the job you first got after your studies and feel sort of ok with it. Or maybe you switched jobs and let go of your dream because things just happened differently than you expected.

This book will help you re-energise, re-visit and re-create your dream. The purpose of this book is to coach, mentor and help you re-focus and re-invent your life.

This book is a self-discovery book. It will help you find your path, use your knowledge and experience to chart a course towards your dreams and ambitions. This book will enable you to recognise your talents and energies to enjoy your life, appreciate who you are and become successful according to your definition.

In this book we introduce the concept of self-engagement at work, in business and life. This new approach will help individuals to use their talents and live a full and satisfied life. In turn this should lead to "Full of Life" teams and organisations with employees and leaders who are self-engaged. We have been training, coaching and mentoring people on self-engagement during our combined experience of over

40 years. We will share stories of self-engaged people who we have come across. We hope that these stories will encourage you to share your experience on our LinkedIn and Facebook communities.

We begin with two stories that have strongly impacted our lives and taught us the meaning of "Full of Life" living.

Angela's Journey

Angela is a single mum; she is a tough professional engineer working in a male-dominated environment. She has raised her 21-year-old daughter by herself.

Her daughter Victoria attended an anniversary with her college friends. The happy occasion quickly turned and became their worst nightmare on the way back home. A drunk driver hit their small car. The drunk driver survived without a scratch but took the life of one of the boys in the car and left Victoria with many broken bones, brain damage and long partial recovery of more than two years.

Angela struggled with the mental and emotional pain of seeing her daughter fight for her life. As a friend of Angela, it made me want to do something, so I started coaching both mother and daughter.

It is easy to become extremely negative, bitter and blame the drunk driver, the government, the world and God for everything that happened.

Now five years later Angela is living in a different apartment, has a new job, got a scholarship to go back to university, and study for a masters in her passion, "sustainable development". Her daughter finished college, has a job which she enjoys and as a family, they are closer than ever before, they both are happy, working hard at making their dreams come true.

Lina's Path

Lina, born to a farmer in rural India, is the youngest among nine siblings. A daily 5-mile barefoot walk to school was challenging, yet she kept on studying. With a bachelors in education and a masters in Hindi language, she became a professor in a small city with a big dream to inspire and positively impact lives.

She had an arranged marriage with an aspiring journalist – Sylvester and moved with him to Mumbai. Their humble beginnings had her sharing an apartment and sleeping in the kitchen. Life caught up, and through great personal sacrifice, they purchased a small home in which their first son was born – Ashirvad.

Success seemed to continue their way as they moved into a larger home, in which their second son was born - Amit. As the kids grew, the family had an amazing fellowship and saw a lot of success. Abruptly life almost came to an end fifteen years ago when Lina was diagnosed with breast cancer. Challenging *chemo and radiation therapies took their toll on Lina. She suffered from bone problems, diabetes, needed heart surgery and was on constant medication.*

Today at the age of 63, she enjoys life more than ever and sees every day as a gift. She is extremely active, visiting the poor, the sick and needy. She is a leader in the local church community. The focus in her life continues to be 'making a difference in her community, her family and to herself.'

THE PATH TO A FULL AND FULFILLING LIFE

Angela and Lina went through traumatic experiences which made them rethink and change. What makes people who go through such an experience re-invent their lives? What makes it harder for people who have a good life to find meaning, purpose and satisfaction? Why do we need to get to a position where we have nothing to lose, in order to finally change our life?

As we go along, we will tell you more about what Angela and Lina did to change and rewire their brains. It will show you how powerful our mind is. Just read on, and you will come to know and believe us when we say – "If they can do it, you can do it too!"

STEPS ON THE PATH TO LIVING A FULL LIFE

People who are "Full of Life", do this in a million different ways and at any age. We all have different needs, likes and dislikes, priorities, circumstances, personalities and goals. We are all unique, so it is no surprise that our paths are also unique.

Therefore, there is no one size fits all recipe to be "Full of Life". You need to create your unique path. Look at people who are successful in creating an extraordinary life, who can find enjoyment in what they do, every day. What do these people have in common?

Through our life experience, we see that such people are generally positive. They believe in being able to make a difference, and they are passionate about what they do. They are a "good fit" for their passion and continually develop new skills and new interests. They are curious, dedicated and somehow, understand what to do to get there. They just know and naturally follow a simple process. During our research and work as trainers with individuals from over a thousand organisations, we created a process that we are confident will get you on the path to living a full life.

THE FOLLOWING STEPS ARE INVOLVED IN THIS PROCESS:

Move towards – "love what you do"

1. Reboot Yourself
The first step is to start each day in a positive frame of mind. You can develop habits that will help you to "love what you do". This part also explains the difference between being happy and being fulfilled. It will move you towards loving what you do.

Move towards – "do what you love"

2. **Understand Who You Are**

   Once you are positive and "love what you do"
   then it's time to begin your journey to "do what
   you love". You start by truly understanding
   yourself. Reflect on your likes and dislikes, your
   talents, behaviour, and personality. Discover
   your values and core beliefs to boost your self-
   esteem and be proud of who you are.

3. **Understand What You Want**

   The next step is to understand what you want to
   do and who you want to do it for. Reflect on your
   purpose and passion to find out what makes you
   feel good and drives you. List your values and
   live by them each day.

4. **Understand How You Get There**

   Finally build courage, commitment, reduce fear
   and start your transformational journey. Choose
   a planning method and develop an action plan to
   move in the right direction. Understand the Full
   of Life model and diagnose what is missing in
   your life. Build good habits, break bad ones and
   implement the change to transform your life.

Follow this process to live the life of your dreams at any
stage of life. You will make a difference for your
customers and colleagues, and positively impact the
world around you. You will leave a legacy, share your
story and help others to live the life of their dreams.
You only have one life and limited time, enjoy it and live
life to the fullest. Take action and begin your
transformation.

INTRODUCTION: ACTION ITEMS / SUMMARY QUESTIONS

Visit fulloflifebooks.com to download your Full of Life Workbook. Write down the answers to the below questions in the workbook.

a. What is your definition of living a full and fulfilling life? If there was one wish you could make, what would you change or what would you wish for yourself?

b. "Joie De Vivre" is French for .... What do the French mean by that, and how do they practise this? What is your view about this way of living?

c. Describe the key steps to living a fulfilled life. Which one of these will be the key to success for you? Which one will be hardest for you to take?

- PART 1 -
Reboot Yourself

"Change your thoughts, and
you change your world".

~Norman Vincent Peale

HAPPINESS AND FULFILMENT

Happiness is a mindset. It is about adopting a more positive frame of mind in all your actions. To achieve this is a relatively straightforward process. It is about focusing on the positives to generate a feeling of happiness. It requires effort each day to sustain this positive mindset.

Fulfilment is a much deeper level of feeling good about yourself. When you "Do what you love" you are continuously appraising three key questions. The first one is about understanding who you are, your identity. It includes understanding your internal strengths, talents, interests, capabilities, likes, dislikes, beliefs, values and limitations. So it takes time to reflect who you are and increase your self-awareness.

The second question involves using your identity to understand what you want, your purpose. It includes understanding your ambition, passion and calling. Just knowing what you want and why you want it, is still not enough.

The final question is about using your identity and your purpose to define how you get there, your mission. It includes building the courage and commitment to begin your transformational journey. Selecting and implementing an effective action plan will move you towards your goal.

Reflecting on these questions is a continuous process. As we develop, achieve and transform, we start living a more fulfilled life. The difference between being positive and fulfilled is clear. To discover the path to success in your life, career and business and overcome any obstacles, you require a positive mindset.

REBOOT YOURSELF – KICK-START YOUR JOURNEY

Rebooting yourself is the first step in getting ready for the transformation journey. This step is important if you feel negative about your work or life. Rebooting involves becoming aware of how a negative mindset affects you. It suggests new strategies and quick wins to become more positive and happier. During our workshops and training programs, we find this to be a critical step for most people. Evaluating your current mindset, and making small adjustments, creates positivity and helps you deal with a rapidly changing world.

THE WORLD HAS CHANGED

"Our economy is based upon people wanting more; their happiness on wanting less." ~Frank A. Clark

Internet and smartphones have led to a digital society that is disrupting our lives. We have information at our fingertips, know everything instantly, problems at home, rumours at work, and drama from anywhere in the world. Repeated access to negative news and events impacts our mindset. Being fully informed often results in subconsciously feeling anxious and negative. A negative mindset just does not work for us.

The first thing we learn when technology does not work is to reboot - turn it off and back on. Similarly, it is time to reboot your mind and fill it with positivity. A reboot will transform your level of satisfaction in everything you do. It gives you an opportunity to see and do things differently.

As authors, we will provoke you to think about all the influences that affect your mind. We use short stories and coaching questions to help you reflect and make changes.

TECHNOLOGY AND LIFESTYLE

Rita's Nomophobia

After many years of marriage, Rita was born to her parents. As the only child, she was pampered and given all her hearts desires. Rita asked for a cellphone at a very young age, and as had been the tradition in the family, her request was granted. At the time her parents could not have imagined that granting this request would send their daughter to rehab.

It all began with social media and gaming. Her parents noticed that Rita was on her phone even at the dinner table. When confronted, she came up with myriad excuses. Things escalated one weekend when she was grounded for being on her phone during a family get together. Rita started sweating, her body was trembling and she felt dizzy. An ambulance was called, and she was rushed into the emergency ward.

Rita was sedated, and the tests run on her all came out negative. As she woke up the next day, she asked *for her phone. Upon receiving it, she seemed to be feeling fine and was discharged that evening. Few more repeat incidents led her parents to realise that at the age of 16, their daughter had Nomophobia. Nomophobia is the irrational fear of being without your mobile phone or being unable to use your phone.*

She spent months at an Adolescent Treatment Center and thanks to her perseverance and treatment she is now fine.

Reflect on this story and think about your own lifestyle.

- How often do you use your phone and other technology?
- How much uninterrupted time do you have with friends and family, without technology present?
- How much control do you have over the use of your phone and technology?
- How would better control of technology positively impact your mindset?
- What guidelines could you set and live by for the use of technology?

MARKETING AND ADVERTISING

What Do You Value And Why?

John watches Tim, his 6-year-old nephew with a big smile, playing with an old cycle-tire and a stick. A classic toy for kids living in villages around the world. John is back in his home-town on vacation from his 9 to 5 job as an accountant in a big city. John starts laughing and pointing at Tim, who immediately stops playing and walks slowly away from John. John calls out to him and asks him "why are you playing with junk?" Tim chirpily replies "This is my speed-wagon!"

John lovingly explains to Tim that he should focus on studying and not waste his time playing with junk. If he studies, he can go to a good college like his uncle John. He can then move to a big city and work for a big company. He would have a good salary, buy a nice house and buy his kids real and expensive toys like this 'Action-Figure'.

He hands out an expensive Action Figure to Tim and explains that he can now be happy playing with a real toy rather than with junk.

"When we buy what we want, we are temporarily happy because, for a brief period, we actually stopped wanting, and thus experience peace and happiness" ~Adyashanty

Reflect on this story and think about what you value.

- What impact do marketing and advertising have on what you want?
- What was your last big purchase? Was it a shared experience (dinner, holiday) or personal item?
- How did it make you feel and for how long? What did you really want from this purchase? What do you value?

- How does awareness of what you value help you when making your next big purchase?
- What will you do to balance the impact of marketing and advertising with what you value in life?

THOUGHTS AND FEELINGS

Velcro And Teflon

Two people from the same family, Velcro and Teflon had to deal with the covid19 pandemic. Velcro was watching the news 24 hours a day and talked to his friends about what might happen and how terrible the situation was. He heard and shared a lot of horror stories about people all around the world, and the impact of the virus on their lives. He was afraid of losing his job and did not sleep well. He found himself going to the supermarket buying vast quantities of toilet paper, just in case. He saw the shelves going empty and people getting angry. This virus was threatening his life, surely the end of the world was near.

Teflon was equally affected by the pandemic. He stayed updated with the latest information to ensure he was safe. To overcome his fear, he talked with his friends and shared jokes related to the virus. He had virtual meetings online and worked from home. He exercised at home doing yoga and volunteered to help those who could not look after themselves. He planned to start a new online business related to his line of work. Life would change and never be the same after this.

Velcro saw that Teflon was not affected and was concerned for his safety. He approached him with data, great stories and rumours. Teflon was hooked by Velcro's arguments and quickly changed his behaviour.

Negative thoughts are like Velcro in our brains. We tend to dwell on them, they stick, and we find it hard to let go. The opposite happens to happy and positive thoughts. Happy thoughts slip away, it is like they are like coated in Teflon. They do not stick in our brain, and before we know, we focus again on the negative.

Dalai Lama Wisdom

The Dalai Lama is the exiled religious leader of the people of Tibet. Tibet was invaded in 1950 by the Chinese. Since then Tibetans are systematically discriminated against and mistreated. After a peaceful protest in 2008, Tibetan monks were violently beaten, many were injured, and some gave their lives for an independent Tibet.

The Dalai Lama responded by getting more media attention, visiting world leaders and trying to influence them to stop the occupation.

When the Dalai Lama speaks, he seems so kind and in

control. A journalist asked him once: "How can you be so kind and controlled while knowing that your people are being killed?"

His response was amazing: "It is not that I am not saddened by what happens to my people, I just choose not to entertain these thoughts and let them rule my life, I treat them as shooting stars – let them go as quickly as possible, so they do not poison my brain." His response is an excellent example of controlling your mindset. After all, it is your choice what thoughts to entertain!

Reflect on these stories and think about your thoughts

- What thoughts (positive or negative) occupy your mind on a typical day?
- What emotions/feelings do negative thoughts trigger?
- What emotions/feelings do positive thoughts trigger?
- How does this affect your mood, your day and your life?
- What can you do to stay in control of your thoughts?

EXTERNAL ENVIRONMENT

A Day At Work

Olivia started work a few months ago. She was full of enthusiasm because her job would positively impact the retail sales staff by improving their knowledge and skills. Unfortunately, once she started working, she found that the company culture focused on individual performance and internal competition.

Olivia still managed to get people together, despite her line manager and the business unit manager. She set up team meetings to assist staff in the sales and service of high quality and expensive items. Team training was actively frowned upon by some of the managers – salespeople should sell instead of having meetings.

To cope with the negative atmosphere, Olivia introduced a simple technique. In her head, she gave each manager a cartoon character name: Big Bad Wolf, Scrooge McDuck, Gyro Gearloose, Dewey, Huey and Louie they were all there.

Seeing people as cartoon characters, she often just smiled. She just stopped reacting to outbursts from the managers.

Reflect on this story and think about your environment

- On a scale from 1-10, how do you rate your current environment? What makes this you give this rating?
- How does this impact your thinking or your mindset?
- What would you like it to be?

- How can you remain positive in your environment?
- How would this positively affect your environment?

ASSUMPTIONS – HARD WORK

Karoshi

Takehiro enjoyed his childhood. Life was good, living close to the sea. With great parents and an amazing brother, he had a great time. After university, he joined a large company in Japan.

He had to get used to the company culture, frequently working long hours. The company is always on his mind, even when he goes out to have fun with colleagues. To get the results and make his sales targets, Takehiro usually works until 11:30 pm and starts the day at 8:00 am. No time for romance and relationship, his life is all about work and recovery during the weekend.

Today is Wednesday night, he misses family, misses the sea and decides to call his mum. After a few minutes, he starts crying, and the last words his mum heard were: "I am so tired – I cannot think, I cannot feel my body, I just want it to stop."

Takehiro was found dead the next day collapsed on his desk, the 4th death by working too hard for this company.

The Fisherman And The Businessman

There was once a businessman who was sitting by the beach in a small Brazilian village. As he sat, he saw a fisherman rowing a small boat towards the shore having caught quite a few big fish. The businessman was impressed and asked the fisherman, "How long does it take you to catch so many fish?" The fisherman replied, "Oh, just a short while."

"Then why don't you stay longer at sea and catch even more?" The businessman was astonished. "This is enough to feed my whole family," the fisherman said.

The businessman then asked, "So, what do you do for the rest of the day?" The fisherman replied, "Well, I usually wake up early in the morning, go out to sea and catch a few fish, then go back and play with my kids. In the afternoon, I take a nap with my wife, and when the evening comes, I join my buddies for a drink, we play the guitar, sing and dance throughout the night."

The businessman suggested the following to the fisherman. "I have a PhD in business management. I could help you to become a more successful person. From now on, you should spend more time at sea and try to catch as many fish as possible. When you have saved enough money, you could buy a bigger boat and catch even more fish. Soon you will be able to afford more boats, set up your own company, a production plant for canned food and own a distribution network.

By then, you can move out of this village and to Sao Paulo, where you can set up your HQ to manage other branches."

The fisherman continues, "And after that?"

The businessman laughs heartily, "After that, you can live like a king in your own house, and when the time is right, you can go public and float your shares on the Stock Exchange, and you will be rich."

The fisherman asks, "And after that?"

"After that, you can retire, you can move to a beautiful house by the sea, wake up early in the morning, catch a few fish, then return home, have a nice afternoon nap with your wife, and when evening comes, you can join your buddies for a drink, play the guitar, sing and dance throughout the night!"

The fisherman was puzzled, "Isn't that what I am doing now?"

Reflect on these stories and think about your assumptions regarding hard work.

- When do you push yourself and work hard? How does this make you feel?
- Are you giving up happiness now for happiness later?
- What other areas of your life are affected due to your hard work?

- What would be your ideal activity and ideal work-life balance?
- What can you do to be happier now?

ASSUMPTIONS – COMPETITION

My First Race

Do you know the very first race you lost? I still remember the first time I lost a race – it was ice skating in the Netherlands, I was probably 6 or 7 years old.

Ice skating races are a part of school sports. I was full of good intentions, dressed for the occasion, skates on and ready to race — a short sprint, like 100 meters at the most, 6 of us starting at the same time.

The start was ok and filled with excitement, as I got to the half-way line my novice legs lost balance, and I fell and lost big time.

I vividly remember that I cried not because of the pain of falling but the pain of losing. After that experience, I hated skating and competitions in general.

Although people say I am quite competitive, I don't enjoy competition, to me, it is a sure way of ensuring someone is getting hurt.

Peter's Dream

Peter is eighteen and in his last year of high school. He is ready for the final week of exams. Today is a tough one, the math exam; he takes the bus to school. When he arrives at the bus stop, the bus door closes in front of him; the bus leaves without him. His friends in the back of the bus are laughing.

Peter panics, really worried he will be too late for the exam. Feeling anxious, he starts running after the bus and somehow makes it on time. His friends see him coming – totally drenched in sweat.

When he sees everyone with their bag, he suddenly realises he forgot his. No calculator, no ruler, no pen and pencil - he panics once again. Even worse, when talking to one of his friends, he discovers that he forgot to study a main part of the exam topic, arghhhhh why is this happening?

He walks into the exam room, knowing he will fail, and then suddenly he wakes up.

It is more than 20 years ago that Peter passed his last exam, he graduated and had a great career, but these nightmares about exam stress are still bugging him, traumatised by the stress they created.

Reflect on these stories and think about your assumptions regarding competition and stress.

- How often do you compare yourself with others? What effect does that have on your mindset?
- When do you compete and who do you compete with? How does this make you feel?
- How important is winning for you? How do you deal with the stress of failure?
- What would be your ideal competitive environment?
- What can you do now to feel more positive about competition?

ASSUMPTIONS - MONEY

Are You A Member Of The Club?

A well-known businessman lived a luxurious lifestyle. However, he was not satisfied. He saw his servants working and singing happily. He was jealous, why was he, a very wealthy businessman unhappy and gloomy, while his servants had so much fun. He asked them "Why are you so happy?" The servant replied, "Sir, I am a simple servant, my family and I don't require much – just a roof over our heads and warm food to fill our tummies."

The man was not satisfied with that reply, and later in the day, he sought the advice of his most trusted business advisor. After hearing his woes and the servant's story, the advisor said, "I believe that the servant is not part of the 99 Club." "The 99 Club? What exactly is that?" the man inquired.

The advisor replied, "To find out, you just need to place a bag with 99 gold coins at the servant's doorstep." The businessman was so curious that he decided to do it. When the servant saw a bag lying at the door one morning, he took it into his house. He opened the bag and let out a great shout of joy. "So many gold coins!"

He began to count them. After several counts, he was shocked that there were only 99 coins. He wondered, "What could've happened to that last gold coin? Surely, no one would leave just 99 coins!" He looked everywhere he could, got his wife and son to count as well, but that final coin was elusive. Finally, exhausted, he decided that he was going to work harder than ever, to earn the last gold coin and complete his collection.

From that day, his life changed. He became overworked, grumpy, tried to save as much as he could, and blamed his family for spending too much and not helping him make that 100th gold coin. He worried about the 99 coins and just wanted to save enough to get the final coin. He stopped singing while he worked, and often spent time recounting the coins.

Witnessing this transformation, the businessman, became even more curious. He summoned his advisor, who explained that the behaviour change was due to the servant joining the 99 Club. He explained, "Some people have enough to be happy but are never satisfied because they always want more and strive for that one extra coin. They keep delaying their happiness and say to themselves: "when I have this or that, I will be happy for life."

The moral of the story: We can be happy with what we have, but the minute we see something bigger and better, we reduce our happiness by wanting even more!

My Investment

At one time in my life, after selling our house, we paid the mortgage off and had money left over. I bought shares to invest the money. As a responsible investor, I checked the share market every day, which completely changed my mindset. When the market was up, I had a good day, and when it was down, I had a bad day.

I understood then that having money can also cause a lot of stress and pressure. It is very easy to become unhappy and depressed when losing money - even if you have enough money to live comfortably.

I feel that people who can be satisfied with what they have, who can be grateful, spend time with family and friends, who can be positive and smile each day – have it all.

"Happiness Is Not Having What You Want But Wanting What You Have" ~Rabbi Hyman Schachtel

Reflect on these stories and think about your assumptions regarding money.

- How worried are you about having more money? How much money and stuff is enough?
- How do your assumptions about money drive your daily actions? How does that impact your happiness?
- Define what would be the ideal situation about money and stuff in your life?
- What is your plan to stop worrying about always wanting more?
- What actions will you take to be happy and satisfied with what you have and still achieve your goals?

MINDSET – MAKING THE RIGHT CHOICE

Angela's Choice

Challenged by her daughter's accident and all the resulting events, Angela could choose between two mindsets: positive or negative.

Angela can choose to be bitter, unhappy and blame the stupid drunk driver who caused the accident. She can question why it had to happen to her daughter. Blame others for her financial problems, and blame herself for not looking after her daughter. She can blame the justice system for letting people get away with murder. She can feel sad that her daughter won't be able to graduate with her friends and be bitter that her daughter might never be the same bright, smart lady with promising career prospects. It is natural to become bitter, find sadness and embrace a negative mindset in such a challenging situation.

Alternatively, Angela can choose to be happy that her daughter is alive and be thankful that they can share this experience which brought the family closer together. She can be grateful for a supportive boss who allows her time off to see her daughter in the hospital. She can be happy that many people visited her daughter and care about her. She can be positive that doctors have the technology to fix severe problems. In short, she can choose a positive mindset even in a terrible situation.

Mohammed's Mindset

Mohammed is a hard-working supervisor at a manufacturing plant. Today his boss comes to him and asks him to do some overtime to get an urgent order out the door. Mohammed has a choice – he can think one of two ways.

Option 1: Mohammed thinks the boss is picking on him; why does the boss always take it out on him; it is just not fair. He always gets more work than the others, why does he have to do everything? Is it because he has a different skin colour or does the boss feel threatened because he is currently doing his MBA?

As a result of his thoughts Mohammed feels picked on, he feels treated unfairly, just because the boss hates him. As a result of his feelings, he is very negative towards his work. He frequently takes shortcuts and actively tries to sabotage the quality of the products sold, that will teach his boss!

Option 2: *Mohammed thinks that his boss trusts him to do a great job. He thinks he was selected because of his skill and efficiency. The boss knows he can use some extra pay, to fund his MBA expense. He feels good about being always the first one to be selected.*

As a result, he takes great pride in his work and makes sure he does it to the highest possible standard. He does not want to let the customer or his boss down!

Your life is defined 10% by what happens to you and 90% by how you chose to react.

Reflect on these stories and think about the choices you make.

- Describe a bad experience in your life or work. Did you choose a positive or negative mindset in this situation?
- How did this mindset affect your feelings and your actions?
- In the future, what positive thoughts will you choose when going through a bad experience?
- What actions can you take to choose a positive alternative? Can you learn from bad experiences?

- What habits can you adopt to ensure you will make the right choice?

YOUR HAPPINESS HABITS

It is natural to be positive. No one comes into this world with a negative mindset. Negativity is something we learn. You can be happy, healthy and deliver extraordinary results. It all starts with your mindset, assumptions and choices.

Making small changes can lead to significant differences when repeated often. When we consciously focus on creating positive choices, our mindset and our actions will change. Turning these small changes into habits will transform you. Let us look at a few proven habits that will move you to "Love what you do".

"Positive thinking changes the way we behave. When I am positive, it not only makes me better, but it also makes those around me better." ~Harvey Mackay

HABIT 1: PRACTICE GRATITUDE

Everyone can practice gratitude, people who have everything and people who have virtually nothing. Gratitude is a thankful appreciation for what you receive, whether tangible or intangible. With gratitude, you acknowledge the goodness in your life. Gratitude often helps people to connect to something larger than themselves as individuals, whether to other people, nature, or a higher power. It is more than feeling thankful: it is a deep appreciation for someone or something that produces long-lasting positivity.

Everyone can develop more gratefulness. You can be grateful for being a son or daughter, for being a father or mother, for having beautiful children or grandchildren, for being alive, for being able to see, for having a job, for being able to work. We all can be grateful for a million things.

The best way to build a gratitude habit is to start a gratitude journal. Simply write down in a notebook the things you are grateful for – and try to pick new things every day. Just write it down – one page each day, explain what you are thankful for and what that means to you. It only takes minutes and will make a big difference to your mindset. Oprah Winfrey did this for more than ten years, every day!

"Gratitude can transform any situation. It alters your vibration, moving you from negative energy to positive. It's the quickest, easiest most powerful way to effect change in your life — this I know for sure."
~Oprah Winfrey

Read the story below to understand the impact of being grateful.

Be Grateful!

At the age of 64, Lina attended the wedding of her niece in her hometown. This event was a long-awaited wedding in the large family and had 50 of her close and direct relatives attending. The highlight for Lina was travelling, spending time with, and even dressing up in the same attire as her two older sisters who are aged 68 and 72 years. The trio was gleaming with joy all through the 6-day Grand Indian Wedding.

Early the next morning, Lina wrote in her gratitude journal. She was in tears as she read an entry from 15 years ago when she was diagnosed with cancer. Her tears were of joy as she felt truly grateful for being alive and with her family.

Lina still takes a lot of medication to stay healthy. Her diet is restricted, and travelling is tough. Her attitude of gratitude and the habit of a daily journal keeps her positive all the time.

HABIT 2: BE PROACTIVE

This habit may sound like a cliché, but it's the most common training need in organisations. Being pro-active is about taking responsibility for your actions. Even in bad situations, pro-active people are able to respond ("response-able"). This means you focus on the things you can control. Reactive people, on the other hand, often blame their environment for their behaviour.

The best way to build the habit of proactivity is to be action-focused. Actively participate, be aware of your environment and stay focused on what you can do. Do things that solve the issue rather than just talk about it. Show initiative, use action language like 'I can', 'I do', 'I will'. Hop in the driver's seat instead of being a passenger. Recognize that you can't control the things that happen to you, but you can control your response in every situation.

"Happiness, like unhappiness, is a proactive choice."
~Stephen R. Covey

Read the story below to understand the impact of being proactive.

Be Proactive!

It was spring season in Perth Australia when the 17-year-old Melissa Fokkema woke up, feeling "weird" and "numb". She woke up her mother, and both noticed purple-brown bruises all over Mel's legs. Mel rushed to the hospital, diagnosed with meningococcal disease. Her treatment was a drug-induced coma. Doctors were unsure if she would ever wake up again.

In time Mel awoke from the coma, the disease had ravaged her body. Mel had to have her hands and legs amputated. Many operations, including skin grafts, followed. Grateful for being alive, Mel was determined to build a normal life. Physiotherapists and occupational therapists worked with Mel to strengthen her body. She spent about nine months in the hospital before moving back home.

Mel left the hospital with prosthetic legs, a hook-like hand replacement for one arm, and a muscle-activated arm for the other. In time Mel learnt how to do many things with her new arms, including cook, type, apply make-up, work a digital camera and play the keyboard. In 2007 Mel got a special driver's license, and a car modified to her needs. Mel uses her prosthetic hands to work the car's hand controls.

Mel said during an interview: "Pretty much everything has changed, it's a whole new way of living, a different way of doing things. I had to accept that things would be difficult for the rest of my life. That was the hardest thing to adjust to because you're not going to get a break from it. It's a constant everyday struggle."

With all the huge changes, challenges and difficulties Mel faced, she is now inspiring others. By being proactive, she recovered from her illness, studied at university and became a primary school teacher. She is currently a Health Promotion Officer for the Amanda Young Foundation (AYF), speaking to people about how to prevent, identify and treat meningococcal disease.

HABIT 3: STAY MOTIVATED

This habit is about being enthusiastic and interested in what you do. It is about understanding the big picture and your contribution to the overall goal. It is about understanding why you do things. For instance, the bricklayer who is helping to build a cathedral instead of just laying bricks. The janitor in NASA who is helping to send people to Mars instead of just cleaning the bathrooms. When you understand the impact of your work, you feel positive despite the task sometimes being unpleasant.

To be motivated, you need to feel proud of what you do. Habits that help you do this include: Making a list how each task helps others. List down how your actions contribute to the overall objective. Always do your best, deliver quality, be on-time. When you are motivated, you inspire others and become a role model.

> *Happiness comes from doing something important and feeling proud of your contribution.*

Read the story below to understand the impact of being motivated.

Which Day Of The Week?

Imagine you wake up in the morning; you wonder what day it is, a work-day or a weekend day? After a few minutes, you suddenly realise it is the weekend. Wow, you feel great and excited, you hop out of bed feel energised and look forward to the rest of your day. You make yourself a cup of coffee, grab the newspaper and start to read – on the top of the page it says "Wednesday" – arghhhhh – how is this possible? You just found out it is a workday!

HABIT 4: BE HEALTHY

Your ability to practice gratitude, be proactive, stay motivated and positive link to a healthy lifestyle. A healthy lifestyle consists of maintaining a healthy body and a healthy mind. Healthy habits include exercise, sleep, nutrition and curiosity.

Exercise

If pharmaceuticals could patent the effects of physical activity through a pill, it would make them squillions. Incorporating exercise in your daily routine will give you more energy, sharpens your thinking, hones your focus, boosts memory, reduces stress, enhances creativity, elevates mood and improves sleep.

I do not have time for exercise is not a valid excuse, a 2008 Bristol University study found that people who exercised before work were happier, more resilient, manage time better and coped better with their workload. Even on days, they did not exercise; they did not feel guilty and maintained a positive mood reflecting their regular exercise habit.

"Regular exercise is about as close to a magic potion as you can get." ~Tich Nhat Hanh

Read the story below to understand the impact of exercise.

A Profitable Exercise

Tina was never overweight; she was just at the right BMI all her life. She started working at an early age, got married early, had children early in life and by the age of 30 she was a mother to 2 children aged 6 and 8. Her life had become a routine, wake up, get ready, run to the office, come home and cook, then off to bed. She had begun to feel depressed and was irritable most of the time. She felt her boss hated her, her husband did not love her as much and her children were apathetic towards her.

The neon red sign of GYM always glowed at her face on her way back home. From the giant glass windows, she could see people in their running shoes, music in their ears, sweating it out on the cardio machines. One fateful day she decided to enter the gym to check it out! She could see women like her who were not overweight, pumping iron and they all looked really happy!

She decided to enrol, even though it would be tough to take time out of her busy schedule to hit the gym 4 – 5 times a week. Within the first week, she could feel her depression lift!

She had an amazing idea while at the gym to quit her job and start on her own. She decided to study to become a fitness instructor and became a nutritionist sometime later. Today she runs her own successful business that employs, an army of fitness instructors and nutritionist across various gyms.

Sleep

A good daily routine includes enough rest and sleep. It will deliver better mood, cognition and a feeling of physical and mental wellbeing. Sleep consolidates long term memory and allows us to forget irrelevant information, it makes us more alert and stimulates creative and innovative thinking.

Humans sleep for anything from 5-11 hours, with the average being 7 hours and 45 minutes. In general, we need between 7 and 8 hours of uninterrupted sleep.

Read the story below to understand the impact of sleep.

Young Raj

Raj loved to sleep! He would go to bed early and wake up as late as possible. On weekends he would sleep through the morning and wake up for Brunch! During a coaching conversation, he realised that he had lost his enthusiasm, and now found himself behind on two critical goals.

His biggest challenge was making time for these goals. With a job where he spent over 9 hours daily and his love for gaming and movies, he had no time to spare. During the second coaching conversation, Raj realised that he should reduce his sleep time to achieve his critical goals.

While his sleep was precious to him, he had to weigh it against what he wanted in life. He started using the latest sleep app. This app, when kept near his bed, monitored his sleep cycles. It had an alarm that would ring when he was in Light Sleep, instead of traditional alarm clocks that ring at a fixed time. (even if you are in Deep Sleep).

Raj achieved his first critical goal within six months. He is happier, feels more enthusiastic and looks forward to attaining his remaining goal.

Nutrition

Most people know which food is nutritious and good for their body. Nutrition is essential, it fuels our body. What we put in our mouth is directly related to our output and energy levels. Even behaviours are affected by food and eating habits. For instance, some people get irritable, while others lose energy by eating unhealthy food.

Stay positive and build a habit of eating healthy. Eat a balanced diet that will supply you with enough minerals, vitamins and energy. Besides food, we need plenty of water throughout the day. So start each day by drinking a glass of water. Eating good food and taking the time to replenish your fuel stores is a most enjoyable habit. It is an excellent way to stay in control and increase your wellbeing.

Read the story below to understand the impact of nutrition.

Anna's Gift

Anna is again in trouble. Her parents just don't know why she is not eating well. They both love food and are obese. They don't understand why Anna is so slim, how is this possible? She just does not want to eat the beautiful pizza's, burgers, ice cream and puddings. What is wrong with her?

At the nutrition centre they explain the problem. After asking a lot of questions the doctor understands and invites the whole family to join him for lunch in the in the audio room. They sit down in nice comfortable chairs around a large table and look around the room. It is full with speakers, large and small, in the ceiling the walls and the floor. The doctor says I will show you what is wrong with Anna, it is not easy to explain so I will let you experience it.

The doctor picks up the phone and orders some food, plates with fresh fruit, strawberries, pineapples, bananas, mangos and other tropical fruits are brought in. When they start eating, they hear the most beautiful music from the speakers, as if they are in a garden with fruit trees. They can hear the birds sing, the bees buzz and the wind through the trees.

Next the doctor orders a plate of seafood, mussels, crabs and fish arrive and as soon as they start to eat, they hear the beautiful sounds of the sea, the waves crashing on the beach, the sea birds chirping in the wind.

The next dish the doctor orders is plate of fast food, pizza, burgers, fries and ice cream. As soon as they start eating, the music screams extremely harsh manmade sounds like a noisy factory. They need to cover their ears, it is painful!

When they leave the audio room the doctor explains. Anna is hearing what she eats. When she eats natural foods, she hears the beautiful harmony of nature's sound, when eating processed foods, she hears a cacophony of harsh sounds like a noisy factory. That is why Anna looks does not eat everything put in front of her, she has a special gift, she hears what she eats.

From that day onwards, the family replaced pizzas, burgers, puddings, and ice creams by fruit, vegetables, and fish. These days, the whole family looks fantastic, and if you meet one of them, they will surely ask you their favourite question: "What did your dinner sound like today?"

Curiosity

As children, we were curious, exploring everything within reach. We wanted to go on voyages, take on quests and slay the dragon. Even as adults curiosity, helps us to view new challenges and situations with excitement. When curious, we welcome change as an opportunity to grow. Unfortunately, we often lose our sense of curiosity over time. We stop asking questions, start to make assumptions, and jump to conclusions. Staying curious is like actively brushing our teeth - it prevents decay.

Build a habit of curiosity. Break your routine to see life from a different perspective. Write down the things you want to learn, try and do. Talk to different people, ask questions to discover their story! Be a great listener. Take a class, find something you want to master. Travel, remove yourself from your daily routine and comfort zone to inspire curiosity. Smile, be open, and curiosity will come knocking.

The more curious we are about the world around us the more open we are to learning and remembering other things as well.

Read the following story to understand the impact of curiosity.

Curious Tom

As soon as his little feet landed on the sand, Tom started running! He saw a girl flying, and she looked so happy. He tried climbing on the swing but fell down the first time.

The sand cushioned the impact, he tried again, and on the 3rd attempt he got on! He now wanted to figure out *how he could fly like the girl next to him. He moved his body ahead hoping that he would magically start flying and he did.*

His dad gave a little push from the back and Tom was soon soaring! He was so happy and screamed – higher dad, higher!

KICK-START YOUR DAY

Reboot and kick-start your journey, make the right choice each day. Your life today is essentially the sum of your actions. How in shape or out of shape you are, how happy or unhappy you are, how successful or unsuccessful you are, are a result of your actions. Habits are simple, repeated actions. Do them every day to become more positive. When you change your habits, you transform your life.

Begin your transformation by waking up early each day. Create a morning ritual and begin your day in a positive frame of mind. Research shows that many successful people wake up early. Not convinced? Have a look at the following list:

Howard Schultz	Starbucks	4:30 am
Ursula Burns	Xerox	5:15 am
Sergio Marchionne	Fiat/Chrysler	3:30 am
Bill Gross	Pimco	4:30 am
Richard Branson	Virgin	5:45 am
Indra Nooyi	Pepsico	4:00 am
Dan Akerson	GM	4:30 am
David Cush	Virgin America	4:15 am
Tim Cook	Apple	4:30 am
Bob Iger	Disney	4:30 am
Irwin Simon	Hain Celestial	5:00 am

Jean-Martin Folz	Peugeot	4:00 am
Brett Yormark	Brooklyn Nets	3:30 am
Gerry Laybourne	Oxygen	6:00 am
Padmasree Warrior	Cisco	4:30 am
A.G. Lafley	P & G	5:00 am
Paul Polman	Unilever	6:00 am
Tim Armstrong	AOL	5:00 am
Helena Morrissey	Newton Investments	5:00 am
Frits Van Paaschen	Starwood Hotels	5:30 am
Steve Reinemund	Pepsico	5:00 am
Anna Wintour	Vogue	5:45 am
George HW Bush	USA President	4:00 am
George W Bush	USA President	6:00 am
Condoleeza Rice	USA Sec of State	4:30 am

TV show host Oprah Winfrey, Apple's CEO Tim Cook, Twitter's Jack Dorsey, Virgin's Richard Branson all get up early in the morning.

YOUR MORNING RITUAL

If you want to "Love what you do" then take up our 28-day challenge. Do all or some of these 10 actions each day for the next 28 days. Personalise the challenge to your current life situation. The key is to have a morning routine that sets you up for the entire day.

1. Wake up 1 hour earlier
2. Drink a large glass of water
3. Do some exercise – take a quick walk/run/yoga
4. Relax - listen to music, do some meditation
5. Practice gratitude – write in your gratitude journal
6. Stay motivated – list how your actions help others
7. Stay curious - read, learn, smile

8. Be proactive - plan for the day
9. Be proud – be on time
10. Be healthy – prepare and eat healthy food

We challenge you to do this each morning. If you think this is too much, select some items, experiment, but start early. Whatever you do, start each day with a positive mindset. Make it manageable and achievable.

Happiness Is A Choice!

PART 1: ACTION ITEMS / SUMMARY QUESTIONS

a. What is your definition of Rebooting your life? Why is this necessary and what is involved?

b. Do a mindset check now and after the 28-day challenge to see the difference! Review the statements below and rate yourself on a scale from 1-5 (1=Not at all and 5=Absolutely)

1. **Technology & Lifestyle:** (Not at all) 1 2 3 4 5 (Absolutely)
   I am in full control of my time spent using technology and social media.

2. **Media & Marketing:** (Not at all) 1 2 3 4 5 (Absolutely)
   I only buy things or experiences that I personally value.

3. **Thoughts & Feelings:** (Not at all) 1 2 3 4 5 (Absolutely)
   On a typical day, the thoughts that occupy my mind trigger positive feelings and emotions.

4. **External Environment:** (Not at all) 1 2 3 4 5 (Absolutely)
   I always stay positive, even in challenging situations.

5. **Hard Work:** (Not at all) 1 2 3 4 5 (Absolutely)
   I love the work I do and have an ideal work-life balance.

6. **Competition:** (Not at all) 1 2 3 4 5 (Absolutely) I set my own standards and do not feel stressed when compared with others.

7. **Money:** (Not at all) 1 2 3 4 5 (Absolutely) I am happy with what I have and work towards my goals.

8. **Choice:** (Not at all) 1 2 3 4 5 (Absolutely) I make a conscious choice to be happy every day.

9. **Gratitude:** (Not at all) 1 2 3 4 5 (Absolutely) I am grateful to be alive and journal every day.

10. **Be Proactive:** (Not at all) 1 2 3 4 5 (Absolutely) I focus on what I can control and show initiative to solve issues.

11. **Motivation:** (Not at all) 1 2 3 4 5 (Absolutely) I feel proud of myself and see how my actions contribute to the overall objective.

12. **Health:** (Not at all) 1 2 3 4 5 (Absolutely) My lifestyle includes daily healthy habits (sleep|exercise|nutrition|curiosity) which keep me positive.

Download the workbook, transfer your results to see your mindset score, and understand what it means.

c. Start the 28-day "reboot your life" challenge tomorrow morning. Track your progress on the happiness habits tracker in the workbook.

d. One thing I can change, to make each day better is _____. Make a commitment to do it

Who Are You?

"The most difficult thing in life

is to know yourself."

~Thales of Miletus - a Greek philosopher

MOVE AHEAD

After starting the 28-day kickstart rebooting program, you already see the benefits of starting with a positive mindset. Getting up earlier and following your morning routine makes you feel positive. You start to appreciate life, see the small things which make life special.

It is easier to **"Love What You Do"** get involved and do your best. It makes you feel good about yourself. You are ready to start the process to find your dream activity and reach the ultimate **"Do What You Love."**

If you did not start the reboot, don't delay, give it a go – after all, what is the worst that can happen? You can go back to your previous life if you do not like the results. Just commit and give it at least 28 days to feel better and appreciate the change.

Wake Up!

It is a crisp autumn morning; Yana wakes up to the Forest Glade tune on her Sleep Cycle Alarm. It's 6.00 am, and she has been waking up early for a few weeks now. Her self-talk has moved from 'another day at work' to 'today is going to be exciting'.

Yana worked as an architect for one of the large construction firms in her city. She led many large projects for her company and through 8 years of hard work has moved up the corporate ladder. Yet she felt something was missing. She was not sure if this was all she could do with her life.

After her early morning jog, she came home and wrote in her Gratitude Journal. She browsed through all her entries from the first few weeks and had a eureka moment. She was grateful for her career but lacked autonomy and freedom in her projects. If only she knew what to do with this insight?

EXPERIENCE A FIVE-STAR LIFE

Five-star experiences in hotels and restaurants are carefully designed, well thought out, and nothing is left to chance. Five-star people do the same; they spend the time to understand their strengths and try to use their unique talents and gifts continually. Building a five-star life takes effort and time; the first step in the process is understanding yourself. This includes a deep understanding of your talents, strengths, beliefs, values, stressors and typical behaviours. When you align your activities with who you are, life becomes more fulfilling. So, let's start by understanding who you are.

Five-star living starts with understanding who you are.

- PART 2.1 -
Your Personality

*"When you are content to be simply
yourself and don't compare or compete,
everyone will respect you."*

~Lao Tzu,TaoTe Ching

What is personality?

When you introduce yourself - what do you say? Most people identify themselves with their profession, their nationality, or their family situation. They introduce themselves, as a Lebanese Canadian, an engineer, a father of three beautiful children - but is that really who you are?

Understanding your personality is the first step to understanding who you are. For centuries researchers have examined human behaviour and found that they can categorise people into different types. Researchers refer to these types as personalities, preferences or temperament.

"Parents matter but they don't make a difference, DNA is the major systematic force that makes us who we are"
~Robert Plomin".

Personality development

Dr Robert Plomin is a psychologist and professor of behaviour genetics at the Institute of Psychiatry, Psychology and Neuroscience at King's College in London. In his latest book "Blueprint: How DNA Makes Us Who We Are", he describes the link between DNA and how this influences traits, strengths and behaviours.

One of his famous studies is about identical twins who were separated at birth and given up for adoption in separate foster families. He made startling discoveries many years later when he observed these identical twins with almost identical passions and behaviour traits.

If you think that the upbringing of children, their nurture, determines who they are or become, you better think again. More evidence shows that genes are equally or maybe even more important than upbringing.

Dr Plomin shows that our genetic blueprint, our personality influences almost everything we do; it determines for a large part, who we are. Virtually every psychological trait you can measure has a genetic basis. That is the most important lesson learned from over twenty-five years of twins' studies.

No, you cannot blame your genes for being who you are and just blame your parents and grandparents for everything that happens to you. You can learn most things, but some come easy while others are much harder to learn.

"Find a wave that helps you and ride it!" ~Chris Barez-Brown

NATURE VS NURTURE

Your natural ability to learn things like music, writing, math and many others have a large heritable basis. If you can find out which abilities are in your genes, which traits are accessible to you, it will make life easier. If you know which ones are built-in and easy to learn you have a great advantage. It allows you to focus on natural abilities. Developing them is like swimming with the stream. In his book, he discusses the importance of "going with the grain" of your nature rather than fighting it.

Most people think that genetics set you up and make a big difference at the start of life and as you grow up nurture takes over and becomes more important.

This might seem logical at first but is not true. Your genetic make-up flourishes later in life because you tend to be in control of your environment. You create an environment where your inherited traits can flourish.

People tend to quickly accept heritability and "swimming with the stream" when talking about physical characteristics. If your two-meter tall son or daughter wants to join a basketball team, it sounds all very logical, but if they tell you they can't do math or music, you suddenly talk about discipline and working harder. Deep down we all know about talents and gifts. When children get introduced to math, music or sports at school, some like it and naturally lap it up and excel, while others must work very hard to pass.

We are all individuals, we make our own choices, but to reach the same level, some must work much harder than others. Some are more inclined to show addictive behaviours like alcoholism; others are more likely to become obese. If you have these heritable characteristics, it does not mean that you are destined to become an addict or obese. You are always in control of yourself. It is very simple if you don't drink alcohol you can't become an alcoholic.

Heritability of characteristics, traits, behaviours and interests are identified by combinations of thousands of genes; this simply means everyone is different.

"Spending too much time focused on others' strengths leaves us feeling weak. Focusing on our own strengths is what, in fact, makes us strong." ~Simon Sinek

PERSONALITY AWARENESS

Awareness is about understanding; reflection will bring awareness and understanding related to different personality elements. Awareness includes both self-awareness and situational awareness. Self-reflection, feedback from others and shared discovery, play an essential role in developing awareness. This is all explained by the Johari Window.

Fig 1: The Johari Window

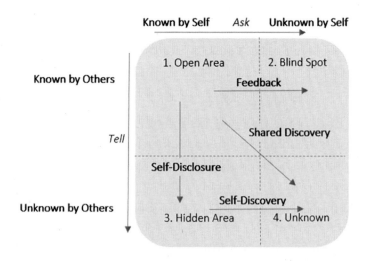

The Johari Window is a tool created by Joseph Luft and Harry Ingham in 1955. It compares what is known/unknown by self against what is known/unknown by others. It is a great model to use because of its simplicity and because it can be applied in a variety of situations and environments.

The Johari window helps you to understand how to improve awareness and build better relationships. The key to improving relationships is to increase shared understanding. This can be done by asking for feedback or disclosing private information by telling others.

The Open Area(1) is shared knowledge, what is known by self and by others. Creating a large open area – sharing more information about yourself and receiving feedback from others will reduce the Hidden Areas(3), Blind-Spots(2) and Unknowns(4). Doing this consistently will result in more general awareness, less misunderstanding and better, more open relationships.

Self-disclosure, asking for feedback, self-discovery and shared-discovery are all important ways to deliver a larger open area of shared knowledge. When there is more shared knowledge, there is more understanding, more empathy and trust.

Do You Know Rita?

Rita is a colleague, and I guess she is one of those people who you find in every organisation. She is pushing it lately, by coming in late three times last week. The week before, she was late every day! Instead of 9:00 am Rita feels it is ok to show up at 10:30. Sometimes even later, just before the coffee break.

I talked with the others in the department, and we agreed, Rita is just lazy, she wants to do as little as possible, does not take on any responsibilities, and we end up having to do her work. I don't think anyone likes her. Still, she is close to the boss, so that is probably how she gets away with this.

Rita just arrived at the coffee break. We all sat there, stopped talking and just looked at her. She burst out crying!

After sobbing for a while, she told us that her husband was diagnosed with stage three cancer. The initial cancer treatments were not working well, and now treatments were becoming more intense. Her husband was hospitalised two weeks ago.

This meant that she had to go to the hospital early in the morning. It was the only time he was feeling awake enough to chat. She asked us for some understanding.

We were stunned. We had no idea! Everyone in the team felt for her and offered to cover for her in the morning. Why did she not tell us before?

What just happened? (in terms of the Johari window)

PERSONALITY ELEMENTS

Building a better understanding of oneself is equally important. The Asha window (Ashirvad Lobo and Hans Horlings 2018) is based on the Johari window. The focus of the Asha window is increasing self-awareness and having a better relationship with yourself.

Behaviours and actions show your personality and preferences to others. Still, it is not that easy to determine personality types, since we do not behave consistently in the same way. We change our behaviours and actions in response to the environment and our mood. Personal beliefs, talents, values and core needs are driving behaviour, either consciously or subconsciously. It requires personal reflection and effort to become more self-aware. You must take time to determine these drivers as they make you who you are. The Asha Window uses the basic framework of the Johari window and adds the critical personality elements.

Fig 2: The Asha Window

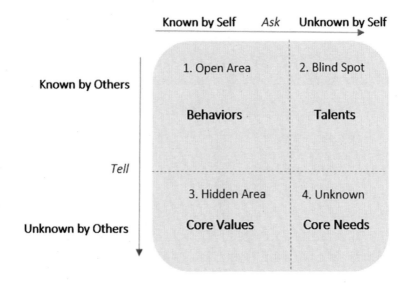

Behaviours

Behaviours are known by self and others this is because most behaviours are readily observable. Day to day behaviours combine to create patterns which are recognised as a typical personal style. Most people are aware of how they act, others close to you, are undoubtedly aware of your behaviours. As relationships deepen, you become more comfortable showing your real self, which makes it easier for others to recognise typical behaviours.

Talents

Talents are often blind spots as they tend to be more visible to others than self. Others tend to spot our undeveloped talents and encourage us to further develop them, they see our potential. Also, we are so used to our current abilities that we often take them for granted. We should have the courage to ask and accept feedback from others to further understand and develop our natural capabilities.

Core Values

Most core values and beliefs are known to us, but not directly to others. These are the rules we live by, they determine the choices we make; they are principles. We rarely tell people our internal behaviour rules, because we might not even be aware of them. The only time we show our values to others is when we are pushed to take a stand. This happens when they cross your principle rule, your line in the sand. You might even act subconsciously on these rules. Increased awareness of your core values helps you to be consistent in your behaviour. When you are consciously aware of your core values, you are also able to make positive changes to your internal rules.

Core-Needs

Core-needs are the least visible both to self and others. Clarity about core-needs is very powerful. Becoming aware of your core-needs helps you understand and accept your true self, your identity. It leads to being in charge of your life by embracing your uniqueness. Continuous self-reflection and reflective feedback from the people closest to you can help you uncover your core needs. Coaching, mentoring and mindfulness are great tools in this process.

The remainder of this book will help to uncover and build awareness of your behaviours, talents, values and core-needs. Together these elements will make it clear who you are and define your unique identity.

"The only thing I recommend is never trying to be someone else. I always tried to be myself - the reason people are successful is because they are unique." ~Ellen DeGeneres

PERSONALITY MODELS

It is better to focus and develop natural strengths, interests, traits and abilities and go with the stream than trying to swim against it. In short, it is just smart to spend time to understand who you are, and what comes naturally to you. Understanding who you are, takes time, self-reflection, an open mind and is a process of discovery. No test will exactly explain who you are, because you are unique.

Personality tests are designed to gather information about temperament, character traits, decision-making methods, communication styles, behaviours, and attitudes towards life, work, education, recreation and people. This information helps you to understand why you think, feel and behave the way you do, and why people behave so differently when faced with the same situation.

When you understand personality types, it will raise both self and social awareness. You will grasp the strengths and weaknesses of each personality. Recognize why you are attracted to some tasks and people and why you find others tedious or boring. When your choices and behaviours align with your personality type, everything in life starts to make sense. Life becomes a lot easier; you have more energy, better health, and your relationships become more fulfilling.

"Do What You Can, With What You Have, Where You" Are." ~Theodore Roosevelt

Now I Understand!

I delivered many personality assessments to people during the last twenty years. Understanding personality preferences always makes a significant impact. Often participants say my husband or my wife needs to do this!

When I went through a 3-day in-depth accreditation workshop to understand personality, it changed me. For the first time in my life, I realised that it was ok to be me.

I suddenly understood that it was ok to be different; I was craving freedom, variety, change, action, excitement and hated strict rules. Others liked strict rules, security, safety, systems, routine, and hated surprises.

In my view, understanding who you are should be compulsory in every school – it will help people question, explore and accept themselves and others.

**Don't Treat People As <u>You</u> Want To Be Treated,
Treat People How <u>They</u> Want To Be Treated.**

PERSONALITY ASSESSMENTS

There are many personality, temperament and behaviour models. Some are more than two thousand years old. Key theorists in this domain are Carl Jung, David Keirsey and William Marston. Over the years their models were integrated in various personality assessments. A google search on personality assessments will come up with some 267 million results.

People are unique, it is important that you don't use personality typing to stereotype others. Human behaviour is far too complex to predict behaviour accurately. Personality typing can be used as a tool to gain more insight through careful reflection. Don't just accept any assessment result, use it as a way to discover your own behaviours, talents, core values and core needs.

THE FOUR PERSONALITY PORTRAITS

We have used our understanding of personality models to create four portraits: People-Focus, Process-Focus, Action-Focus and Knowledge-Focus. The following section describes these four portraits in detail. Read them carefully and visualise which one is most like you and which one is least like you.

PORTRAIT A: PEOPLE-FOCUS

You are warm, supportive and care about people. You tend to find meaning and significance in life through relationships. You find it easy to share feelings and value harmony, authenticity and cooperation. You need to be with others, seek their approval and value their encouragement and support.

You use intuition and gut feel to understand what other people need. Committed to help others, you see their potential and want them to grow. You are imaginative and creative, and your strengths include the ability to show sincere concern for those around you.

You avoid conflict, have a tendency to be too compliant, and can be unwilling to say no. This may result in trying to do too much and set unrealistic goals. Your strong people focus gets you too involved and tends to lead to poor time management and slow decision making. As an empathic listener, you like to resolve disputes, inspire and motivate others.

You like to make new friends and entertain others. Your concern for others, and flexibility to meet their needs, makes you a valued team member and bridge builder. In return you just want to be respected for who you are.

You are stressed by people who have a secret agenda and those who are two-faced or dishonest. You dislike conflict, which you take very personally. You enjoy life when you feel connected and work to become a better version of yourself.

"Let's Do It Together, Everyone OK?"

PORTRAIT B: PROCESS-FOCUS

You are very responsible, have a strong sense of duty, delivering what is required. You are very loyal to your family, team or organisation and find it easy to submit to the culture, hierarchy and traditions. Your need for stability, predictability and a sense of order forces you to be highly organised.

You create and follow a plan from start to finish, follow step by step instructions, clear rules, and regulations. You create order through planning to meet deadlines and get things done. You are dependable and have a strong sense of right and wrong.

Because you want to avoid uncertainty and disorder, you have a tendency to reject change and might come across as stubborn or inflexible. By constantly worrying about what could go wrong, you become negative and expect too much from self and others. As a responsible, planner, organiser and executor you get things done which makes you an excellent and dedicated employee.

You like clear responsibilities, rules, systems, procedures and objective measurements. You like to finish a job well and are known as skilled and always prepared. You appreciate objective measures.

You are stressed by frequent change and surprises. You set high standards for yourself and might feel overwhelmed by everything you believe you are responsible for. You enjoy life most when there is a clear separation between work and the rest of your life.

"Let's Make a Plan and Do It"

PORTRAIT C: ACTION-FOCUS

You look for change and variety and can act at a moment's notice. You are independent, competitive and work well under pressure. You crave freedom to make decisions and need to be in control of your destiny. You are observant and appreciate the beauty around you.

You trust your impulsive ways of doing things, take initiatives, and make pragmatic decisions. You are highly skilled, do things quickly, without supervision. You are good at reading the situation, adapt easily, using the right tools to achieve desired outcomes.

You tend to lose interest, become bored quickly and may leave projects unfinished. You don't like details, abstract ideas, theories, and extensive research. You can be pushy, impulsive and often act too quickly to get things done.

You like to use your creativity and can find many new ways to get the job done with whatever resources are available. You can be very entertaining while delivering a skillful performance. As someone who craves change, you like to be continuously stimulated and love variety. This makes you great at driving new initiatives and selling new ideas.

You are stressed by strict rules and the need to do everything according to set procedures. As an action-focused person, you dislike routine, and get stressed by a lack of variety and change in what you do. You enjoy life when you have the freedom to pursue your dreams.

"Let's Do It Now"

PORTRAIT D: KNOWLEDGE-FOCUS

You are someone who investigates and asks questions to make sense of things. You make improvements, set high standards and focus on concepts and principles. You need to know, master the data to feel competent. You value knowledge and being recognised as the expert.

You work best when given the time and space to understand the relevant facts and theories. You analyse and think through complex problems, and come up with solutions. Clear thinking, along with using precise words and deliberate language are your strengths.

You might come across as cold and impatient, be seen as someone who is too analytical, often giving complicated explanations. You lose others' cooperation, when you don't share the details, and just focus on the big picture. You hate incompetence and tend to be a perfectionist.

You like theories, models and abstracts to find patterns that explain the past and the future. You trust logic rather than emotions. You appreciate expertise and like to find all the information before making decisions. You are on a quest to deliver high quality and will fight for what you believe in. You are happy to work by yourself and have enough patience to dig through complexity.

You get stressed by people who make quick decisions based on gut feel rather than logic. You enjoy life when given the time to research and develop your knowledge.

"Let's Analyse It First and Do It Right"

Behaviour Fingerprints

I am Action Focused, I require freedom, of course, I also show some other traits like caring for people, valuing and supporting others. I don't like conflict, but deep down I need freedom, variety and action. I get bored quickly by a job my wife does – too much routine, not enough excitement. I think that rules are good, but sometimes can be broken. My favourite holiday includes adventure, hiking, sailing, not knowing where we go next, what we will do and when we move on.

My wife is organised, a loyal employee and likes security predictability, clear organisation and schedules. She is very organised in her teaching – the year is split up in 24 teaching weeks, each week with clearly defined content. She has high expectations for herself, her students and has a strong sense of duty. She always finds it hard when students fail to do what is expected of them. She is focused on tasks and strict about following rules. She gets stressed quite easily and is often worried about problems that lie ahead. Her favourite holiday is a cruise, booked at least six months in advance, knowing exactly where she will be each day. Since she is a processed focus person, convincing her requires a plan and structure. It might take a long time for her to get used to a new idea.

My son needs to know; he likes to find out things, the perfect person to have on a quiz team. He knows all the useless facts, why the sky is blue, why green tomatoes are better fried and so much more. If you want to convince him you must come with facts. He works with logic and likes computer programs. He will read the whole report sent to him before going to the meeting because he needs to know and makes decisions based on logic and facts and does not want to look bad. He is clearly a knowledge focused person.

My daughter is also action focused; she is a musician, plays in different bands, does some private tuition and works at a call centre. She always has new ideas, new initiatives. She is action focused, doing things, entertaining people, making some money and not too worried about life. She is flexible, likes adventure, and spur of the moment things. Convincing her is more about feelings and gut.

EVERYONE IS A NATURAL MIX

You now have an idea which portrait looks most like you. However, to get a more accurate picture you should ask others, who know you well, to assess you. Show them the portraits and see what they say. Self-analysis might not be enough; there is always value in hearing what others have to say.

You are a mix of all four types, one comes more naturally than the others. Some people are a little bit of all and very close to the middle, while most are more extreme in one or two colours. Your personality is a mix of learned and natural behaviours. This explains why siblings can be so different.

People are unique, a blend of the four types, you can use each of the four types when the situation requires it. For example, you choose to write with your left or your right hand. One has preference over the other. One is easier, effortless and feels more comfortable than the other. It is the same with these four personality types. One comes easier, feels more natural than the others. Trying to figure out your mix of preferences is a process, don't try and work out what you want to be, but look at what comes naturally.

ANOTHER PERSONALITY VARIABLE

Even people who have the same mix are different. One of the reasons for this difference is how much we value the company of others. Some people love to go to social events as it energises them, while others feel drained after a social gathering and would rather be by themselves. This is because some people are extrovert, some are introvert and others are a bit of both. People who are a bit of both, so-called ambiverts find it easy to understand both extroverts and introverts. It is difficult for an extreme extrovert to understand an extreme introvert, hence it is very important for you to know what you are and how this affects you.

The main difference between introversion and extroversion is linked to energy. Extroverts gain energy when they are with others, while for introverts this takes energy. Introverts recharge when they are by themselves, while for extroverts being alone is draining and takes energy.

UNDERSTANDING INTROVERTS

Introverts (or those of us with more introverted tendencies) tend to recharge by spending time alone. They lose energy when being around people for long periods, particularly large crowds.

For introverts, to be alone with their thoughts is as restorative as sleeping, as nourishing as eating. Introverted people think things through before they speak, they enjoy a small, close group of friends, and one-on-one time. They also need time alone to recharge. Some of the below pointers help you to understand introverts.

Quick pointers about introverts

- You need people to respect your privacy and alone time.
- You prefer private meetings, instead of public forums
- You need time to observe any new situation
- You need time to think and often don't give instant answers
- You tend to withdraw and be quiet when interrupted
- You need advance notice of expected changes in your life
- You need warnings to finish what you are doing
- You like to be taught new skills privately

- You need a few best friends, with similar interests
- You dislike and do not need to make lots of friends
- You want people to respect your introversion

"Don't think of introversion as something that needs to be cured. Spend your free time the way you like, not the way you think you're supposed to." ~Susan Cain

UNDERSTANDING EXTROVERTS

Extroverts (or those of us with more extroverted tendencies), tend to gain energy from other people. Extroverts find their energy disappearing when they spend too much time alone. They recharge by being social.

Extroverts are energised by people. They usually enjoy spending time with others, as this is how they recharge. An extrovert likes to make eye contact, smile, maybe chat if there's an opportunity. As an extrovert, that's a small 'ping' of energy, a little positive moment in the day. Some of the below pointers help you to understand extroverts.

Quick pointers about extroverts
- You need respect from and by others
- You like compliments in the company of others
- You like encouragement from others
- You want to explore and talk things through with others
- You like to surprise and entertain others
- You need time to meet others

- You need to dive right in
- You like to have different options
- You like physical and verbal gestures of affection
- You like to show others you can do it

"Extroversion is an enormously appealing personality style, but we've turned it into an oppressive standard to which most of us feel we must conform". ~Susan Cain

UNDERSTANDING AMBIVERTS

Since introverts and extroverts are the extremes of the scale, most of us fall somewhere in the middle. Many of us lean one way or the other, but there are some who are quite balanced between the two tendencies. These people are called ambiverts.

Ambiverts exhibit both extrovert and introvert tendencies. Being a bit of both means they generally enjoy being around people, but after a long time, this will start to drain them. Similarly, they enjoy solitude and quiet, but not for too long.

Ambiverts recharge their energy levels with a mixture of social interaction and alone time. This balance can be a good thing. For example, a study by Adam Grant found that ambiverts perform better in sales than either introverts or extroverts. They know when to push and when to hold back, when to speak up and when to shut up.

Enjoying Christmas

Christmas is family time in Holland. We don't do presents; this is done early in December at Saint Nicholas. No, Christmas is all about peace, understanding and appreciating each other.

Last year I asked my daughter for her plans at Christmas. She replied – on Christmas day we will go to my boyfriends' family in the south of Holland. The whole family will be there; it will be great to see everyone. She then planned to go to the north of Holland on boxing day to spend time with my wife's family. Another large family gathering, traditional meals and a great time together.

When I asked my son the same thing – he answered that he just bought a great book, which he saved especially to read over the two days off. As an introvert he looked forward to time off, spending two days just by himself.

As an extrovert, I find it very hard to accept his need for being by himself. I feel that he does not have friends, and is often lonely. In business, introverts are often taken for granted. They might be better managers because they think before they say something and focus on facts. The extroverts that make the most noise tend to get the most attention.

I believe that many extroverts find it very hard to

understand introverts and vice versa. That is why we need to understand what it means to be extrovert or introvert.

THE POWER OF SHOWING WHO YOU ARE

We completed hundreds of training sessions on this topic and used personality assessments to give people more awareness and insights. It is always one of the most exciting and appreciated part of the training. As seasoned trainers, we think people gain so much from becoming aware of who they are. It affects their relationships with others, at home and work. It affects how they see themselves and for many it is a real "Aha" moment; they suddenly understand why.

When you understand who you are, it makes sense to choose a job or career that fits with your personality. Think about how much structure you need or want? How much freedom do you want? Do you want to work inside or outside, with people or data, use logic or gut feel, enjoy change or want routine? There are so many options. In our view, you will feel much happier in an environment that fits with your personality and preference.

"I had no idea that being myself could make me as rich as I've become. If I had, I would have done it a lot earlier." ~Oprah Winfrey

When you understand who you are, understand deeply what makes you unique, you will no longer feel inferior or feel ashamed of who you are. You will embrace yourself, and become proud of your unique characteristics. You will see them as strengths and accept yourself. You will set your boundaries and live your values without being apologetic.

You will become vulnerable, and this takes courage and might feel uncomfortable. You will become brave enough to show who you are, without feeling ashamed of it.

Making your own choices will give you confidence and allows you to live your life in the way you want. You find it easier to speak up and follow your dreams.

Confidence, authenticity, outspokenness and decisiveness are all characteristics that combine to deliver personal presence. When I met the late Nelson Mandela as part of a small gathering in Sharjah, I suddenly realised what "presence" means.

Personal presence is difficult to define but easy to recognise. People with presence carry themselves in a way that turns heads. When they talk, people listen. When they ask, people answer. When they lead, people follow. When you understand who you are, you develop personal presence which will assist you to grow, follow your passion and succeed.

"let go of who you think you are supposed to be and embrace who you are, come alive and show the power of wholehearted living." ~Brene´ Brown

PART 2.1: ACTION ITEMS / SUMMARY QUESTIONS

a. Why is it important to become aware of your preferred personality type?

b. Ask five people who know you well to give you feedback by email. Ask for honest feedback, how they see you, what are your key strengths and weaknesses in their eyes.

c. Why is it that some people like change and thrive in chaos while others like routine and clearly defined systems and processes?

d. Do the personality, ambition and social style questionnaires in the full of life workbook.

e. Define how you add value to your work, what you do well and what makes you the right person to do this.

Your Core Beliefs

"We don't see things as they are,

We see things as <u>We</u> are".

~Anais Nin

YOUR PERSONAL FILTERING SYSTEM

You have now understood yourself a little more and are aware about your personality traits and preferences. It is time to go a bit deeper and understand your personal filtering system. We see everything through this system. This system is created and updated based on experiences, actions, and habits. It determines how you perceive the world around you. Your filtering system interprets what you see and controls how you react.

For instance, you might enjoy rain and look for holidays where you get to experience rain, or you might hate it and try to avoid rain on your holidays. You might see a puddle as something you need to avoid or something you just have to jump into.

The culture and situation you were born into affects your personal filtering system. The people around you, your parents, family and friends together with the rules at home, school and work have a large influence on how you perceive things. Your core belief system is the guide to your behaviour. Understanding who you are requires a good look at this filtering system. Your core beliefs influence who you are and how you behave.

Little Abdu

Two-year-old Abdu is experiencing both chaos and fun at his friend's birthday party. All his friends are around, and he is getting to play unsupervised. A loud thud and crashing of glasses suddenly catch the adults' attention. Someone has clumsily run into a table that had juice and glasses on it.

The host is embarrassed and does not want to make an issue about this; the parents are embarrassed and hope that it isn't their child who caused this mess. One of the parents asks, who did this? Sweet little Abdu smiles and promptly puts his hands up admitting his mistake.

His parents' storm in, grab him and pull him out of the party. Abdu is crying and wailing but to no avail as he is now being taken home and then sent to a corner. What will Abdu now believe about being honest and owning up to mistakes?

CORE BELIEF BASICS

Core beliefs are beliefs about yourself, other people, and the world you live in. You see them as absolute truths, and they sit deep down, underneath all your surface thoughts. Essentially, core beliefs determine how you perceive and interpret the world. They are present in your subconscious. When something happens, your mind will consult your core beliefs which will try to keep you safe and protect and defend you against the world. For example, when you see a dog showing his bare teeth, you might interpret this as friendly, the dog is smiling at me or aggressive, the dog is ready to attack me. Your core belief system determines the way you react.

Your core belief system is mostly shaped early in life based on input from others, especially your parents. If you have been told throughout childhood that you are a capable, lovable individual, you are likely to grow up seeing yourself that way. Similarly, if you have been told you are useless, then in your own head, you may never amount to anything. These kinds of remarks end up as building blocks for your assumptions about yourself.

Feelings also affect our core beliefs. Losing a skating race or failing an exam might make you feel like a failure. This feeling can enter your beliefs system as "I am just not good enough". Emotional trauma caused by being humiliated or bullied is widespread and strongly influences your core belief system.

Experiences feed our core beliefs. We are very good at recognising patterns and instinctively drawing conclusions from our experiences. If you burn your hand on a hot stove, you are unlikely to touch it again. Your beliefs system has been updated based on this experience. This update influences your actions and keeps you safe.

Over time your assumptions, feelings and experiences, harden into a set of core beliefs. These often take the form of hidden truths, about ourselves, other people and the world around us. Core beliefs are compelling. You accept them as true and live your life without being fully aware of them.

Core beliefs are neither good nor bad. They are what they are. However, some beliefs limit you, while others broaden or extend your behaviour. Therefore, it is important to become aware of your core beliefs and how they develop.

Core beliefs develop early in life. They involve child-like thinking patterns. This thinking lacks the insights and understanding that comes with greater life experiences. It tends to be simple, black-and-white thinking since as children, we find it difficult to deal with complexities.

Growing up does not automatically mean we change our child-like core beliefs. Therefore, as we become adults, we should examine whether our core beliefs still include these child-like thinking patterns. We can then consciously change them to healthier, more adult thinking styles.

What Is Your Emotional Age?

Psychological or emotional age is different from physical age. Have a look at the following thinking and behaviour patterns. How do you think and respond?

Child-like Patterns	Adult-like Patterns
Blame others	Solve the problem
Lies and deception	Deal with reality
Attack the person	Attack the problem
Poor impulse control	Self-control
Immediate gratification	Delayed gratification
Demand attention	Give attention
Bullying behaviour	Assertive behaviour
Stereotype and prejudice	Fairness and tolerance
Self-centred	Modest
Subjective thinking	Objective thinking

Anger and aggression	*Compromise*
Mistakes=failure	*Mistakes= learning*

After looking at the above list, you might find that you still have some childish thinking patterns. These thinking patterns affect your core belief system and can be changed. The first step to change is to understand the elements of the core belief system.

CORE BELIEF CATEGORIES

Core beliefs fit into three main categories. Beliefs about yourself, beliefs about others and beliefs about the world. Have a look at the following examples:

- Beliefs about yourself: Thinking you're a loser or an achiever.
- Beliefs about others: Thinking that everyone is out to get you or they are here to support you.
- Beliefs about the world: Believing that opportunities are limited or that the world is full of opportunity.

Beliefs about yourself

A core belief about yourself is always about you. It is in an "I" or "Me" statement. For example, "I am the greatest", or "I am stupid". These are also referred to as self-beliefs and are assessments we make about our own capability. Our self-assessment is often confirmed by people or actions around us. So you may say, "Look, it's true! I am stupid!"

Beliefs about others

A core belief about others takes a similar format but is a statement about others. For example "People are trustworthy" or "People never change". Naturally if you believe this it will affect how you treat people. Trust and building relationships work both ways. If you trust others, it will be easy for others to trust you.

Beliefs about the world

Beliefs about the world are our internal generalized views about the world, such as "The world is safe" or "The world is not safe". Depending on what you belief, you might feel positive or experience ongoing anxiety and fear. You will make choices based on what is 'safe' over what you truly want. In extreme cases you may never let your guard down and might miss out on life. This belief can also affect beliefs about yourself and others since you are likely to believe that "everyone is trustworthy" or "everyone is out to get me".

COMMON CORE BELIEFS

Many core beliefs are black and white, and in our mind, are outright truths. Have a look at the following common core beliefs , both positive and negative are listed below:

POSITIVE	NEGATIVE
✓ People can change	✗ People can't change
✓ People like me	✗ Nobody likes me
✓ I am smart	✗ I am stupid
✓ I am a good parent	✗ I am a bad parent
✓ I look good	✗ I am not pretty
✓ I am beautiful/handsome	✗ I am ugly
✓ I am clever	✗ I am not clever

✓ I am resourceful	✗ I am no good
✓ I am a hard worker	✗ I am lazy
✓ I am successful	✗ I am a failure
✓ I am fantastic	✗ I am useless
✓ I am perfect for that job	✗ I am not good enough to get that job
✓ I will find the right partner	✗ I'll never find the perfect partner
✓ It is ok to be who I am	✗ I must be perfect
✓ People like me	✗ People don't like me
✓ People are kind	✗ People are unkind
✓ I am always happy	✗ I'll never be happy
✓ It will turn out ok	✗ If anything can go wrong, it will
✓ I like mixing with new people	✗ I am not good at mixing with new people
✓ I am valuable	✗ I am worthless

It is often hard for people to state their beliefs, since they are implicit. After reading the list of beliefs, you might be able to reflect on some core beliefs that profoundly affect you. What you believe will not just affect you, but it will define you.

CORE BELIEF EFFECTS ON THE SELF

This might be a good time to introduce you to Carl Rogers (1902-1987). He was a humanistic psychologist who agreed with the main assumptions of Abraham Maslow and his hierarchy of needs (explained in part 3). Rogers defines Maslow's self-actualisation statement in more detail.

Rogers claimed that for a person to "grow", they need an environment and core-belief system that provides them with *genuineness*, *acceptance*, and *empathy* and that without these three ingredients relationships and personalities will not develop as they should. Much like a tree which will not grow without sunlight, water and nutrition. According to Rogers humans have one basic motive, self-actualisation, which is the tendency to fulfil one's potential and achieve the highest level of 'human-beingness' you can.

SELF-ACTUALISATION

Rogers regards self-actualisation as a continuous process rather than a destination or a goal. He describes self-actualising people as curious, balanced and interesting to know. These people often become high achievers in society.

The Self-Actualizing Person's Characteristics

1. Open to experience: *both positive and negative emotions are accepted. Negative feelings are not denied, but worked through, rather than resorting to defence mechanisms.*

2. Existential living: *in touch with different experiences as they occur in life. Able to live and fully appreciate the present, not always looking back to the past or forward to the future.*

3. Trust feelings: *feeling, instincts, and gut-reactions are trusted. Regard decisions as the right ones, and able to trust oneself to make the right choices.*

4. Creativity: *creative thinking and risk-taking are features of a person's life. Not playing safe all the* *time. This involves the ability to adjust, change and seek new experiences.*

5. Fulfilled life: *a person is happy and satisfied with life, and always looking for new challenges and experiences.*

Central to Rogers' theory about self-actualization is how we view Self, which he call the "Self-Concept". According to Rogers, the Self-Concept includes three components: Self-Worth, Self-Image and Ideal-Self.

Self-worth

Self-worth (or self-esteem) is sense of how much you value yourself. A person who has high self-worth has positive core beliefs about himself or herself. This person is confident, able to face challenges and accepts failure.

People with extreme high self-worth are over-confident, and act like they are Gods' gift to humanity. They feel superior, do not accept failure and are not open to advise from others.

People with very low self-worth lack confidence, avoid challenges and end-up being very defensive and guarded around others. Self-worth has a lot to do with your core beliefs and how you see your actual and ideal self.

Self-image

Self-image is simply how you see yourself. Our core beliefs create our self-image. At a simple level, you might perceive yourself as either good or bad, beautiful or ugly. Self-image affects how you think, feel and behave in the world. An example of an unhealthy self-image is someone who suffers from eating disorders like bulimia. Their distorted self-image leads to an obsessive desire to lose weight through self-induced vomiting or fasting, even though they might be very skinny already. Self-Image and Core-Beliefs are directly linked to each other and impact who we would like to be.

Ideal-self

The ideal self is the person who you would like to be. This version of you includes your ideal personality, beliefs, ambition, and values. Understanding your talents plays an important role in developing your ideal-self. As you move through life, your ideal-self is updated through new insights and self-awareness of your personality, core beliefs and core values.

Self-Concept

Your self-concept is dynamic; it is changing due to a changing self-image and ideal-self. You can mould your self-concept through coaching, self-reflection and continuous development. New experiences, new insights, newly accepted or changing core beliefs, adopted values and developing talents will drive your continuous process of self-actualisation.

Asma's Story

Asma had two sisters and a brother. When she was young, her mum always told her that it was a pity that she was not a little more like her younger sister. Her younger sister was always regarded as the pretty one.

Naturally, this affected Asma's self-worth and self-image. Asma tended to wear trousers and behave like a boy and play with the boys. She never used make-up and would not dress-up like her sisters. She just accepted and believed that she was not pretty enough.

As a teenager, she decided that she just had to be the smartest. Her ideal-self was defined by becoming an oilfield engineer. So, she studied hard, graduated and got a job as an oilfield construction engineer, mostly working onsite in the desert.

Even in her twenties, she believed that she was not desirable. When her younger sister got married, Asma thought she was just not made for marriage. She finally got married and had a child. When her husband left her, she blamed herself.

She changed to an office job, to be able to look after her daughter. Her self-image improved and as she became proud of being a single mum. She brought her daughter up on her own, despite all the obstacles. Her daughter did well at college and turned out to be a smart and beautiful girl.

Now twenty years later, she has one of the highest paying jobs, in a man's world as an engineer. Her parents, sisters and brother are proud of her achievements.

She surprised the guys at the annual company outing by dressing up and liked the attention she received. She now begins to believe that she is good enough. Her self-worth improved a lot when she received awards for being the best engineer. Her sister helped her to get ready for the event, and she got a lot of compliments at the awards ceremony.

Her self-image and ideal-self are now very close together, and her self-worth is at an all-time high. She feels good about being who she is and the life she currently has. She recently went back to university to complete her MBA. She is proud of her work, her daughter and her achievements – life is good!

YOUR SELF-BELIEFS

From the story you can understand that core beliefs have a direct impact on the way you perceive the world and interpret what happens. They colour your judgments of self and others. Negative core beliefs have a significant effect on our self-concept: self-worth, self-image and ideal-self.

A negative core belief might look something like this: "I *am not good enough.*"- People would not like me if they knew the truth about me. Behaviours resulting from this might include not going to that party because I don't know anyone there and will feel nervous and shy.

A similar but positive core belief might look like this: "I *am capable and competent.*" - I can do my job well, and my colleagues appreciate that. Behaviours resulting from this belief might include eventually asking for a promotion or a raise because I know I am worth it.

IDENTIFYING YOUR CORE BELIEFS

Now that you understand the influence of core beliefs, you might be open to identifying your personal core beliefs through the core belief inventory tool.

A way to uncover your core beliefs is to answer the core beliefs questionnaire in the workbook. It will analyse the core beliefs which are most critical to your self image, which include:

"I am Worthy"
Indicates how valuable you believe you are as a person

"I am Safe"
Indicates how safe you believe you are as a person

"I am Competent"
Indicates how competent you believe you are

"I am Powerful"
Indicates how much you believe you are in control

"I am Loved"
Indicates how nurtured you believe you are as a person

"I am Autonomous"
Indicates how independent you believe you are

"I am Treated Justly"
Indicates if you accept what you get as fair/reasonable

"I Belong"
Indicates how secure and connected you are to others

"People are good."
Indicates how likely you are to trust others and expect them to behave positively towards you.

"My standards are reasonable and flexible."
Indicates how you judge your own and others' actions

The Core Belief Inventory is a guideline and a starting point to identifying your core beliefs. You can use it to start the process of reflecting on your thoughts.

AWARENESS OF YOUR THOUGHTS

Most people take their thoughts for granted. No one teaches you how to be aware about your thoughts or reflect on what you think and why you think it. Many people mix up thoughts with feelings and emotions. Feelings and emotions are usually identified by one word which describes a sensation or a collection of sensations. For example, feelings of love, happiness, gratitude, guilt, jealousy, or anger. Thoughts are different. They consist of many words. They are your self-talk and describe what is running through your head. For example: "*My partner is pre-occupied.*"

Some people experience thoughts as a running commentary inside their heads. Others see them more as words printed on a page. Some thoughts can take the form of images, for instance, when you think about a past experience. Memories are a type of thought, so is rehearsing a speech in your head, preparing to ask a question or doing a mathematical equation.

Automatic thoughts are the thoughts that pop up instinctively in response to something. For example, when someone cuts you off while you're driving, an automatic thought might be, *"What a jerk!"* When you realise you've had that thought, you can challenge it, by thinking, "Maybe he just didn't see my indicator."

It is good to practice reflecting on your thoughts. Ask yourself - does this thought help me or hinder me? If you find that it is negative or hinders you, then ask yourself: "Is this thought based on facts, is it just an assumption or am I jumping to a conclusion?". You will see that most of your negative thoughts are just assumptions or invalid conclusions. This technique keeps you continuously aware and helps you to become more positive and less reactive.

DIVING DOWN

The "diving down" technique, involves following each thought down to its origin, the underlying assumption or belief.

To begin, think of a frequent thought, feeling or idea, for example: "*I procrastinate too much.*" Now ask yourself, "What does that say about me?" The answer should say something about you as a person, such as "*I'm lazy*" or "*I'm scared I will fail*". Now ask yourself again, "What does that say about me?" The answer might be, "I'm weak," or "I am a failure". That might be your core belief, or you can ask again, "What does that say about me?" and answer "*I am just not good enough*".

A similar process can be followed to understand your beliefs about people and the world. Start with a thought about people, for example "I can't trust my manager". Now ask yourself "What does that say about managers?" a few times, until you arrive at the core belief about trust and people.

When you have identified one or more unbalanced beliefs, you can begin a dialogue with your inner-self. The first step is learning to be aware of your thoughts. Once you recognise that you are having automatic thoughts in response to your core beliefs, you can start to deal with the situation in more adult ways.

EMPOWERING & LIMITING BELIEFS

The four-minute mile

For hundreds of years, people held the belief that it was impossible for a human to run the mile in less than four minutes. It just could not be done. You would die instantly, be too exhausted; it would be too painful and too extreme for your heart to cope.

In 1954, Roger Banister broke this imposing belief barrier after doing a lot of physical and mental exercises. He achieved the 'impossible' by breaking through the four-minute barrier. The greatest aspect of this breakthrough was what it did for others. Within one year 37 other runners also broke it.

His experience provided others with a sense of certainty that they too could do the "impossible". The year after that, 300 other runners did the same thing!

Every day you hear people recite excuses why they can't do something. Most of which are limiting beliefs. People with limiting beliefs have restrictions; people with empowering beliefs get stronger, more successful, and have a greater sense of what they are capable of.

Our beliefs limit us, and often, these beliefs come from others. Don't let anyone tell you that you can't or that you aren't good enough.

If Rosa Parks let people tell her that she didn't deserve to sit in the bus just because she was black, how would history be affected? The truth is, we still don't know what humans are capable of. It is hard to break the beliefs, assumptions and rules others have. The least you can do is set yourself up for success by not being influenced by what others say.

Kyle Maynard climbed Mount Kilimanjaro as a quadruple amputee, this was done through empowering beliefs. You can have a greater sense of what you are capable of by accepting empowering beliefs and by testing the generalizations that come from your beliefs.

Do not accept limiting generalisations. Instead, see what is possible, teenagers who become millionaires, people running marathons well into their nineties, black presidents and female prime ministers who are under

34 years old. Anything is possible, and it starts with your core beliefs.

It is tough to test your core beliefs because they are subjective. You can, however, test the rules that you derive from these beliefs. Core beliefs almost always result in rules by which you live your life. Most of these rules are self-protective, designed to help us avoid pain, and disappointment.

If, you have a restrictive belief like "*I am a failure*", your rules could include the following:

- ✓ Never try something hard, because it will lead to failure.
- ✓ Never ask questions or challenge the opinions of others, because others know more than me.
- ✓ Never expect to get ahead, because I am not good enough.
- ✓ Never try out for a sports team, because I will fail.
- ✓ Never quit a job, because I might not get another job.

In your head, breaking one of these rules might lead to a disaster. For example, what if you tried hard, and still failed? There would be no escaping confrontation with the negative core belief, "I am a failure". So, the rules protect by merely helping you to avoid situations in which you might fail.

On the other hand, if you have an empowering belief that "I *can do anything*", your rules could include the following:

- ✓ Always try hard and make the best of any situation.
- ✓ Just start, do not procrastinate – you will learn what is required on the way.
- ✓ Change is good and taking risks is part of life; in the end, it will all work out.
- ✓ Invest in yourself, build new skills, new experiences.
- ✓ Always be curious, take the initiative, experience new things and situations, embrace change.

Enabling beliefs, help us to have a growth mindset. On the contrary restrictive beliefs create self-protective rules. Unfortunately, living by these restrictive rules means you may not reach your true potential.

YOUR CORE BELIEF RULE BOOK

Over time we have developed an unwritten rule book. This rule book is written by the ink of our core beliefs and leaves a strong impression on our value compass (a tool we will introduce later in Part 2.3). In our experience as coaches, we have seen our clients benefit from making the ink in this rule book visible.

You can do this by going through a challenging yet straightforward tool we call 'The Rule Book", you will be able to identify the rules coming from a particular core belief and change them to your advantage.

The Rule Book Tool

STEP 1: Write down your core beliefs on a piece of paper. Review this chapter again if you are still unsure about your core beliefs and do the core belief inventory in the workbook.

STEP 2: Pick one of your core beliefs and go through the below questions. For Example: "I Am Worthless". Read the question list below and pick some questions which seem relevant – be honest!

- How do I deal with other people's anger?
- How do I deal with other people's withdrawal or their rejection of me?
- How do I deal with mistakes I make?
- How do I handle stress, problems, or losses?
- How do I express my needs?
- How am I at trusting others?
- How do I express my opinion?
- How do I express my anger?

Example

If my core belief is "*I am worthless.*" I might choose the following questions:

- How do I deal with other people's anger? – answers:
    - o I try to keep the peace.
    - o I stay quiet or withdraw.

- How do I deal with stress/problems/losses? - answer:
    - o I avoid making decisions.
    - o I procrastinate taking action.

- How do I express my needs? – answers:
    - o I hint rather than ask directly.

- I don't ask for help but sometimes get frustrated when others don't guess what I want.

- How do I express my opinions? – answer:
  - I don't disagree unless it's someone I know well.

STEP 3: Now move on and make a list of potential disappointments or catastrophes, things that might happen if you were to break the rule.

Example

My list of potential catastrophes, things that might occur if broke the rule look like this:

Rule to break	Catastrophic prediction
I need to try to keep the peace	The other person will get angrier. It will be my fault, and the relationship will end.
I don't make decisions or take action	I will do the wrong thing or make matters worse

Once you identify your core beliefs, the Rule Book Tool helps you figure out what rules your inner self has made to protect you from facing that belief. The tool also helps you acknowledge the fears – the catastrophes – that these rules avoid. The next step is changing your core beliefs.

CHANGING YOUR CORE BELIEFS

Changing your core beliefs is also a step-by-step process. A tool to do this is given in the full of life workbook with detailed instructions. Ideally, it helps to have a coach guide you through this entire process. Review a brief summary of the steps below.

STEP 1: Choose a core belief you want to change.

Focus on one of the rules that is dictated by that belief. Pick a rule that allows you to test the core belief directly. It is a good idea to choose a relatively low-fear rule to start with. Select a rule that you want to consciously break. Think of it as an experiment. The outcome of breaking the rule should be measurable. It should have a clear behavioural result, and not simply a subjective feeling.

Example

"Don't make decisions" would be a good one to test. It will be easy to see the outcome and feel any changes that result.

STEP 2: Write down the catastrophic outcome and decide your experiment

We often follow our rules since we fear the terrible outcome of breaking them. In this step list the catastrophic outcome associated with your rule. Finally, end by deciding on the experiment you will conduct to try to break your rule.

Example

Rule: Don't make decisions

Catastrophic outcome: I will do the wrong thing and make it much worse. I will regret my choice.

Experiment: When something goes wrong, create a step by step plan for how to solve the problem, and immediately take the first step.

STEP 3: Do the test.

Try out your new behaviour and collect data on the outcome. Write your results in a prediction log given in the workbook.

Example

Actual outcome: I followed my steps and figured out the problem. I resolved the situation, perhaps not entirely, but it was not idiotic.

Personal results: I feel proud, gratified and slightly more confident because I have accomplished this. I think I will be more motivated to take action again.

STEP 4: Repeat step 3 for this rule and come up with tests for other rules, record your results.

We have used this tool as part of many coaching sessions. Reality is not always quick and simple. It often requires some experiments and feedback from the coachee. For example:

Experiment 1: I tried and failed, and XYZ happened, but something good ABC also happened.

Experiment 2: Things get better.

Experiment 3: Total Failure.

Experiment 4: Things get much better, and over time I can write the final actual outcome.

STEP 5: Rewrite your core belief in the form of an affirmation.

If it is a "Self" core belief, write it in the first person. Keep it simple and short. Then think of new recommendations to replace the old rules. New core belief: I am capable, I am worthwhile.

Example

Old rule	New Response /Affirmation
Keep the peace	I can cope with conflict.
Don't make decisions or take action.	I have good judgment. I can solve problems

"Just as your car runs more smoothly, requires less energy to go faster and farther when the wheels are in perfect alignment, you perform better when your thoughts, feelings, emotions, goals, and values are in balance." ~Brian Tracy

YOUR NEW CORE BELIEFS

As you can see, it is not a quick process to update and change the childlike core beliefs we hold on to. However to grow and mature as a person, you need to reflect, challenge yourself and let go of your old, negative and unexamined beliefs. Now you need to start living your life consistently in line with your personality and your core beliefs, regardless of the environment or situation. The next chapter will show how values and principles can assist you to be yourself and start living the life of your dreams.

PART 2.2: ACTION ITEMS / SUMMARY QUESTIONS

a. Why is it important to reflect on your core beliefs? How will knowing your core beliefs affect you?

b. Define new beliefs by going through the described process.

c. Create some clear affirmations to help you cement new beliefs which are more positive and beneficial to you.

d. How do these new beliefs affect your ability to do your work? What will you do differently from now on?

Your Values

"When you live your values, you will define yourself from within rather than by people's opinions or by comparisons to others"

~Stephen Covey

VALUES AND BELIEFS

Values and beliefs are important to us, we use both to guide our actions. Beliefs define how we see the world, they colour our perception. Values are our principles, the standards and the rules we live by.

We use both values and beliefs for decision making. As discussed in the previous part, beliefs originate from past experiences and are based on the culture and environment we were brought up in. Making decisions based on beliefs alone can be risky, since beliefs are based on past experiences, and may not apply in the present or future.

Values are the rules we live by, they define our behaviour in the present and future. They are related to our needs and what we value.

Psychologists define beliefs as the building blocks of our conscious thoughts. Beliefs influence our values, so it's important to be aware of your beliefs first and work to change any limiting beliefs before reviewing your values.

Values don't always go in line with beliefs. A good balance between values and beliefs is important. Values help you to take the right decisions and your positive beliefs will ensure you take them in the right context.

VALUES DEFINE YOU

Values are powerful instruments of personal growth as they help us surpass our limiting beliefs. Awareness of values and living your values can help you become who you are and live a more fulfilled life.

Rohan's Self-Discovery

Rohan was brought up in the suburbs of a big city in India. Both his parents had a very tough up-bringing.

As Rohan was growing up he was told to finish the food on his plate, because 'food is precious'. He played with his friends in simple and worn-out clothes while they were all well-dressed. When he asked why, his parents repeatedly told him to be grateful for what he had, since they did not even have these clothes when they were growing up. Rohan understood the message: 'be grateful' loud and clear.

His friends often made fun of him and some would refuse to play with him and even call him names. He noticed that those who were dressed well and had pocket money were treated nicely by others. In Rohan's mind a realisation began to sink in 'I am inferior to others' and 'people are judgemental'. Rohan's parents tried to motivate him by telling him that one day he would have a nice office job and would help elevate the family. Rohan believed, 'my family depends on me'.

Rohan's parents worked hard to send him to a English language school, and then to a good university. While in college Rohan was approached many times by the college festival committee since he was great at singing. Rohan would always decline, thinking to himself 'how can I perform in front of so many people'. Rohan valued 'praise' but deep down he believed 'he was not good enough'.

After graduating Rohan started working as a sales executive in a large bank. His manager told him to upgrade his wardrobe. He would be speaking with high-income group prospects, so he must be dressed well for the job. Rohan valued 'simplicity' but he understood that his job required him to show up as someone different.

Rohan also valued 'money' and 'ambition' since he knew that his family was depending on him. He worked long hours every day and would often visit clients in the weekends. Within 6 months there was another job opportunity that would pay him 20% more. Rohan knew that he had a lot more to learn in his current job, yet money was important so he made the jump. Rohan did this a few times till his salary was nearly 3 times his starting salary in just 5 years.

Rohan was now deputy manager at a large bank and was asked to present to a group of High Net-Worth Individuals (HNI). These HNI's were CEO's and wealthy businessmen. Rohan was nervous, he never did a presentation like this before. He would have had opportunities to present in his previous jobs, but every time just before it happened, he jumped to a better paying job. Rohan was so nervous to speak to this large crowd that he declined to make the presentation.

He knew it could be a 'career limiting move' and was ready to face the consequences. Rohan was not satisfied with his life and did not understand why!

Rohan's story shows how values are influenced by beliefs. His values were 'praise', 'simplicity', 'money' and 'ambition'. He valued 'praise' because he believed 'I am not good enough'. His values of 'money' and 'ambition' stemmed from his belief 'my family depends on me'. Rohan needs to become aware of his limiting beliefs and how they influenced his values. His value of 'simplicity' seems to conflict with the values of 'money' and 'ambition'. This conflict leads him to work in an environment where he does not feel fulfilled. To improve his situation, he can work to change his limiting beliefs and consciously create values that are aligned with each other.

Our life choices such as being part of an event, changing jobs and our work-life balance are all influenced by our values. Values are unique to each person and drive our decisions, actions and behaviours. Some people value stability, while others value flexibility. Some people are humble while others value status.

Values should be aligned with each other to consistently guide our actions. For example, if you value honesty and dependability, then you do your best to demonstrate that you are reliable and speak your mind. If someone requests your support, you will be straightforward and say yes or no. If you agree to help, then you give it your best because they are counting on you.

Values are based on your principles, they are a roadmap that guides you through life, but they can change as your life changes. For example, when Rohan was a student, he would never waste food. As he became a deputy manager, had money to spare and had to watch his weight, his value might change. Similarly, a footballer's values may change once he retires and becomes a coach.

In summary, our values are important. They shape our lives, we define success and failure based on our values. As coaches, we find that most people never take the time to consciously become aware of, select and live their values. Doing this will enable them to live a full life.

WHY ARE VALUES IMPORTANT

Values exist whether you are aware of them or not. If you are not aware of your values you might unknowingly violate them and feel miserable. It is important to become aware of your values so you can honour them. You can live with integrity knowing that you are standing up for what's important to you.

We all have values, but we don't always back them up with our actions. I can tell myself and others that I value adventure, but if I spend my days at home and my holidays in local resorts then my behaviour tells a different story. You feel greater fulfilment if you choose to live according to your values.

Research shows that people make choices based on emotions and not on facts. Marketing and advertising thrive on this fact and often get us to buy things we do not really value. Knowing and living your values help you make fact-based decisions. When you do this, you weigh each choice against your values before making a decision. This results in living from the inside-out rather than being influenced and living from the outside-in.

In life, we face problems and have to deal with challenging people. In such situations, our decisions are often driven by external influences. We tell ourselves "just this once" and do things that are not in line with our values. Values serve as a guide in decision-making. By using values, you start making better long-term choices that are in line with what's important to you.

Living your values helps to bring consistency in life. When you embrace your values, people expect a certain standard from you. This builds integrity, improves trust and helps you build relationships. For example, if you value timeliness, you are always on time for meetings and social events. Therefore, people will rely on you, to deliver critical projects on time and your friends will call on you to drop them to the airport.

Everyone is different and their values are unique. If what matters to you is different from what matters to people in your organization, you are in a value conflict. For example, if the people involved in your project don't value timeliness then you find yourself in a stressful situation. You might even face this value conflict with family and friends. Knowing your values helps you set clear expectations and stand up for what you believe in.

TYPES OF VALUES

Before we begin the process of uncovering and living values, it is useful to know that there are different types of values. These include accidental values, aspirational values and core values.

Accidental values are the most common ones. These values get formed automatically by our beliefs and our environment. If you have never consciously thought about your values, a few of your values may be accidental. For example, a young accountant loved to party with his friends during university. He brought his accidental values of fun and impulsiveness into work. During a coaching session, he realised that these values do not apply to his job.

Aspirational values are those values that we need to succeed in the future. We might currently lack these and know that having these would significantly improve our life. For example, the young accountant aspired to be precise and organised in everything he did. This would help him to become an excellent accountant. Aspirational values drive us to improve ourselves and become better. It is good to select a few important aspirational values that you like to apply in your life.

Core values are deeply ingrained principles that are backed up by our actions and behaviours. They are inherent and show up in our day to day lives. For most people, core values stay the same throughout life. Very few people are consciously aware of their core values. For example, the young accountant might have core values of integrity and accuracy. These may have formed over the years by the choices he/she made. These values would show up with friends in college, with family and at work.

UNDERSTANDING YOUR VALUES

Knowing what is important to you, helps you live in harmony with your values. For example, if you value fairness but work for a company that does not pay minimum wage to its blue-collar workers, how much internal stress and conflict would you feel? And if you don't value spirituality, and your partner is devout and religious, how would that affect your relationship?

In these types of situations, understanding your values can help. Knowing your values is like having an autopilot or compass that guides your actions. This is exactly why we call the next tool "The Value Compass."

The Value Compass

You are in a dense forest, and you have no idea how you got there and are desperate to find your way back to civilisation. You have seen enough reality shows and movies to have some idea of what could help you, and what dangers may exist. You start looking around and see a green duffle bag with a message on it - Act or Die!

What is the one thing you wish this bag would have?

Perhaps a working satellite phone? To your utter dismay, all you find in this bag is a compass and a note.

The note describes that the compass is unlike any you have seen. It is voice-activated! You simply say 'Hey Compass' followed by a question and it will tell you exactly what you need to do, to survive.

All you need to do is follow the instructions to get out of the wilderness and survive. Thrilled to have this device - you shout 'Hey Compass' and you wake up!

Waking up from such a dream could leave you with mixed emotions. Happy for finding yourself safe and cosy in your bed, yet you are sad for not having a voice-activated compass. A special tool that would tell you exactly what you need to do in a crisis.

'What guides you in tough situations?'

The Value Compass ensures that actions are guided by, deep personal values. Acting, behaving and living by values makes us feel alive each day. We choose to use this compass and live from the inside-out rather than compromise on our values.

"When your values are clear to you Making decisions becomes easier" ~Roy. E. Disney

Outlined in the next pages is the path to discovering, prioritising and changing the values on your compass.

This tool helps to bring these values to the surface, prioritise and use them to make the right decisions.

THE VALUE COMPASS PROCESS

STEP 1 - Identify your values

There are two ways to discover your values. The first one is with a coach through some coaching questions. The second one is to review a list of values and ask yourself which words on the list resonate with you the most.

Values Coaching

Values coaching is a deep and meaningful experience. It is designed for those who want to really understand who they are and what they value so they can make better decisions. Read the five questions given below and record your responses in the full of life workbook.

- Think of your most amazing life experiences. Which values were you honouring?
- Think of a time when you had a serious personal conflict. Which values were you fighting for?
- Think about the times when you took a stand. What were you standing up for?
- Think about the people you admire or look up to. Which of their values resonate with you?
- Think of a time when you were most proud. What values contributed to feeling this sense of pride?

This method of identifying your values relies on real-life experiences and helps you uncover rather than select your values. Once you have a list of values from the above questions it's time to move to Step 2- Prioritising values. If you struggled to arrive at the list with the above method, don't worry we have a simpler method listed below.

Values List

Values are best discovered using the coaching method. However, if this is your first time thinking about your values you can review the complete list of values given in the full of life workbook. Here is a short list of values:

Accomplishment, Accuracy, Adventure, Balance, Bold, Calm, Collaboration, Commitment, Directness, Daring, Discovery, Empowerment, Excellence, Fairness, Flexibility, Focus, Gentleness, Gratefulness, Growth, Health, Honour, Humour, Independence, Innovation, Integrity, Knowledge, Learning, Loving, Loyalty, Optimism, Orderliness, Perseverance, Productivity, Recognition, Respect, Resourcefulness, Safety, Simplicity, Spirituality, Tact, Tolerance, Trust, Understanding, Unity, Vitality, Wisdom.

The above list gives you some values. Use the full list provided in the workbook to uncover your values.

STEP 2 - Prioritize your values

At this stage, you must prioritise to arrive at 3 - 6 values that form your "Value Compass". The best way to do this is outlined below.

1. List the values identified in Step 1 on small A5 or A6 Cards and stack this list facing down. Pick

one card at random and place it on your right hand (The Right Choice)

2. Pick up an alternative card in your left hand and ask yourself which value would you say YES to and which would you say NO to (this is the hard part, imagine you had no other choice!)

3. Keep doing this, till you go through the entire stack. You would then have your topmost value. (your North)

4. Finally, to prioritise the remaining values, ask yourself "In your world, if everyone (including you) had to follow three rules, what would they be?"

   Pick three other cards based on the above question. You now have your East, South, and West!

   During this stage you might think 'This is hard', 'I can't do this', 'Why do I have to choose?'. If these are your thoughts, then you know you are on the right track. The short-term pain of this process will lead you to the long-term gain of having a Value Compass.

STEP 3 – Change your values

Going through the above process will lead you to your core values. These values got you where you are today, but will they take you where you want to be? You might realise now that some of your values are accidental. You can choose and change your values if you want. The way to do this is to identify the accidental values that hold you back and replace them with aspirational values that will move your forward.

For example, an experienced manager had been trying for a while to move into a leadership position. The company required 360-degree feedback and an online assessment. He had tried a few times and never got through the first round. During a coaching session, he realised that his current value of 'humility' was holding him back. So he resolved to replace 'humility' with an aspirational value of 'ambition' to get the promotion.

Changing your values involves experimentation. What should you choose to become more successful? Go back to Step 1 to arrive at 1 or 2 aspirational values for your future. Add them to your value compass and start consciously living those values.

LIVING YOUR VALUES

Having found your Value Compass, you need to commit to applying this knowledge for the next fortnight, month, year or even life. The best way to live your values is to weave them into everything you do. Ask yourself a question every time you need to make a choice. 'What would I, who Values (Insert your Value) do in this situation?'.

Based on your values, you will end up with 3 to 6 questions that you can ask yourself when you feel lost in the wilderness of your personal and professional life. The value compass is a guide. For example, when I was thinking about writing a book. I asked myself "what will I do?" I want to make a difference – writing a book was the answer. It is what inspired me to co-author this book.

Another way to ensure you live your values is to communicate them often. Don't feel shy to tell someone why you do something based on your values. Stand up for your values in your personal and work life. Put your values in your email signature, on your desk or in your home. This constant reinforcement will help you stay true to your values.

Using your values during conflicts is a great way to ensure you are living your values. For example, Hans split up with a business partner and move out of a profitable business due to a value conflict. His partner values quick sales and revenue while Hans valued customer service and long term relationships. This showed up in the way they would deal with customers. Hans was unhappy with the customer complaints and his partner was unhappy when revenue was delayed due to customer service or relationship building. Hans lived his value by choosing to step out of the business.

You are on your personal journey; your challenge is: "Do I want to live each day by my values or let other people's values define each day?"

Meet Rameez

Rameez is a Key Account Manager for a system manufacturing firm. He has been in sales and account management for 15 years now. He is valued within the organisation, promoted, and the management appreciates the work he does and his customers remain loyal.

There are a few situations at work and in life where he feels unsure about exactly what to do. Some of them described below:

At Work

A client is making a demand that is outside the contract, and his colleagues from the service department are asking for his support to ensure the client pays for spare parts.

At Home

His family is asking that they go on a vacation and he has an individual goal to save money for his personal development. He also wants to improve his health, but his work schedule leaves him choosing junk food on most days.

Rameez decides to use the value compass exercise to figure out the best thing to do in these situations.

Step 1 - Identify: Rameez has gone through the coaching questions and is also reviewing a list of values (can be found in the full of life workbook). At this stage, he is tempted to pick many of the values as they all sound nice! He reminds himself of the three types of values – accidental, aspirational and core *values and sticks to only eight from the list.*

Step 2 - Prioritise: Now the tough task of prioritising begins!

1: He writes down his eight values on separate A5 size cards.

    a. Accountability
    b. Respect
    c. Compassion
    d. Making a Difference
    e. Humility
    f. Expertise
    g. Faith
    h. Control

2: He picks a random card with his right hand (Humility)

3: He picks another card with his left hand (Control). Asks himself – Which would I say Yes to and which would I say No to? He keeps the value that he will say Yes to in his right hand (Humility)

4: He picks another card with his left hand (Make a Difference) and continues with this tough process until he is only left with one card (Respect)

5: Having found his Top most value (Respect), he is now seeking to find the other top values. He does this by asking himself "In my world if everyone including me had to live by three rules what would they be?" He reviews the seven remaining cards *and picks another three values to arrive at his top 4 values (Respect, Humility, Trust and Accountability)*

Step 3 – *Change your Values: Now Ravi has to review his list of values to see what is missing? What else should he value to find more success in life? Which of his values are accidental and are actually holding him back. He realizes that Humility is an accidental value based on his upbringing. It worked well for him so far in life. However today it is holding him back as he is not able to market himself and his work within the organization. He adds ambition to his list of values and makes an action plan to live his value of ambition at work.*

Knowing who you are by understanding and living your values changes your behaviour, actions and decisions. You come a step closer to understand your identity

YOUR IDENTITY

Combining awareness of your personality, beliefs and values will help define your identity. To cement this understanding, ask yourself these questions:

1. What are my greatest assets?
   What do I excel at, what am I good at?
   Why do I think so?

2. What are my core beliefs?
   Come up with some key affirmations

3. Why do I get up every morning?
    What is important to me, what do I value?

Spend 5 or 10 minutes on each question every day for a week. Everyday write it down without reviewing the previous day – use a new page every day.

Why? Because the mind has a way of working out the answers in your subconscious, when you ask yourself a question give the mind some time, let it work it out – talk to others about it, and you will see you will get clear answers. Just keep writing it down until you are satisfied.

DEFINE AND REFINE YOUR IDENTITY

Most organisations have a Vision, Mission and Values Statement which hangs next to the reception desk. Some even print it on their business cards. The aim is to ensure that everyone in the organisation understands it and acts in the same way.

As individuals we should also identify ourselves – The question "who are you" is not easy to answer if you have not thought about it. After you have invested time to deeply understand yourself through your personality, your values and your beliefs it is time to create a "*Personal Identity Statement*".

This statement should clearly articulate who you are; it should be authentic. It can acknowledge your positives as well as include some negative areas you are trying to improve and want to work on. It should combine key characteristics, beliefs and values. It can include your principles, interests, and what you stand for. It is really up to you what you want to include or exclude.

An identity statement can be long or short. It is intended to give you a clear view on who you are and brings together your personality, your values and your beliefs. As authors, we share our deeply personal identity statements below.

Hans Horlings

Strengths: Working with people, inspiring others through facilitating, training, coaching, mentoring and speaking engagements. My ability to accept last minute changes, being flexible and adaptable. Due to my impulsive nature, I sometimes take too many risks.

Values: Adventure, Optimism, Authenticity and Action. I value the ability to make a difference and making the most of every situation.

Beliefs: I believe that people are generally good and trustworthy. I also believe that people are often underdeveloped and undervalued and capable of doing much more when truly challenged and motivated. Finally, I believe that we all can make a difference and that we are in control of our own lives.

Identity Statement: "I am an individual who loves adventure, change and the freedom to act. I believe that most people are able and willing to improve their lives when given the opportunity and confidence to develop their innate talents. My purpose is to help people to invest in themselves, make the most of their lives and positively touch the lives of the people around them. To facilitate this, I focus on continuously seeking new adventures to develop myself, share my knowledge and build relationships to improve people's lives in any way I can. I am grateful for everything I receive and all the people close to me who keep me grounded and allow me to make a difference."

Ashirvad Lobo

Strengths: As someone with a very high people and action focus, I love to collaborate with people. I am driven, ambitious and caring. Due to my focus on doing the right thing for others, I often take too many opinions into account before making a decision.

Values: Challenge, Making a Difference, Dynamic, Humble, Leaving a Legacy and Accountability.

Beliefs: If you don't grow you die, everyone wants to and can learn and improve, God is in each person I meet.

Identity Statement: "I firmly believe if you don't grow you die, I am passionate and driven about learning, teaching, coaching and mentoring. I collaborate and care for people, to help them to learn and improve. Since God dwells in each person I meet, I am humble in my dealings. I aim to improve my decision making so that I can make a difference in this world. This would be seen by the legacy I leave behind as a dynamic, challenging, husband, father, facilitator, author, speaker and coach."

YOUR INNER SCORECARD

Warren Buffett, CEO and chairman of Berkshire Hathaway and the most famous investor lives by a golden rule which he calls the inner scorecard. The inner scorecard is made up of your own values, dreams and principles, while the outer scorecard is made up of others' values, dreams and principles. Success can be found by following your inner or outer scorecard.

According to Buffet if we live by an outer scorecard we want success and admiration from others, what they say about us is important. While if we live by an inner scorecard we want success and admiration from ourselves, by following our own principles, values and dreams.

"The big question about how people behave is whether they've got an Inner Scorecard or an Outer Scorecard. It helps if you can be satisfied with an Inner Scorecard."
~Warren Buffett

He goes on to say that fulfilment and happiness comes by following an inner scorecard. Living by an outer scorecard might make you feel good when you receive praise. However, once you realise that this praise is undeserved, you feel dis-satisfied and feel like you let yourself down. For example, if everyone says you are the best, but deep down you know you do not deserve this, you will not feel happy, fulfilled or satisfied.

Warren Buffet lives his life according to his inner scorecard, regardless of his wealth he still lives the same way, follows the same rules, lives in the same house and dresses the same way and regularly visits the same restaurants as thirty years ago. Unfortunately, most people chase praise and recognition from others and are driven by their outer scorecard rather than their inner scorecard. They start to behave differently when they get praise from others, and let go of their own values and start to accept the values of others.

You need to learn to behave in a way as if if you knew no one was watching. There's a simple word for this: Authenticity, be yourself. The way to get there is to remember the Inner Scorecard and start grading yourself accordingly.

LIVING YOUR LIFE WITH AUTHENTICITY

You now understand who you are and how to consistently live from the inside-out. It is time to make decisions in line with your personality, beliefs and values, take new actions and start new habits. The best thing is to look back on all your experiences. Different environments and types of work help you to decide and evaluate what your unique skills are and what uniquely fits with you.

No experience is a waste of time; understanding what you don't like is also valuable. Just complete the part 2.3 action items on the next page and move on to a systematic process to understand what you would love to do. Part 3 will help you define your ideal job, find your passion and understand your calling and will move you closer towards your dream life.

PART 2.3: ACTION ITEMS / SUMMARY QUESTIONS

a. Why is it important to define your values? How will knowing this effect your life?

b. Define your Values by going through the described process in the workbook. Pick 4-6 key personal values you are prepared to live by.

c. Try and live your values by making decisions in line with your values – ask yourself, is this in-line with my values?

d. How do these values affect your ability to do your work? What do you have to do differently from now on?

e. Create your own Personal Identity Statement. Share it with your family and close friends and seek their feedback.

What Do You Want?

"The World needs dreamers, and the world needs doers. But above all, the world needs dreamers who do."

~Sarah Ban Breathnach

A WORLD FULL OF CHOICES

This part of the book builds on who you are and helps you become aware of what you want. Living a full and fulfilling life is about making choices which fit with your personality, beliefs and values. Choices in life relate to many different areas like work, leisure, relationships, home, health, religion, among others. Each person is unique and has different areas of importance and different priorities. The key is to start making your choices in the most critical areas first.

Most people make basic choices on what to watch, where to go or what to do in the weekend, rather than making choices related to redesigning their life and finding a deep connection between who they are and what they do. Unfortunately, most people live from the outside-in making choices pushed by their environment and do not take the time to live from the inside-out, making choices related to who they are and how they can live a life with purpose and meaning.

People change jobs to earn a little more or have better prospects in the future. Some are lucky and discover their calling almost accidentally. Most people do not even want to dream and think about how to live from the inside-out. Most just let life happen and do not take the time to pro-actively design their life.

It takes time and effort to define what you want and to design your life. It takes courage to look inward, reflect on your experiences, and try to find and live the life of your dreams. It is now time for you to embrace who you are and look at what you want in life. When you do, your life is the most exciting adventure you can imagine.

Embrace Who You Are

To me, understanding "Who You Are", felt like a liberation. For the first time in my life, I realised that it was ok to be myself, that there was nothing wrong with me.

I suddenly understood why I craved variety in everything and always wanted action. Sure, I still had to work on some of my limiting beliefs, but this understanding made me feel good about myself.

It gave me the confidence to be different from my colleagues, set my values and choose a path that was quite different from everyone else.

I started to come up with new initiatives, volunteered for duties, which others viewed as undesirable. I stepped out of my comfort zone and started learning new skills and took on new hobbies and met new people.

My job started to change. I took on more and more responsibility for things I liked and slowly started to move away from the type of work I did not like. I added real value to my job and myself – I was making a difference.

Looking back, it all started to happen almost automatically after understanding myself.

"Don't die without embracing the daring adventure your life was meant to be." ~Steve Pavlina

MAKE CHOICES ALIGNED TO WHO YOU ARE

The key to success in your career, business, and in life is to understand yourself, what you want, and work diligently towards it. It requires a large dose of courage, investment in yourself and a determination to follow your dreams and your heart. When you do, you are on a path, a path where you unleash your personal power and make an impact in this world, any way you choose.

Doing something that comes naturally to you is a pleasure. When you are interested in something, you get more knowledge about it, develop your skills further and become the expert. You become passionate about that activity. The activity can be anything. It can relate to your profession, a hobby or a sports activity.

You can use the tools in this part of the book to understand the choices you have to design an extraordinary life. Start by understanding your needs and wants. Define what success means to you and then look at the decisions you need to make. The next step is to understand and build your passion. This is done by reviewing your strengths and talents and by reviewing your experiences in life so far. At the end of this part, you will discover your calling, your mission and purpose. The key to discovering what you want is to reflect on your choices.

Back To Reality

Amy felt inspired to chase her dreams. Brave and full of hope, she decided to do it. She quit her job and applied for that dream job. It felt wonderful, empowering and exciting.

A year later, Amy was feeling utterly defeated. It just didn't work. She hustled hard to get the job that would send her overseas to work for women's rights. A series of unpaid internships, applications and emails led to nothing. It was incredibly frustrating. She began questioning if it was worth it. Following these dreams, when you end up feeling so defeated.

When I talked to Amy, six months ago, she told me something wonderful happened. She woke up early one morning, sitting outside, with a mug of hot coffee, cuddled between her hands, she looked at the sunrise. Orange and yellow streaks were painting a brilliant early morning sky. She felt the sun on her face, and as she sat there, with none of her dreams come true yet, she realised that it was ok. Alive and healthy, she was grateful for the opportunity and the new experiences. She realised that even if her dreams never came true, she would still be ok and thankful for the opportunity.

She realised that she was making choices that would continue to help her achieve her dream. She understood she could only control her actions and *should not feel defeated by external circumstances. This realisation was so liberating that she keeps trying to pursue her dream.*

FOCUS ON WHAT YOU CAN CONTROL

You know that things don't always turn out exactly as you want. Life has its twists and turns, ups and downs. External circumstances have an impact on life, whether you like it or not. The trick is to focus on what you can control. This gives you a better chance to get there and move in the right direction.

Living a full life is all about understanding that you are in control. You make choices and take steps towards making your dreams come true. You become pro-active and excited about the progress you make. You start to see opportunities because of your mindset changes. You will find a way to make your dreams come true.

The dream is exciting, but it is the journey that counts. Get involved in the journey and adventure of your own life, discover your purpose, laugh at yourself, enjoy your relationships. Like Amy enjoy a quiet morning with the sun on your face and a cup of coffee or tea in your hands, feeling good about who you are.

YOUR LIFE IS AN ADVENTURE

Life is a unique adventure. Embrace this adventure, accept that your life is continually developing. What your adventure looks like should be defined by you. Young people find it easier to dream, they see footballers, pop stars and actors and almost instantly build their adventure. It is hard for them to realise how much hard work is involved. Many adults find it hard to dream, saying it is not realistic, I am not in control.

Everyone is in control of their own life. You shape your life by the choices you make. This does not mean it is easy, but when you design and follow your path, it will give you fulfilment.

"I start early, and I stay late, day after day, year after year, it took me 17 years and 114 days to become an overnight success" ~Lionel Messi

You already understand that you are unique. As a unique individual, it is logical that your life should also be unique rather than standard. Craft a unique path, using your unique talents, which gives you meaning. A path like this is an adventure; it comes from within and becomes your unique "normal".

Life is shaped by many experiences, trying different things, learning and growing along the way. It might not fit with the expectations of those around you, what counts is that it is a life shaped by you. Let's explore this through some life-adventure stories.

Living The Dream

Guarded by a colonial fort, the "Sweet River" called Rio Dulce has a beautiful lake 'Izabel'. This is where many sailors spend time in the winter to get out of the hurricane belt.

Upon the banks of the Rio Dulce, lies a handmade and simple bar. Sitting on moss-filled poles, The Shack is under the biggest bridge over the Sweet River. The owner, Pete, an ex-sailor, settled here after sailing around the world. He now serves beer, simple food and tells great stories. His customers are friends, and he lives a carefree lifestyle.

This is where Nitzan and his long-time buddy Shai were hanging out. Like most sailors that visit The Shack, they are self-sufficient. A water-maker, solar panels, wind generator, inside a safe hull and rig allow them to live on the water. Nitzan and Shai live a simple life, on less than $500 a month. They feel fulfilled living a carefree life. They enjoy their freedom to go when and where they want. They have great relationships, no worries and a million-dollar view.

The adventure started in the minds of four friends at the tender age of 16. They agreed to save money to buy the perfect boat. All four set off to live this dream when they finished their education. A "normal" life caught up with 2 of them. One got a steady girlfriend and planned to get married. Another stayed for three months and realised this was not for him. He needed to get a stable job and a "normal" life.

Nitzan and Shai were still living their dream. They had lived on board for the last five years. Worked now-and-then on other people's boats to make enough money. A five-star life as a sea-gipsy was a *great adventure.*

They told me, it took them around six months to become true sea-gipsies. During this time, they settled down and got rid of the pressure to have a "normal" life.

Like Nitzan and Shai, some people want to live close to nature and do not need a lot of wealth to live a full life. Some work to make the world a better place. Others are entrepreneurial and start a business. Many are just proud to be employees and do a great job. Few just do what they love and become famous by mistake rather than by design. Everyone who lives a life uniquely shaped by themselves is on an exciting journey.

Raha Moharrak's Adventure!

Raha Moharrak, the youngest of three, born in Jeddah, Saudi Arabia graduated from the American University, Sharjah. She loves sports, but as a young woman, practising sports did not fit into the traditional values.

Her dad explained to her that she should do more lady-like things. Raha convinced her father that she loves physical activity. When a friend told her about a holiday to climb Mt Kilimanjaro, she begged her father to allow her to go. He did not understand why she wanted to walk so much, sleep in a tent, eat basic rations and put herself through this misery. Finally, he gave in, and this first trip was the start of many to come, as she became a passionate mountain climber.

Following her passion, Raha became the first Saudi woman to climb and reach the top of Mount Everest, the highest mountain on earth. Raha is now a famous woman in the Middle East. She regularly gives talks about passion, courage and following your dreams. Was it easy? No, says Raha! - "convincing my father and family to let me climb was as great a challenge as climbing the mountain itself!"

Was it worth it? Raha says: "Yes! Especially when a thirteen-year-old girl tells you that she is taking up cycling because of you. It means you make a difference for someone else, which to me is more important than fame and recognition."

Raha was aware of what she wanted and found a way to make it happen. Her father still does not understand why she wants to go through mud, snow and ice, but he understands that climbing mountains is her passion!

BE EXTRAORDINARY, NORMAL DOES NOT EXIST

When I was young, a "normal" life scared me. In my view it included getting married, buying a house, a car, having children, a dog, a full-time job and a few weeks holidays a year. These choices came with commitments, like a mortgage, a car loan, weekend duties like lawn mowing, car washing, dog walking, child care and regular family visits. My carefree ex-student life would instantly change. I was not ready for a "normal" life, so I got married and moved to the other side of the world.

In New Zealand, I felt free to design our life the way I wanted it. I met people who have an incredible career as a ski instructor, windsurfer, handyman, gardener, dog walker, travel guide, journalist, sailor, event organiser, wedding planner, athlete, musician, artist, park ranger, and so many more.

I realised that we don't have to work in an office. Most people who have a so-called "normal life" may not be living the life of their dreams. You can carve your own normal based on your personality, background, strengths and values. You can shape it by your job, living condition, family and current situation.

"Normal is nothing more than a cycle on a washing machine". ~Whoopi Goldberg

David's Normal Life

David, spent five years in Holland, while his wife worked a high-profile job at the giant oil conglomerate Shell. This allowed him to follow his passion for golf. He managed to set up a golf academy in Rijswijk.

Unfortunately, her reassignment to Shell UAE meant they had to relocate. The family moved to the UAE, and David decided to spend his time studying for a masters in psychology and human behaviour, inspired *by a desire to understand his autistic son better.*

David continued his passion for golf and started organising golf trips for ex-oil workers. People who retired from oil-related jobs, who wanted to enjoy life and regularly catch up with old friends, playing golf around the world. A great example of how to use your passion to make a living.

David completed his Masters at age 42. The title of his final thesis was: "What is normal?" Yes, living with an autistic son makes you look at life differently. Both from his perspective, his wife's perspective and their son's perspective, the conclusion was: "There is no normal" – everyone's life is unique, with unique circumstances.

THE FIRST STEP TO AN EXTRAORDINARY LIFE

Courage is the first step to live a life designed by you and aligned with who you are. Do you have the courage to change and embrace your great adventure? Courage might be as simple as starting to do the exercises in the workbook. Courage develops as you begin to design your new life. As expats, living away from family, making the step to immigrate to another country takes courage, but this does not happen instantly. It took me five years of talking to friends and family, visits to the library and the New Zealand Embassy before we decided to go.

For me, the fear of regret of not having done it was always greater than the fear of stepping into the unknown. Just start the process, take the first step, be courageous, create and follow your dreams. If it is not what you expected, change again. You learn from every experience, and every change brings you closer to your five-star life.

"Twenty years from now you will be more disappointed by the things that you didn't do than by the ones you did do. So throw off the bowlines, Sail away from the safe harbour, Catch the trade winds in your sails. Explore. Dream. Discover." ~Mark Twain

See your life as a great adventure, with ups and downs, short cuts and dead-ends. Embrace the adventure and you will eventually find your path and taste that "Joie de Vivre" – and feel "Full of Life". A life designed by you, just right for you.

Life is an adventure defined by you, it is whatever you want it to be. You have to decide what you need and want. We suggest you take some time to think about it, make your decisions, live and embrace that unique adventure called life.

Understanding Needs and Wants

"Money won't make you happy...
but everybody wants to find out for
themselves". ~ Zig Ziglar

UNDERSTANDING NEEDS AND WANTS

Everyone has wants and needs, which are different from each other. Wants are desires for things that we would like to have but which are not necessary. Needs are a must for our survival, things such as food, water and shelter. However, to most people wants seem like needs.

Needs are easy to understand, they are indispensable. The reality, however, is that for most people, the line between needs and wants is blurry. This is because most of our decisions are made subjectively using emotions rather than objectively using logic. For example, working to earn money provides for both our needs and wants. Some people see work as a need, they work from nine to five or longer to meet their requirements. Others work part-time only. Some do not want to work full-time, while others have more than one job. It is important to understand what you need, what you want and what you value.

What Do You Call Success?

Out of all my friends from high school, only one followed the same path of mechanical engineering, a year of internships, followed by a university study in business as myself. He grew up on a farm. He was very focused, a good soccer player, hard worker and extremely ambitious.

When we left university, he had one main goal: "retire before reaching my forties". I guess we all have these ideas, retiring when thirty-five or forty slowly turned into fifty, fifty-five or sixty. It finally becomes retirement when a state-pension will allow you. I even know many expats who forever claim they will do just one more year. I guess it is a bit like defining when people are "old" – I used to think forty is old, then fifty, and sixty, but I now believe eighty is old.

When I left for New Zealand, we lost contact. Through the internet, he reached out to me some 20 years later. He told me his story. He did very well, became the logistics director of a large retail chain in Europe. His job required him to almost live on planes and in hotels. He regretted not being able to spend much time at home with his wife and children, which eventually lead to an amicable divorce.

He kept his promise to himself and retired before his fortieth birthday. The company offered a lot of money to stay two more years, but "he was done with it" he just had enough. He reflected as follows: "I blame myself for my divorce, not being able to see them, not being part of my children's lives is unforgivable."

He now lives in Thailand, with his Thai girlfriend, they have a comfortable life. On most days he spends two hours in the gym and an equal amount of time in the bar. Yes, he retired early, but he did not seem very fulfilled. He reached out to many school friends but found almost all still working.

Sometimes our goals for career, status and money go against our desire to become fulfilled. Understanding what is essential for you, and finding a balance helps you enjoy your wealth and success. It comes down to priorities and understanding your needs and wants in each area of your life.

To answer the question 'what do you want?' in order to live a fulfilling life, you need to answer four key questions:

1. What do you need?
2. What do you want?
3. What is your passion?
4. What is your purpose?

WHAT DO YOU NEED?

Maslow's hierarchy of needs is one of the best-known theories of human needs and motivation. It was introduced by Abraham Maslow in his 1943 paper "A Theory of Human Motivation" and his book Motivation and Personality. He suggested a hierarchy since he believed that people are motivated to fulfil lower-level needs before moving on to other, more advanced needs.

As a humanist, Maslow focused on learning about what makes people happy. He believed that people have an innate desire to be the best they can be. So he created a hierarchy of needs that includes five levels.

Needs at the bottom of the pyramid are basic physical requirements, including the need for food, water, sleep, and warmth. Once these lower-level needs are met, people can move on to the next level of needs, which are for safety and security. As people progress from their basic needs, they look to meet their psychological and social needs. Like the need for family, connection, esteem and feelings of recognition.

According to Maslow, a person finds meaning by doing important things. This drives personal growth and discovery throughout a person's life. Maslow believed that needs are similar to instincts and play a significant role in motivating behaviour.

The first four levels in the pyramid are so-called deficiency needs. Satisfying these needs is essential to avoid unpleasant feelings. Maslow termed self-actualisation as a growth need. This need does not stem from a lack of something, but rather from a desire to grow as a person.

While the theory shows a clear hierarchy, these needs do not always follow a standard progression. For some people, the need for creative fulfilment may supersede even the most basic needs. Studies of people in extreme poverty show that while people are mainly motivated by food and shelter, they still experienced love and connection with their community.

It is generally accepted that self-actualisation is the desire to become the best you can be. Satisfaction, happiness, wellbeing, fulfilment are all expressions of living a life aiming for self-actualisation. There are some critics of Maslow's hierarchy since there was little research supporting it. However, the hierarchy of needs is well-known and used across fields.

Many studies put the hierarchy to the test. These studies have validated Maslow's theory of human motivation. However, many found that motivation is not necessarily hierarchical. People from cultures all over the world reported that self-actualisation and social needs were important even when the most basic needs were unfulfilled.

After spending years reading books on the subject of motivation and observing humans throughout our lives, we feel there are a few real needs, some of these are:

- Have enough food/drink, feel satisfied
- Have a place to sleep and feel safe
- Have a relatively healthy body, feel well
- Have a few close relationships, feel good
- Have some regular physical activity, feel alive
- Have access to nature, feel grateful
- Have a purpose, feel needed
- Have recognition, feel appreciated

Most of these things do not cost a lot of money. However, it seems that few people understand this. Most people go through tremendous struggles to obtain more money and more things, always more, never enough.

THE ROLE OF MONEY

When we ask 'What do you need?' in our workshops, there are always people who say money. Will money really make you fulfilled? There is nothing wrong with wanting money, but most likely what you want, is what money can do for you. Money is important and can buy you pleasure, prestige, time, freedom and reduce worry and anxiety about the future.

When money is the only thing that is important in life, it often does not lead to more fulfilment. Do you secretly wish you could make enough money, so you never have to work again? Because you just want more time for yourself, less stress, and a little more freedom. Most people can make a living with less stress and more freedom.

We quickly get used to a particular lifestyle, standard of living, and standard of luxury. We get influenced by the rules of the people around us. We quickly adapt and adopt similar practices and patterns. Being busy, making a career and accepting a stressful existence to move up the ladder is a norm.

When you look back in time, you used to be able to live in different circumstances and levels of luxury. Many young people find it easy to take a year off or dedicate part of their life to going overseas for a good cause. They are happy to get paid with food and lodging. They help people set up an eco-business, assist nature parks, help poor people, or assist those in need because of natural disasters. Somehow these initiatives seem irresponsible as we get a little older.

Most see money as a sure path to happiness and satisfaction. After all, our role models of success are rich and lead seemingly perfect and enviable lives. Most people want to be rich and think it will solve all our problems and make us fulfilled. As a world society, most of us are better off than ever before, and at the same time, we are less happy and less satisfied than ever before. Research shows that money helps in giving you options but can equally stand in the way of living a full life.

The latest findings suggest that money doesn't fulfil basic psychological needs. When you value money above other things, it actually may decrease your happiness. Researchers found that the pursuit of money makes people engage in social comparisons, which leads to increased stress. This is especially true for those that link their self-worth with financial success.

People want money to do something that it cannot. Money can meet your physical and safety needs. It can make life very comfortable, and it's much better to have money than worry about money. However, fulfilment, self-esteem, and happiness are psychological needs that money alone cannot meet. These are met by an inner feeling of competence, having close relationships, being appreciated, having a sense of freedom and living with a purpose. It is good to reflect on how important money is for you, how much money do you need and how much do you want? How does it affect your level of fulfilment?

PAIN, PLEASURE AND FULFILMENT

The pain and pleasure principles, developed by Sigmund Freud, suggest that we all crave pleasure and want to avoid pain. We find ourselves always looking for something new, novel or more exciting. We make decisions and have beliefs that will keep us away from pain. So, when looking at your wants and needs, it is important to consider how your need for pleasure and avoidance of pain influence your choices.

The pursuit of pleasure, virtual or real, can lead to choices that take you away from a full life. A quick Google search for "Child uses a parent's credit card" will show many stories of children spending unbelievable amounts to avoid pain and gain virtual pleasures. More research will show the most significant users are not kids but adults who want to escape. Most try to get in the virtual world, what they cannot get in real life.

Virtual Meets Reality

Tim has reached Castle Level 7; he has an army of Barbarians, Elves and Dragons. He plays non-stop and sneaks time to play when his parents are not looking. All his friends in High School play this game, and they spend a lot of their social time talking about it. Most of his friends have overtaken him since they bought the 'Gems Pack'!

Tim has tried hard to convince his parents, but they 'Just don't get it'. They would never spend real money, they worked hard for, to buy fake virtual gems in a game! Tim decides to borrow his mother's credit card and buy the biggest Gem Pack available! The Gems he bought go into speeding up build time, buying precious resources like gold, wood, stone, an elixir to name a few.

He realises the Gems Pack is over within a day, so he does this again and again. He is soon at Level 9 castle and well above his friends. He feels great showing off his virtual achievements. Life is good, till the day his mom receives a credit card bill of 7000 USD for the Gems Pack.

Do you look for pleasure, quick gratification, or are you looking for fulfilment? Fulfilment is much more than chasing pleasure. It is about your real interests, your purpose, and feeling good about what you do. Reflect on what is more important to you before you take action.

Design your life rather than letting things happen. Create a path, define what you need and want in each area of your life and work towards it. Define what success means to you. Then set priorities and find a balance. So, start making decisions and design your life around your most important areas.

*"**Some people dream of success, while other people get up every morning and make it happen.**"* ~Wayne Huizenga

UNDERSTAND WHAT YOU WANT

Tim Kreider wrote an article in the New York Times called, "The Busy Trap" – in which he describes how we are suffering from self-imposed busyness as a status symbol. Busy is good, and people feel guilty when they are not – and not just at work!

Besides work, people have too many appointments, too much action, too many obligations, classes and activities. Not just adults but children too, everything is carefully scheduled and planned around all the other activities. A more relaxing life is possible, it is a choice people can make.

Tim gives an example of a friend who left New York City and is now living in an artist's residency in a small town in France. She describes herself as happier and more relaxed. She feels like she is in college again, going out with a large group of friends, having coffee in a café, so much more relaxed.

The article concludes with: "being busy is a state we collectively force one another to do." Are you caught in the 'busy' trap? If you understand what you really want, there might not be a need to be busy all the time.

Seeking The Elusive Work-Life Balance

One of the most common questions we get asked as coaches and trainers is about how to improve Work-Life-Balance. When asked further about the concern, in most cases, it seems people are so busy with work (that they don't enjoy) they want to somehow find a balance by spending time in life (doing the things they enjoy). Most people find this hard because of increased work demands and the requirement to do more with less.

A participant who gave the most interesting response to this question was a consultant and trainer by profession. She said she never found a need for Work-Life Balance. She enjoyed her work, which seemed like suffering to other trainers. Some of the sufferings she enjoyed was travelling 10 – 15 days in a month, being away from home and family, eating hotel buffets, spending time on early morning and late-night flights. Her work and the impact it had on people's lives was fulfilling enough to make the suffering enjoyable.

When she was home, she ensured she spent quality time with her spouse and her daughter. One of her rules was to never work on a weekend. She spent quality time on her hobby of strategy gaming. She dedicated time to personal development by reading on flights, doing online courses in the evening in hotels. She was 100% fulfilled in her work life, and 100%

fulfilled in her personal life. Hence the question of Work-Life Balance never came up!

"There's no such thing as work-life balance. There are work-life choices, you make them, and they have consequences." ~Jack Welch

TAKE CHARGE OF YOUR LIFE

Most people have a clever answer to the interview question, "Where do you see yourself ten years down the line?" As a coach, having asked this question to 100's of coachees, the results are fascinating. Most are quick to share their ambition of growing within or outside the company. Some want to leave and start their own business. As coaches, we help people dig a bit deeper by asking, what actions are you taking towards achieving this? The answer is almost always the same. I am too busy to take any steps towards my ambition.

For many people, life is repetitive the "work-eat-sleep, repeat" lifestyle, with some weekend relief. Life is not exciting and fulfilling. People no longer feel in charge, and end-up feeling empty inside. How do you stay in charge and true to yourself?

It starts with understanding what you value in the most important areas of your life. Some people have two, while others select ten. It is up to you, pick the most important areas in your life and define what success looks like for each. Have a look at areas like Career, Relationships, Finance, Spirituality, Health, Personal

Growth, Leisure and Living Environment and see which are important for you.

Career

This includes your main activities like employment, business or volunteering. Most people look for freedom, growth, exposure, comfort, purpose and skill development in their career. What do you want in your career?

Relationship

This area can include relationships with family, friends and significant other. People look for open communication, intimacy, fairness, shared responsibility, respect, trust, support, honesty and responsibility in their relationships. What does success look like for you in this area?

Finance/Money

This includes the importance of money and your financial situation. People look for lifestyle, financial goals, savings, income, independence, and required buffers. What do you want in your finances and how much do you need?

Spirituality/Religion

This area is about connecting with a higher being. This could include religion, morals, ethics, belief, daily and weekly practices, meditation, reflection and charity. What does success mean to you in this area?

Health

This is about self-care and includes exercise and physical activity, body mass index, nutrition, rest &

sleep, emotional and mental health, mindfulness. What does success mean to you in this area of your life?

Personal Growth
This area is about self-development both in your personal and professional life. People focus on continuous learning, emotional intelligence, skill-building, investment in yourself, reading, conference visits, new hobbies and interests for personal growth. What does success mean to you in this area of personal development?

Leisure/Fun
What does success in fun and leisure look like for you? It might include holidays, travel, reading, social time, games and events.

Living Environment
Your living demands related to a house, home, location, interior décor, garden fall in this area. What does success look like for your living environment?

To stay in charge and feel you are in control of your life, you need to take initiatives in each area and work towards success as you see it in that area. Become active and setting goals and priorities in each category will also create a balance.

The 'Propeller of Life' is a tool that helps you to make those decisions. It guides you to make choices and set priorities.

THE PROPELLER OF LIFE – TOOL

The Propeller of Life is a coaching tool to uncover and focus on important areas of life. It is like a real propeller, that transmits power by converting rotational motion into thrust. Similarly, this tool helps you to understand what propels you forward. You can use the tool to access the energy that will thrust you towards achieving your most important goals.

A functional propeller can have one or multiple blades. Multiple blades are most common because this helps reduce vibration and improves balance. Similarly, in our life, it helps to uncover more than one driving force so that life also feels balanced. The number of blades is a choice that you have to make.

Elated Tom!

He had an Ivy League degree and was excited to begin his career as a financial analyst at a large investment bank. He had a clear ambition to be the head of analytics within ten years at a Fortune 500 company.

Eight years later, Tom was head of analytics at a Fortune 50 company. He had made headlines in the financial industry. Tom owned an apartment in a nice neighbourhood, drove a fancy car and was at the top of his game. From the outside-in, Tom seemed very successful.

While talking to his coach, Tom shared that he felt

'empty inside'. He wasn't sure why he felt this way. He began to question whether life was only about career success.

ARE YOU FEELING EMPTY INSIDE?

Have you ever felt like Tom? Most people feel like this at some stage. One probable reason for this 'Empty Inside' feeling is a lack of clarity about what is important in your life.

Tom seemed to have followed his passion, with eight years of singular focus. Yet he felt 'empty inside' as he needed clarity on other things that energise him. Thus, a more balanced approach could have left him with a greater sense of fulfilment. How would it help to have a more balanced approach to life?

Life moves at a quick pace, and we are busy doing things. External influences often make us lose clarity on what is important. Life looks like a rusty propeller or one with bent blades, that has lost its effectiveness.

When you were a child, you were full of enthusiasm about so many things. You had a shiny propeller with so many blades. As time passed, you got busy focused all your energy in one area. Your blades became misaligned, dirty and rusty. It is time to reflect and consciously make choices. Set priorities to clean, polish, and inspect your blades. Use the Propeller tool to

- Clarify the important areas in your life
- Evaluate fulfilment in each of these areas
- Balance the important areas of your life

- Re-energise and find your enthusiasm

THE PROPELLER OF LIFE - PROCESS

There are two steps in the Propeller of Life. This process is also outlined in the workbook along with a template and some examples for your understanding.

STEP 1: Identify Your Blades

Review the areas of life given earlier in the book and decide on what areas you feel are the most important. The workbook uses a five-blade propeller, but you can select any number you want. The only thing that counts is that the categories you identify are the most important parts of your life.

For example, you might change family, friends and partner into two or three separate categories. For most people categories will include activities (work, business) relationships (friends, family, partner), dream areas (self-development, leisure, travel, money) and personal items (ethics, spirituality, charity). Draw your blades on a sheet of paper or use the workbook.

STEP 2: Rate Your Blades

Once you are confident that you have arrived at the most important areas, be honest with yourself. How fulfilled do you feel about each area today? Which blades are bent or out of shape? Review your current level of satisfaction and your desired level of fulfilment in each area. When you look at the desired level of fulfilment, don't be bothered about how you will get there. Focus on, where you want to be. Give each area a score between 1-10. Ten means very satisfied, while one means very dissatisfied. To be able to rate each blade, you really need to know what you mean by satisfied and therefore, how you define success. For example, success for Tom's personal-development is travelling each year to a different country, spending at least a month there to learn about the culture.

Tom scores it 4 because while he travels, he does not take the time to engage, see the sights and learn the culture.

Tom's list looks as follows:

Area/ Blade	Current Level of Satisfaction	Desired Level of Fulfilment
Work	8	10
Finances	7	10
Personal Development	4	10
Health and Wellbeing	6	10
Relationships and Connections	3	10

Tom is feeling empty inside because he scores low in a few important areas. Apart from a low focus on personal development, he also realised that he has no time for his family.

The Propeller tool is also used to take action in the areas where you are off-balance. We talk about this is in Part 4 – How do you get there. The workbook also has the next two steps in the Propeller process to help you bridge the gap.

POLISH YOUR BLADES

As you continuously strive to achieve more, your propeller will get dirty; you need to regularly maintain, inspect, adjust and polish it to get the most out of your life.

Using the Propeller tool is like taking a pit stop to reflect on your life. It can ensure your actions are balanced and take you in the direction you want to go. The choice is yours, gain clarity and work with a balanced approach towards understanding and achieving a full and fulfilling life.

BALANCE, AMBITION AND PASSION

People with a lot of ambition, those who love to work and those focused on a few things will have fewer blades then someone who has varied interests. You can be passionate about one area or passionate about many areas.

It becomes even easier to become passionate when you can combine different areas. For example, combine your entrepreneurial skills, with love for teaching young people and sailing by setting up leadership development programs on a sailing boat. Combine your passion for sports with your job and become a professional tennis player or coach. You can add health and finances to the same passion.

The next part of this chapter will explore how you find and build your passion. Understanding what fits with your personality, your values and your situation is not hard, but it takes time. You need to do many simple exercises and give your brain the time to come up with the answers.

PART 3.1: ACTION ITEMS / SUMMARY QUESTIONS

a. What do you need and want? Make a list of needs and wants.

b. What role does money play in your life?

c. How do pleasure and pain relate to fulfilment?

d. Reflect on your life-so-far. What would you ideally want to change? Do you feel balanced in your life – what could you do to achieve a better balance?

e. Go through the Propeller of Life tool in the workbook.

Finding Your Passion

"Working hard for something we don't care about is called stress. Working hard for something we love is called passion."

~Simon Sinek

The passion myth

The word passion has diverse meanings. Some people think passion is the one thing that you love to do. Others say it is something that drives you to act or gives you meaning. Our research and our experience as coaches and facilitators lead us to a clear understanding of passion and its importance in living a fulfilled life.

To understand what passion is, you need to know what you like to do and where you want to spend your time. You can be motivated to spend time on temporary and quick activities to feel good. These could include watching tv, shopping, eating and getting 'likes' on social media. Alternatively, you can be motivated to do long term activities that will shape you. These things take time and effort to master, and eventually, you can become excellent at doing them. Some examples include art, music, volunteering, teaching, leading and organising.

You can become passionate about almost any activity. Passion is an intense desire you act upon to do these self-shaping activities. Your passion activities will help you grow and become a better version of yourself. The reason why many people claim they don't have a passion is that they spent time on quick, feel-good activities and do not take the time to develop long term passion areas in their life.

In 'Part 1 Reboot Yourself', we focus and explain in detail how you can choose to get more out of life by eliminating the influence of marketing, society and peer pressure and focus on feel-good activities that give quick results. Reread this part and complete the 28-day kickstart your life challenge if you have not done it yet. Get into the right mindset to discover and work on your long-term passion areas.

Some people feel that they just do not know their passion and ask for a quick fix in finding it. Passion is not just about what you want to become. It is about who you want to become. The mystic Sadhguru explains this concept well. He says passion is not about just making a living. It is about doing things that will give you a life. Following your passion means becoming someone that you are proud to be. This means doing activities that will make you feel alive. Passion is not a quick fix. In our workshops, participants often ask, just tell me what my passion is, give me an assessment to find out, and I will start working on it. To understand your passion, you need to look inward and truly understand yourself. Understanding what fits with you, your interests, strengths and talents will enable you to build your passion.

Passion is also often seen as being singular. However, you can be passionate about many things in your life, and these things can change over time. You can be passionate about your work and one or more hobbies at the same time. Many famous actors once loved their jobs like school teachers, telemarketers and even funeral directors. They were passionate about acting as a hobby. Passion often develops and eventually leads to career changes for people. An example of this is Arnold Schwarzenegger, who went from bodybuilding to acting to being a governor.

Understanding your passion will give you the power to be yourself and live a full life from the inside-out. It will release the real you, full of drive and commitment. It is like a renewal when you understand what you are meant to do with your unique talents. There is some pain involved, it takes time and effort to discover and develop your passion, but it is definitely worth it.

THE PASSION PUZZLE

Is Finding Your Passion Bad?

A recent article in the New York Post quoted research from Yale and Stanford to claim that "Finding Your Passion is bad advice" – The key arguments were:

I. Your passion might not make you a lot of money, and as such, it is terrible career advice.

II. Finding your passion is too hard; it is unclear how to do it; there is no one easy recipe.

In a world where everyday bills and vast sums of student loans must be paid, where competition is fierce, setting out to get paid to do what you love is dangerous advice.

Conventional wisdom is: "You just have to accept that life is tough". Give up on your dreams and work to pay the bills. Delay your happiness till the weekends, holidays or until you retire. The alternative advice is "just follow your passion and just do what you love".

The truth is that finding your passion is like a puzzle, with many pieces. The parts of the puzzle represent the various parts of you, like your personality, values, beliefs, strengths and talents. If a few parts are missing the puzzle will never feel complete.

Just as it takes time and effort to complete a complex puzzle, finding your passion can be hard. However, when you live a full life, you allow yourself to love the little things in life. You accept that your life will be an adventure. You see new opportunities all around you.

The trick is not to chain yourself to only chasing your dream. Allow yourself to appreciate the freedom in just having the chance to try. Be open to new opportunities which you find more interesting than your original dream. Adjust, adapt, and explore these opportunities.

Check with yourself and see—would it be so awful if you just kept trying? Would you be happy about all the efforts you put in or sad that things never quite worked as per your dreams? Think about it. How wonderful and exciting is it that you can go off and chase your dreams?

Work the process, not the outcome. Let living fully be your dream. There may come a day when your dreams come true, and it will be the icing on an already magnificent cake. Understanding your passion allows you to focus on that dream.

BEING PASSIONATE MEANS HARD WORK

When you become passionate about something in your life, it does not mean it will be easy. Working or engaging in your passion feels good, so good that it does not feel like work. Feeding your passion is hard work that is exciting, energising and engaging. It is certainly not an event or a box you can check off, after an hour with a coach and not have to think about again.

It is not all happiness either, because, in the process, you will need to deal with the inevitable conflicts and messiness of life. You will need to make tough decisions, set priorities, deal with people you don't get along with, and manage the drama of love, family, and career.

Don't make the mistake of thinking that finding your passion is all about blue skies and sunny days. In real life, finding your passion doesn't mean working only two hours a day and easy money. It is likely to be more effort and more hard work. When you talk to people who are passionate and feed their passion, they will tell you to go for it, because it makes you feel alive!

It might be worth it not to have to divide yourself into two different selves. A nine-to-five self and a nights-and-weekends self. It is worth it to be someone who shows up to work enthusiastically and to experience profound personal growth. It is worth it to have your Mondays and Tuesdays feel as exciting and worthwhile and as your Saturdays. It is worth it to have new projects feel more like exciting challenges than boring assignments. Following your passion, doing meaningful work is knowing that your daily struggles are contributing to something deserving of your time and efforts. Your time at work can be a source of joy, growth, and fulfilment.

Doing the things, you value most in life tend to be the things you have to fight for. So, start fighting to find your meaning, purpose and passion. Enjoy the adventure, open your eyes every day, live your life with ups and downs, enjoy the journey and be thankful for the people you meet, the lessons you learn and the growth you experience.

A Full Life

It's the year 1955 in rural southern India; a second son is born into a family that lives in extreme poverty. A father who works as a farm labourer and a mother as a betel-leaf vendor at the local market. They work hard to make ends meet. Add an alcohol habit of the father into this mix, and you get a recipe for a tough childhood.

By the time Sylvester was 14, the hardworking parents were looking for education opportunities for him. They knew their earning was not enough to feed their five kids and look after their education. The only viable option at that time seemed to be sending their son to join the seminary and become a priest. The seminary would provide education for their son.

Sylvester studied for 12 years in the seminary. He served the poor, educated others and did all forms of charity. He felt a calling to serve as a priest and embrace a religious life. Unfortunately, due to an illness, he could not continue his studies. He left the seminary four years before his ordination.

With a graduate degree in science, he migrated to Mumbai looking for a new life. He found his calling in journalism and started writing about technology. He joined the millions who come to big cities with dreams of becoming affluent and living a comfortable life with their families. He got married to a devout teacher, and they had two wonderful boys. He grew in his career to become the Chief Sub-Editor at the biggest newspaper in Western India. He then moved on to a private news and magazine company, where he rose among the ranks through hard work to become the Regional Manager and Executive Editor of a computer channel magazine.

At the peak of his career, he was only a few levels below the CEO and could have risen up the ranks. But Sylvester felt Empty Inside; he felt the passion within him grow stronger. The desire for leading a life of prayer and community service. A life he had experienced and let go off when leaving the seminary.

He made a tough choice and decided to quit his job! He wanted to live the rest of his life in personal prayer, bible study and helping others to make a difference.

Following his passion meant facing awkward questions at social events, where people would continuously enquire about his decision to quit his *job. Living on his savings, paying for his kids' college, all seemed to be daunting tasks.*

Yet having found his passion, Sylvester's life seemed to have come full circle. At the age of 57, he took another tough decision. He joined the seminary again! He went through an orientation for one year and then studied theology for four years. His spondylitis and his age made it hard to study full time five days a week.

Yet he persevered and enjoyed the process. He became a Permanent Deacon in the Archdiocese of Mumbai (A Deacon is third in Catholic Church hierarchy after Bishops and Priests). He was able to unravel the Passion Puzzle, do the hard work and make tough decisions to live a fulfilled life.

To unravel your passion puzzle, spend time on the things that interest you. Learn to notice what gives you satisfaction. Just like Amy, who pursued her dreams and learnt to enjoy the process. Just like Raha, who worked against all the odds to get to her passion. Just like Sylvester, who found his passion, got back to regular life and then returned to his passion once again. All three of them enjoyed their adventure. They made a choice, worked hard, and sometimes had to suffer and deal with disappointments and overcome them.

HOW DO YOU LIKE TO SUFFER?

Most of us spend over 40 hours a week, nearly three-quarters of our conscious time at work. Therefore, finding something that you enjoy doing is very important. The attitude towards work is a very sad state of affairs. With only 13% engaged employees worldwide, it seems that most people accept work as a form of punishment.

Most people are just not happy with what they do, they work hard, for the weekends, for their annual break or their retirement. In a previous job, many of my colleagues kept on talking about their expected retirement, which was more than 20 years away!

Most of us like to dream about what we want and fail to add the required effort. You might want to be a famous pop-star but are you prepared to put in the ten thousand hours into learning to play the guitar well? We all want to have a fantastic body – but are you willing to spend two hours in the gym every day and adjust your diet accordingly?

Understanding what "pain" you are willing to accept how you will suffer, puts your dream into perspective. It is much harder to answer and keeps you away from just dreaming. Your success involves effort and giving up some things for other things. You might hear advice like "You just have to want it enough!" but in our humble opinion just wanting it is not enough.

If you want the benefits of something in life, you must also want the costs. If you want the beach body, you must want the sweat, the soreness, the early mornings, and the hunger pangs. If you're going to be a business person, you must also want the late-night work, the risks, and the conflicts with people.

If you find yourself wanting something month after month, year after year, and you never come any closer, then maybe what you want is a fantasy. The question "How do you want to suffer?" helps you separate your passion from your fantasy. Choosing your pleasures is easy. The more interesting question is the pain. What is the pain you are willing to accept?

Sailing And Seasickness

I enjoy sailing. For me, that means I must accept working hard to be able to afford to buy a small boat. I must accept that sometimes bad weather will make me seasick. I accept the hard work of cleaning, sanding and painting in the winter, to get my boat ready for the summer. Enjoying sailing also means living in a small space and sometimes having uncomfortable nights. Still, it is all worth it when I experience those moments of pure joy, seeing the sun come up at 5:00 am on a flat sea, seeing only water at the horizon, an unbelievable pleasure.

LOVE THE PROCESS AS MUCH AS THE RESULT

Being in in love with the result alone isn't enough. It is easy to imagine yourself being a fluent Spanish speaker or playing the guitar. You can see the pictures in your head, and you know what it would look like. It is much harder to be in love with the process. Because of that, people repeatedly fail at getting what they want.

There are some things that each of us work hard at and love the process of. For example, learning to sail, being on or close to the water in cold and rain, on a surfboard, in a little sailing dinghy, a catamaran or a large yacht excites me. It is a long climb to the top of your dreams, and you need to like climbing.

When I moved to the Middle-East, I felt passionate about learning Arabic. I tried many times, with books, apps and even classes. I did not succeed, am not even close to succeeding and gave up. Some would say that I wasn't determined enough or didn't have enough belief in myself. The truth is far less interesting than that, I thought I wanted something, but it turns out I didn't - end of story. I wanted the rewards and not the struggle. I wanted the result and not the process. I was in love not with the fight, but only the victory and life doesn't work that way. Only those who enjoy the struggles of a gym are the ones who get in good shape. People who enjoy the stresses and uncertainty of the starving artist lifestyle are ultimately the ones who live it and make it.

Our struggles determine our successes. Therefore, choose your struggles wisely – if you enjoy the struggle, you will succeed. It is all about what pain you enjoy and can put up with. It depends on your personality, your passion and your values – If you choose something that fits with your personality, your talents and your passion – you are going to enjoy the journey. You will reach the heights you are willing to suffer for.

So, if you find getting up an hour earlier is a struggle, ask yourself, will this make me happier in life? It is your choice? My advice: Try it, give it a go, if you don't think it is worth it – don't do it and live your life the way you live it now. If you like the results, keep struggling to get out of bed when you hear that alarm clock. You will be rewarded for it the rest of the day. After a few weeks, you will not want to do any different. Even in the holidays you get up early because you love it!

UNDERSTAND AND BUILD YOUR PASSION

Continuing to live life the way you are will not make you unhappy. However, you may not be realising your full potential. Understanding and building your passion will help you get excited about what you are doing. You will find yourself in a state of "flow" as you build and live your passion. You know that this process is complex, requires hard work, and you will need to decide how you want to suffer. If you are ready to enjoy the process, then it is time to build the courage and take the leap to understand and build your passion.

The methodology described in the book and workbook, if used correctly, will help you discover what fits with you, what you are passionate about and how to develop it further. Follow the steps outlined in the workbook. Take your time, reflect, write things down, review and let it simmer in your head. It will take some time for the answers to float to the surface.

FOCUS ON YOUR STRENGTHS AND TALENTS

You can impact the world through your strengths, talents and gifts. This is important because hard work is not always enough. You may end up spending hours learning a new skill, only to realise you don't have a talent for it. While most skills can be learnt if you give it enough time, gifts are part of you; a gift is something special, something that comes naturally to you.

From our experience as trainers, we have seen the adoption of the strengths-based approach over the last ten years. We used to train people to shore up their weaknesses. Managers would review the weaknesses of their people and create a training plan that would help them become better at dealing with their weaknesses.

Today the focus is on developing your talents and building strengths to put you in a position where you can use these gifts. If you work on your weaknesses, it often goes against the grain. You might do it for a few weeks, but after a while, you give up because you don't like working on your weaknesses. Let's look at a famous example to understand this.

Cristiano Ronaldo

Real Madrid, one of the most successful football clubs in Spain, employed star player Cristiano Ronaldo. Ronaldo was their star striker who made a record number of goals for Real. He was voted the best footballer of the year in Europe and best in the world. He transferred to Juventus and is still one of the best footballers ever.

Imagine the coach of Real Madrid or Juventus focusing on Ronaldo's weakness – defending – and forcing him to train on defence. Ronaldo would just not accept this and leave. He wants to focus and drive himself to be the best he can be, be the top scorer and collect the most trophies.

Training his defensive skills would be in line with conventional wisdom, but that is not why he earns $33 million a year.

You should know your gifts or talents. These are things you will love to develop further, even if it is painful or a struggle. Building your strengths is sustainable and will make a big difference. Everyone has unique gifts, something that is just undeniably "you" and is useful to those around you. It's much more than a skill – it is an ingrained strength fuelled by your deepest passions, and nurtured by an unwavering sense of purpose.

PERSONALITY TYPE, STRENGTHS AND TALENTS

Your personality preferences have a lot to do with your gifts. The combination of preference, talents, strengths and interests make you unique. Are you good with people or better at analysing data? Do you perform well when being surrounded by people, or are you performing better when working on your own? Are you creative or logical? Are you inspiring others? What are your strengths? If you are still unsure about your gifts and talents, review your personality portrait from Part 2 in the book and workbook.

Start with writing down a list of strengths and talents you can think of, ask good friends or family who know you well, to arrive at a list of talents or strengths. In the workbook, you find a list for each type of personality, what kind of activity might suit you. Just go through the list and mark the ones which are attractive to you or those you feel you want to develop.

DO A STRENGTH ASSESSMENT

Numerous, scientifically validated assessment tools can help you determine your talents and strengths. These tools will provide valuable clues. You must be willing to answer the questions as honestly as you can. You can even do a 360-degree strength assessment and ask others about your strengths. It shows you how others see you, and it might provide some more clarity. Just see these assessments as another view, more insights instead of the only truth. The workbook gives you a few options, or you can just google it!

REFLECT ON YOUR LIFE SO FAR

Understanding your strengths, talents and gifts is a crucial step to discovering your passion. Once you have done this using the various methods we have described, it is time to do some self-reflection.

Review your current and past jobs

To uncover your passion, you can evaluate all the jobs you did in the past. Make a long list of all the tasks and activities you did and put them in three columns: positive, neutral and negative. This way you will start to get an idea what part of each job you enjoyed and what you did not enjoy at all. It was amazing to see that one of my first jobs, windsurf instructor in a summer camp in the USA registered my love for travelling, outdoor activities, and working with people. I completed this activity and listed all the positives from the jobs I had. The list looked like this:

Positive

Student interaction	Teach new topics
Explain, large groups	Client interaction
Have an impact on others	Solve problems
Research, learn new things	Presentations
Entertain others, talking	Start new projects
Work within a team	Travelling
Self-directed – no supervision	Long holidays
Outdoor natural freedom	Physical training

Neutral

Material creation	Planning, preparing
Invoicing, Admin	Working set hours
Some rules and regulations	Colleagues Interaction
Repeated tasks – routine	Comfortable

Negative

Close Supervision by Manager	Grading / Marking
Many Meetings	Cold Calling
Not being able to deliver	Sales, make proposals
Strict rules and regulations	Long Meetings
Strict schedules	

When I created this list, I worked as a consultant, corporate manager and educator at a tertiary educational institute. I started to understand that to get rid of a lot of the items. I had to move away from standard education. I started a training department at the university, conducting short workshops.

Later I became a trainer in a training company. This gave me variety, travel and most of the positive elements, while I did not have to do too much of the administrative work. I later started my own training company, but that started to involve a lot of sales – so after five years, I quit and became a freelance trainer.

For me, this was the best decision I ever made. Now I have all the positives and very few of the negatives in my job. I am now doing more speaking and coaching engagements and focus on the topic of this book.

Revisit your childhood

Think back as far as you can, to pre-school days if possible. Think back to times when peers or fears didn't influence you. Back to times when your parents' expectations of you didn't go beyond you playing and exploring in a safe environment. What did you do? How did you fill your days? What activities or experiences created the greatest memories? What was the most fun? Speak to your parents and siblings and ask them these questions. Look for a common thread that with a little reinterpreting can fit your adult world. This will give you insights about your passion.

When do you lose track of time?

When is the last time you lost track of time? Are there activities that you find so engaging that you don't think about time, or eating, or sleeping? Do you have these experiences at work? Do your hobbies and leisure activities fall into this category? Moments of lost time point towards areas of strong interest. Another key stepping-stone on the path towards your passions.

Feedback from others

Insights can be valuable, revealing, endorsing, and reinforcing. Many times, other people's observations have greater clarity than self-analysis that is surrounded by a fog of self-talk. Get feedback from close friends and family, ask them what they think your strengths, skills, and unique talents are. "What makes me unique? What do you think I do particularly well? What is my strongest skill or characteristic?" They may not nail your passion, but they will offer clues.

FOCUS ON WHAT YOU LOVE TO DO

For most, it is frustrating when people ask you "what is your passion?" Because the reality is few people take the time to think about their passion. Most people are passionate about something when they are young. Reasons like work and family pressures and lack of time cause us to let go of our passion. It is never too late to pick-up and find something you enjoy doing. Take on a new hobby, and you never know where it will lead. Start playing an instrument, photography, beekeeping, learning a new language, whatever it is. Do something that will engage you that will make you feel good about yourself, as you start the adventure.

Passion is only the first step. The next step is to link your passion with a purpose bigger than yourself. Doing this will unlock your unlimited potential. You will want to impact the world and make a difference. In short – you will feel a calling. The next part will look at how to activate your passion and release your energy into the world and find your calling.

"Passion is energy. Feel the power that comes from focusing on what excites you." ~Oprah Winfrey.

PART 3.2: ACTION ITEMS / SUMMARY QUESTIONS

a. Why is passion like a puzzle? How do you define passion?

b. What activities are you willing to suffer for? What skills would you love to develop further?

c. What activities do you like to do in your free time, during the weekends, on holiday? How could they be part of the job you love to do?

d. Make a list of all the jobs that come to mind that involve your key strengths.

e. If you could create an entirely new way of living your life, what would it be?

f. Complete the discover your passion exercises in the workbook.

- PART 3.3 -
From Passion to Calling

"I've come to believe that each of us has a personal calling that's as unique as a fingerprint and that the best way to succeed is to discover what you love and then find a way to offer it to others in the form of service, working hard, and allowing the energy of the universe to lead you."

~Oprah Winfrey

WHAT IS PURPOSE?

You can use your talents, gifts and passion to serve yourself or to serve others. Purpose is about your responsibility as a human being, it is about your worldview. People can be happy living for themselves, but true fulfilment comes from responsibly using what you have to support the people around you.

As authors, our understanding of purpose is, using your talents, gifts and strengths for those around you. In doing this, you feel great because you get to be yourself, live your passion and make a difference in others' lives. We both bonded in a common purpose, to help and spread the message of fulfilment to everyone around us. We believe we have the skills, talents and passion to help others live a more fulfilled life and that this would help the world.

Our experience showed us how unhappy and empty people felt living from the outside-in. So, we resolved to help people to live from the inside-out by writing this book, the workbook and through our coaching, facilitation, online learning and keynote speeches. The journey of understanding purpose and living a purposeful life has brought incredible joy and fulfilment in our life. Take the time to go through this process of understanding your purpose to increase your fulfilment in life.

UNDERSTANDING YOUR PURPOSE

Your life's purpose is your contribution. The process of arriving at your purpose involves understanding your gifts and then using them to contribute to the world. To find your purpose, you need to ask yourself certain questions and reflect on the answers.

From my coaching experience, I have seen that crisis is often a time when people are reflective and want to evaluate their purpose. This is because a crisis forces a change in the routine, and as people begin to accept this change, they ponder their purpose in life.

Since purpose is outward focused, it is often hard to look for it inwardly. Finding your purpose is often accidental. When you are doing things that you love and reflect on the impact they have on others, you might find your purpose.

Reading is a great way to find your purpose. Research suggests that people who read are far more connected to their purpose. This can be through religious books, fiction or non-fiction. When we read, we ponder on the lives of others, we get to see their purpose, and this helps us reflect on our own purpose.

Sharing your life experience with others through blogging, writing a book or doing keynote speeches is also a great way to uncover your purpose. The more you tell your life story, the more you begin to reflect on what you really want in life and the contribution you want to make. Therefore, your purpose is as unique as you are.

Since a young age, my purpose came from my Christian upbringing. As I grew older, this purpose evolved, but it was always centred around making a difference. I still have not written down one specific purpose for my life, but I use my talents each day to make a difference. When you understand your purpose and live each day to fulfil this purpose, you will feel a deeper calling.

WHAT IS YOUR MISSION?

The dictionary defines 'calling' as: "a profession or career which someone is strongly attracted to, especially one which involves helping other people".

For some, a calling has a divine component, meaning 'what you were called to do' by the divine. In business, it is called a vision. Almost every company has a mission or vision statement. We feel this should also apply to individuals. So, what is your calling or mission?

As per the definition, a mission should include your purpose, something bigger than yourself. It should include how you make the world a better place, for someone else, not just yourself. This could be your children, your family, your town, city or the world.

It should include your passion, the activity that fits uniquely with you, the problems you solve, using your unique strengths and talents.

Once you start linking purpose and passion, something magical happens. You get energised and ready to take action. When you understand 'your what' and 'your why', you understand your calling. Your calling can be big or small, it could be to become the best parent for your children, or it could be to change the world through a new product or service. Some people do this by making a difference in their community, and others make a difference in their company, city or country. It does not need to be high profile. Your calling could be: 'the best mother', 'a provider for my family', 'a priest' or 'a teacher'.

When you see your job as a calling, you are responsible. It helps you to understand your purpose, you feel proud of what you do, and you give it your best.

Manoj Singh

Meet Manoj Singh. He is a rickshaw driver in India. In a movie about happiness, he starred as one of the happiest people on earth. His job helps him to do something for his customers, pulling his rickshaw gets them to their next appointment. He sees that as his prime responsibility. By doing this he provides for his family, he has a small one-room shack where he lives with his wife and his young son.

His job allows him to provide for his family and allows his son to have an education. His job also serves his community.

Every day when he comes home from work, his son sees him coming from a distance – he runs towards him and jumps on his back, together they make the last meters home. He is a very happy and satisfied man.

Many who are on a mission to impact the world find that they have to do this through starting a movement, a company, an organisation, because there is no organisation yet that has the same mission. If this is the case, good luck and we hope your initiative will be the next big thing.

Google employees want to come up with innovative products to change the world; Mark Zuckerberg wants to bring people together. Elon Musk wants to help the environment. We might not all have the same ambition to change the world, but we all have interests, talents and can do something meaningful. You too can find your calling, wherever you are and whatever you do. We all are here for a purpose.

What we have in common is a need to understand our purpose, our calling. Maybe you already know your calling. For those who don't, let's have a look at some exercises to uncover your purpose, calling or mission. In the workbook, you will find these and others explained with examples. It might take a few days or a few weeks to do them all, but when you do these, you will know what your calling or mission is.

IMAGINE TAKING A YEAR OFF

One way to start thinking about your mission and how you like to make a difference is to imagine what you would do if your boss forced you to take a year off, and asked you to volunteer anywhere in the world. It will get you out of your current environment and will widen your thinking. Another advantage is that volunteer organisations and opportunities usually do have a clear purpose. They are generally very meaningful assignments. Remember this is just an academic exercise to start to understand your calling, you don't actually have to do it to find your real interest areas. If you have the chance, it might be an amazing transformative experience.

GOOGLE "VOLUNTEERING WEBSITES."

Spend a few days googling volunteering websites to find what purpose excites you. What type of work, in what kind of environment? Would you like to work with young people or the elderly, close to home or far away? Would you prefer to teach, build, organise, manage, protect or care for people? What environment would you want to be, close to water, inland or in the mountains? What would you like to work on, development projects, awareness campaigns, video editing, storytelling, programming, marketing, human resources, data analysis, health and nutrition, photography, social media, disaster recovery, or something else?

There are so many great initiatives that aim to make the world a better place. Which one would you want to get involved in, what matters to you? The workbook shows you links to the most popular sites. Make a choice based on what you would like to do and how you can use your strengths and talents to impact the world. How would you like to make the world a better place?

Community-Related: Help schools, special education, special needs, playgroups, elderly care, teenagers in trouble, refugees, immigrants, language learning, culture exchange, re-integration, prison visits, church groups, sports clubs, after-school activities, poor and homeless support, disaster support, special events support, hospitalised children's support or any other community-related activity.

Human Rights: Women's rights, children rights, abused citizens support, gun violence victims, home violence, drug and substance abuse support, homeless support, medical and healthcare support or any other.

Environmental Support: Beach clean-ups, general sweeps & clean-up, plant a tree, energy awareness campaigns, grow your own food, save the (rain)forest, save the oceans, world wildlife fund, local chapters, animal shelters, community initiatives, wellness, conservation, sustainable farming initiatives, sustainable construction, eco-tourism initiatives and many others.

Have a look at the thousands of non-profit organisations, what are they fighting for? What does take your interest? How can you use your skills, talents and strengths?

Go and have a look at websites like "www.idealist.org" and explore how you would love to make the world a better place. Look for your purpose and calling to make the world a better place.

CREATE SOME SPACE TO THINK

You only see the entire forest if you climb up the tallest tree. If you stand at the bottom, you only see a few trees. Create some space in your life so that you have the opportunity to gain perspective. This will help you determine the general direction you should be moving in, which will then lead to a more defined path, and eventually, your personal path. Unclutter your life from activities, people and things to create thinking space.

GO SOLO, FIND YOURSELF

This is the extreme of creating space. If you find creating space in your daily life difficult, or if you have created space and are ready to go to the next level, go solo for a week. Go camping, find a cabin, a deserted island, go sailing - be alone for a week. No distractions, no phone, no television. Start listening. You will overcome the fear of being alone and hear your calling.

CREATE A JOURNAL, WRITE IT DOWN

Write down your thoughts every day. Record observations, intuitions, feelings, revelations, and shifts in perspective. Your journal will begin to reveal patterns, those created by common threads that represent areas of strong interest, honesty regarding feelings, awareness of special skills, and a natural draw toward certain people, places, and purposes.

RELEASE THE GENIE

Imagine that you brush up against a magic lamp, and out pops a genie. The genie says, "I am here to grant you 20 experiences, of your choosing, to be enjoyed sometime in your lifetime." What would your list look like? This list represents more clues. These experiences represent your values, your interests, and your passions. Then try and give yourself at least one of these experiences soon.

RE-ENGINEER YOUR LIFE, JOB OR BUSINESS

You don't have to switch jobs or your profession to find your unique gift. Start by pulling out your current job description. Identify everything you enjoy doing, and everything that you must do but would prefer not to do. Next, identify items that are not part of your job description that you would like to do. Now try to rebuild your job into the "perfect" job. Renegotiate what you can! Making a career is all about finding the job you do not want to retire from. Most people see a career as earning more and becoming the manager or person in charge. I have seen many engineers who enjoyed their job and were great engineers and eventually became lousy and unhappy managers. Stay focused on activities which fit with your strengths, talents and personality.

DEFINE YOUR FAVOURITE TIMES

Do you know the feeling of joyful anticipation as you look forward to a special event or day? Like Christmas morning, or your birthday as a child, or getting ready for vacation, or daydreaming in school on the first warm day of spring. Have you ever had positive butterflies while thinking about a project? Perhaps it's a special project at work, or coaching a soccer team, or fixing up the yard, volunteering at church, organising a golf outing, or looking forward to a quiet day with a book, or preparing for a marathon. Which favourite times represent your gift?

EXPERIENCE SOMETHING NEW

Everyone has something unique to offer. Allow yourself to find it. A fulfilling life will emerge from a conscientious approach to living and using your talent. Follow the methodology used in the workbook to discover your purpose and calling. When used correctly, you will start to see what you were born to do.

Do not deny yourself the joy of finding a fulfilling path and discovering your unique gift. It takes time and effort, but it is worth it. If you get stuck, select a workshop, get a coach or mentor and get unstuck. Just step out of your comfort zone to get a new perspective.

CREATE A 'STORY BOARD'

Put the list somewhere where you can see it every day. Add pictures of your ideal jobs or items, from magazines and photographs from the web. Images stimulate your imagination. Create a large colourful mind map and look at it every day. The brain will absorb it and will start to come up with new ideas.

Paying attention to the things that you believe are truly important to you will give you a deeper understanding of those things. Slowly you will get more clarity. Do this exercise regularly like every 3-6 months and do not be afraid to make changes as you get more insight.

Take time to work through the process and know that, no matter what, you'll be getting closer to where you want to be. It won't happen at once, but opportunities will tend to fall in your lap.

From the time I decided to quit my job, it took me more than a year to stop and start the "Sail Arabia" charity. In that last year as a teacher, I took students on a sailing trip around the Canary Islands. I set-up a chapter of toastmasters international. I helped students to learn to present better. I attended a global youth leadership conference and worked with special needs organisations. I met with many leaders, ministers and social groups to help fund the charity. All this helped me prepare for my new business.

Once you know what you want to do, you will find ways to make it happen. These activities will build your passion, your strengths and your belief.

With a mission, commitment, persistence and the desire to learn more and develop yourself, nothing will stop you. But good intentions and energy are not enough. You will need to take action and take the first steps to make it happen. How to make your dream and your mission happen will be discussed in the next part of the book.

PART 3.3: ACTION ITEMS / SUMMARY QUESTIONS

a. Define your purpose and the impact you want to have in your life, on our world and others.

b. What charity/non-profit organisation would you want to work for if you would have to take at least one year off?

c. Define your dream life, job or business in all the details you can imagine. Describe and write the dream down on a picture board. Use key images, words and items.

d. Imagine being in your dream life, job or business – dream away, every morning or at night – enjoy the time thinking about this.

- PART 4 -
How Do You Get There?

"Choose a job that you like, and you will never have to work a day in your life."

~Confucius

Transforming your life

After rebooting, understanding who you are, and what you want, you are probably very enthusiastic to start your journey. You have the right mindset, know your personality preferences, your talents, your values, your interests, your strengths, your purpose and your calling. By now you have many ideas about what you should do, all you need to do now is act! You might have so many ideas that it is hard to choose what to do first.

What to start with depends on your unique you – your age, unique ideas, passion, courage and your current situation. It also depends on what risks you are willing to take. The aim is to start what you love to do and find a way to earn enough money.

It takes courage to start changing what you are doing today and move toward your dream and fulfil your purpose. Before you start planning and executing, let's have a look at a few transformation truths,

The best investment you can make

No doubt you have heard it before. Investing in yourself means more than just gaining skills or knowledge. When you invest in yourself you become pro-active. You force yourself to think about what to do and to think about what is important for you in the future. If you want to cultivate a habit of investing in yourself you should set aside time and money for self-development.

Brian Tracy suggest to set aside at least 3% of your income towards professional or self-development.

Maybe this is too low. Why not spend 5% or 10% on investing in yourself. Whatever you do, set yourself a goal, investing in yourself is the best investment you can make. The investment mentioned here is an investment by yourself for yourself. Not the workshop or training you must do for your employer to fix some area of weakness or to keep you up to date. So, this personal investment could mean learning something totally new not related to your current job at all. It needs to be something that excites you.

Some people spend $10,000 or more a year on self-development, earn degrees through expensive courses at famous universities. However, it does not have to be expensive. Most famous universities have online courses equivalent to the face to face delivery. Massive Open Online Courses (MOOC's) allow you to spend very little money and invest mainly time to develop yourself. Coursera and Udemy courses are famous examples with thousands of topics in many fields. Just start looking, what do you like, what fits with you and make a commitment. Investing in yourself is a safe investment because all the gains go to you.

THE ROLE OF A COACH AND MENTOR

A part of the investment you make in your development can go to a coach or a mentor. A mentor is someone who has the experience that you want to learn from. Most people look for mentors who are more experienced than themselves. However, a mentor does not have to be someone older or more senior than you. The concept of reverse mentoring means you can learn from people who are younger than you. A mentor can listen to your ideas and challenges and share his or her perspective. Mentoring is a long-term relationship that is focused on development through sharing experiences.

Having a mentor will keep you going when things get tough, because they can relate to your journey and can help you see beyond the current step. A mentor is an expert, a person who will impart knowledge, expertise and wisdom from their subject experience. It helps to select a mentor from various fields of work. This gives you a diverse range of experience and can open your mind to various perspectives.

A coach is a partner, someone who believes in you, who inspires you to maximise your personal and professional potential. The coach will challenge you to think differently by asking questions, listening to you, providing tools and holding you accountable to your commitments. A coach can be your confidante if you trust them. The trust is based on your belief that your coach wants to help you move forward.

Coaching arrangements often take at least six to twelve months and frequently last for years. Initially weekly or bi-weekly meetings, move to monthly and later just as required. When you select a coach/mentor, it is important that you feel comfortable with the person. You can choose anyone as long as they encourage and inspire you, and have the right expertise and experience. There are websites that list certified coaches that might be the right fit for you.

The key is to factor in some time, money and effort for self-development. This is the first step to working on your plan to achieve your dreams and aspirations.

CONSIDER YOUR AMBITION

Most inspiring stories of success, showcase the ambition that people had in life. Pick a book about the life of successful people and often a key trait that distinguishes them is ambition. When we are young most of us are ambitious and often share our hope and dreams with our family and friends. As we grow, based on our personality and core needs the importance of ambition changes.

When you begin your transformation, it is important to reflect on your own level of ambition. As coaches we see ambition as neither good nor bad. It is what is for most people and each person defines the importance of ambition in their life. The difference in the level of ambition was clear for us as Co-authors.

I have been, and still am, very ambitious about my goals in personal and professional life. However, I can sense this level of ambition changing as I grow older and as I shoulder family responsibilities. People that know me, say that I often take on more than I can complete. So, my focus is now towards proper planning to achieve the things that I want in life.

Hans, on the other hand is less ambitious at this phase in his life. He is semi-retired and is happy with what he has in life. He still has goals and aspires to achieve them, however his level of ambition is lower than mine.

This difference in ambition gave us a unique perspective as we wrote this book about being full of life. Decide your level of ambition as you embark on the final stage of your journey towards fulfilment.

CONSIDER THE RISK

After a workshop or reading a book, people are enthusiastic about fulfilling their purpose and starting their journey. Some decide to take drastic steps and quit their job and start a new life. Our advice is to make small changes, invest yourself and get ready for the big leap.

Try something new on the side, and when it looks promising, take a sabbatical, or start working part-time. It will energise you, give you experience and create clarity. Remember finding your ideal job or activity can easily be with your current employer; it might not be necessary to move to another employer or another situation. It might just mean upgrading your skills and moving to another department.

Achieving your dreams by using your strengths and talents is a step by step process. So, you don't need to feel overwhelmed and you don't have to take big risks. Think first, plan next, and finally take action.

Planning And Execution

"All our dreams can come true,
if we have the courage to pursue them."

~Walt Disney

Planning – a step by step process

Having read through Part 3 of this book you are now clear about what you want to achieve. It is now time to get there by setting goals and planning the steps you must take to realise your dreams. Goal-setting is a powerful way to motivate yourself to achieve your personal vision. You will be able to concentrate your effort on activities that take you where you need to go.

To understand how to plan, set goals and take action let's go back to Tom's propeller example. In part 3.1 we described the first two steps, identifying the values and rating each area. Tom understands what he needs to do and which areas need his attention. The next step for Tom is to set a vision, goals and make a plan for each area before taking action to bridge the gap.

Prop tool step 3: set a vision, goals and milestones for each area to bridge the current gap

In the propeller, Tom listed the areas which are important and rated where they are currently and where he wants them to be. His mind is already thinking about how to get there. A few questions he asks himself are: 'What does success look like?' 'What actions do I need to take to get there?' 'What should I start with?' and 'How much time and effort will this take?'

Tom sets a vision for each area in his life and sets a few goals (short-term/long-term) for each area. After doing this he then breaks down his goals into milestones and plans actions to achieve them.

Tom's example on the next few pages is very ambitious, loosely based on a plan and goals from Ashirvad. A less ambitious, more realistic approach is shown at the bottom of each page through Hans' comments.

"Good fortune is what happens when opportunity meets planning." ~Thomas Edison

AREA/BLADE: WORK

Vision:

To be a global role model in data analytics, positively impacting a billion lives

Goal 1:

Become a successful Chief Analytics officer at my dream company within the next 5 years.

Milestones:

- ✓ Increased my close network to 100 people
- ✓ Landed an interview for the position
- ✓ Exceeded department targets by 150%

Goal 2:

Started my own Data Analytics Consulting firm with a 50 million USD Turnover within the next 10 years.

Milestones

- ✓ Created seed capital of 10 million USD
- ✓ Created a business plan
- ✓ Hired the right people
- ✓ Launched the business

Hans' Comments: My vision is to impact 100,000 people through the book and website and ten speaking engagements in the first year.

AREA/BLADE: FINANCES

Vision:

To be debt free and create a fund for my retirement at 45.

Goal 1:

Move to zero debt within the next two years

Milestones:

- ✓ Analysed the current debt
- ✓ Created a personal cash flow statement
- ✓ Increased savings by 50% for 12 months

Goal 2:

Create a Retirement fund

Milestones:

- ✓ Set aside 10% of monthly income for retirement
- ✓ Researched and finalised best investment options
- ✓ Spoke to top financial investment advisors
- ✓ Created a fund of 20 Million USD within the next 15 years

Hans' Comments: My aim is to work 4 months a year, which should pay for living on my modest sailboats. (38ft in the Caribbean and 33ft in European Canals and Lakes). More money would mean more comfort, easier travel and more opportunity to help people while on our journey.

AREA/BLADE: PERSONAL DEVELOPMENT

Vision:

> Be the most qualified, certified mentor in the data analytics domain

Goal 1:

> Complete one certification each year for the next fifteen years

Milestones:

- ✓ Identified top certifications
- ✓ Created a Certification Plan
- ✓ Completed two certifications in first two years

Goal 2:

> Mentor five upcoming Data Analyst every year

Milestones:

- ✓ Created a Mentoring Plan (allocated time)
- ✓ Decided on Mentee Selection Process
- ✓ Picked first five mentors
- ✓ Held a networking meeting for my 50 mentee's after ten years

Hans' Comments: Learn to sail better and learn all the systems on a boat so that I can do most of the repairs. Learn to speak Spanish, write another book, and create online learning courses.

<u>AREA/BLADE:</u> RECREATION

Vision:

> To create amazing moments that act as fuel to my Career and Financial vision

Goal 1:

> Drive/Ride across the entire United States of America within the next ten years

Milestones:

- ✓ Upgraded bike and car
- ✓ Spoke to experts/people who have done this
- ✓ Created a plan for every year
- ✓ Drove/Rode across 50% of the USA in the next five years

Hans' Comments: Sail across an ocean – maybe single-handed. Become an active part of the sailing community. Visit long lost friends around the world over the next ten years. Travel with my wife to see how extraordinary our world is.

AREA/BLADE: CONNECTION

Vision:

To be a committed and dedicated partner and spiritual leader.

Goal 1:

Commit to a relationship and get married within the next three years

Milestones:

✓ Found a suitable partner
✓ Got engaged
✓ Got married

Goal 2:

Become a spiritual thought leader in the church

Milestones:

✓ Completed a detailed bible study course
✓ Spoke at local church events
✓ Spoke at regional church events
✓ Donated 5 million USD within the first ten years

Hans' Comments: Be a good husband, friend and father, spend more time with family and long-lost friends. Understand more about myself. Achieve peace of mind, look deeper into areas like mindfulness, yoga and spirituality. Enjoy stillness and thought.

Goal setting, milestones and visualisation

Many people will react differently to goal setting. Some people live by it, and others hate it. Many use milestones as triggers for visualisation. That is why they are often written as though they already have been achieved. So instead of 'donate 5 million' you would write 'donated 5 million'.

What we ask you to do is to create a system, to find out what is truly important for you. Once you identify key areas of importance, you just need to follow a systematic approach, to bring them to a level 10.

All you do is define what success would look like. You define your vision for each area and define what is required in terms of hard work, pain and suffering to make that happen.

There is no right or wrong way; it is just about understanding what you want and starting to take action in a systematic way. Some people are energised by big, ambitious goals while others like a more achievable approach. It is your choice, use whatever works best for you.

Tom is very ambitious, if you feel less ambitious, that is ok. As long as you believe in your vision and goals for each area/blade and want to strive to make it happen.

Visions are dreams that create the energy to start. So even if the vision seems almost impossible it is ok, as long as you want to work towards it. The goals and milestones should be steps towards realising the vision.

A combination of your vision, goal and milestones can also become your personal affirmation, your mantra, visualising the whole picture – like a storybook.

"My goal was for acting to become my main income. I would say to myself, 'I'm good enough.' That became my mantra". ~Michael Fassbender"

PLANNING YOUR OWN BUSINESS

Sometimes your goals can only be achieved by starting your own business. As an entrepreneur you also create a propeller for the business. You identify the key elements of the business, rate where each blade is now and where you want it to be. Then you create a plan, set goals and milestones for each part and take small steps.

Research shows that most new businesses fail. Many new entrepreneurs make the same mistakes. Starting your own business requires some obvious but often neglected elements. So, it is critical to have clarity on the following elements.

- What problem do you solve?
- Who is your target customer?
- What products /services do you offer?
- How are you going to market your business?

When you have clarity around these four key questions you will know what to do. Use the templates in the workbook to gain clarity and create a plan of action. The workbook has more details and suggestions, so you can quickly see if the business is financially viable.

ACTION PLANNING METHODS

Doing is the fun part, this is why you did all the work of finding out 'Who you are' and 'What you want' and making your 'How to get there' plan. When you start executing it, it will feel that the journey has started.

Your plan will develop, change and grow. Just keep executing and keeping score. Make yourself accountable, keep the promises to yourself. Start living a life full of energy, excitement, meaning and purpose. We have suggested various methods that have worked for us. In the workbook you find templates for these. pick the one that works best for you.

KANBAN PLANNING METHOD

The Kanban personal planning system is a very simple personal planning method. It is a system to manage your professional tasks as well as personal life tasks. It helps you by focusing on the things that you should be doing and control the amount of work you take on. There are two rules: Visualize your work and limit work in progress.

Visualise your work through a three-panel list:

- ✓ To do, the work ahead,
- ✓ In progress, the work you're currently doing
- ✓ The work you have completed.

Having a visual of your work allows you to prioritise and signals the current workload. Make sure you do not take on more than what you can handle. Getting started on Kanban is easy, create a Kanban whiteboard with three panels, to do, doing and done or use a simple electronic version in MS Word, Kanban app or special software.

Just start identifying the tasks that you have to work on in your to do list. If you're using a whiteboard, you can use sticky notes for your tasks. You can also use colour-coding to signify the priority level of each task so that it's easier for your eyes to focus on which ones you need to do first.

When putting tasks from you're the To Do panel to the Doing panel, it is important that you are tackling ideally only one task at a time. This will help you focus more on getting things done than just getting things started. As you finish each task, pull them from the Doing panel to the Done panel. It's that simple!

Make sure the board is visible, prioritise what you are going to work on and update your tasks on the Kanban board to keep the focus. You can use the Kanban method for executing your "Full of Life" projects. Kanban can help you achieve your goals.

AGILE/SCRUM PLANNING METHOD

Scrum is a project management technique originally developed for software development teams. This method works if you don't like long term planning. You work towards attainable short-term goals, and then repeat the process towards another set of goals. The basic principles are very simple:

1. Do what you can with what you have. Do at least some of the steps needed to get yourself somewhere close to the finish line.

2. Constant self-reflection (every morning) through three key questions:
    ✓ What have you accomplished so far?
    ✓ What will you accomplish today?
    ✓ What's stopping you now from making progress?

3. Work towards clearly-defined short-term goals. Set deadlines and time limits for your sub-goals.

4. Block out some time of the day when you can work free from distraction.

The key is to identify what's holding you back, how you can work around it, and where the next few days or weeks should take you. Implement a weekly personal planning session during which you decide which tasks you want to complete in the upcoming week.

FORMAL PROJECT PLANNING METHOD

This method relies on the principles of traditional project management. Imagine making a project charter to become full of life. Like a project plan, you must include all the important sections. To give you some ideas see the list of items in a project plan:

Executive Summary   (your elevator pitch)
Project Overview   (brief overview of your plan)
Objectives   (smart objectives - measurable)

Cost / Benefits	(estimated budget)
Feasibility	(technical, operational, legal, etc)
Justification	(what if you don't do the project)
Estimated Duration	(timing – step by step)
Assumptions	(clarify what assumptions made)
Risks	(manage risks mitigate, transfer)
Constraints	(limitations)
Dependencies	(what to do first, second, third)
Stakeholders	(who to reach out to)
Planning & Schedule	(milestones & activities)
List activity	(for each who, what, when, cost)
Final Decision	(go / no go)

As you can see, it requires a lot of work to create a good project plan. Some people like this detailed approach and it can work for your personal goals. You can take the blades from the propeller tool and make a project plan to achieve them.

Select the method that works best for you. From our experience visualising, goal setting and creating milestones is probably the quickest way to start.

THREE GOLDEN PLANNING RULES

Whatever method or system you use there are three golden rules you should be aware of.

1. Set goals that motivate you

We recommend setting goals that are important to you. If you have little interest in the outcome, then the chances of you putting in the work to make them happen are slim. Motivation is the key to achieving your goals. Achieving your goals requires commitment, so to maximise the likelihood of success, you need to feel a sense of urgency and have an "I must do this" attitude.

2. Set SMART goals

You have probably heard of SMART goals already. But do you always apply the rule? The simple fact is that for goals to be powerful, they should be designed to be SMART. There are many variations of what SMART stands for, but the essence is this – goals should be: Specific, Measurable, Attainable, Relevant and Time-Bound.

Specific: your goal must be clear and well defined. Vague or generalised goals are unhelpful because they don't provide enough direction. Remember, you need goals to show you the way. Make it as easy as you can to get where you want to go by defining precisely where you want to end up.

Measurable: include precise amounts, dates, and so on in your goals so you can measure your degree of success. Without a way to measure your success, you miss out on the celebration that comes with knowing you have achieved something.

Attainable: make sure that it's possible to achieve the goals you set. If you set a goal that you have no hope of achieving, you will only demoralise yourself and erode your confidence. By setting realistic yet challenging goals, you hit the balance you need. These are the types of goals that require you to "raise the bar", and they bring the greatest personal satisfaction.

Relevant: goals should be relevant to the direction you want your life to take. By keeping goals aligned you'll develop the focus you need to live a fulfilling life. Is the goal in line with your Propeller? Is your goal aligned with your values?

Time-Bound: your goals must have a deadline. This means that you know when you can celebrate success. When you are working on a deadline, your sense of urgency increases, and achievement will come that much quicker.

3. Set goals in writing

The physical act of writing down a goal makes it real and tangible. You have no excuse to forget about it. You can use "completed" to show you will have done it by the deadline, or use "will" – don't use "would like to" or "might." – Keep track and re-read your goals often.

"Do. Or do not. There is no try." ~Yoda (Star Wars)

Planning without action is useless. Execute, have fun, do, try and work hard towards your goals. This includes reviewing and adjusting your plan. Remember to celebrate early wins and achievement of each milestone. The templates in the workbook will help you to plan and execute your journey

TRANSFORMATIONAL SUCCESS HABITS

Successful implementation of your plans can transform your life. Procrastination, not being accountable, and not following-up can come in the way of this transformation. You might have good intentions but you now need a successful strategy for creating new habits.

Habits are automatic behaviours, we do them without thinking, like clipping nails, brushing teeth and tying shoelaces. These are successful habits we attained by using a simple strategy.

This simple habit strategy, is practical and works flawlessly. Using it will double or triple your chances of a successful transformation. As an example, let us look at a habit that many struggle with, the habit to exercise.

HOW TO MAKE EXERCISE A HABIT

If you want to create a habit of exercising consistently there are two things you should do.

First imagine what someone who exercises regularly looks like. Make an image in your mind, like an athlete. Now every time you exercise you need to tell yourself you are getting closer to becoming that image. The same method can apply for anything that you want. If you want to be a musician, picture yourself as one of the best musicians. Every time you practice you tell yourself you are getting closer to becoming a musician.

Secondly you have to build the habit slowly. Build the intention habit first, create a habit that will kickstart the activity. A 2010 study of 248 people reported in the British Journal of Health Psychology found that 91% people who planned their intention to exercise by writing down where and when they would exercise each week followed through. While only 35% of the control group, that had to read a list of all the benefits of exercise, followed through.

Conclusion, you need to set a date and time for the new behaviour. Make the intention very clear and make the activity easy to do. For example: Put on your exercise gear and trainers at 7 pm every day for a minimum of 15 minutes. Make the intention clear, write it down, put it in your calendar. Make a commitment to put your gear on every day at 7 pm. You do not even have to exercise. After six or eight week it will be a habit. Then start building in some exercise, maybe go for a walk around the block, bike, run or go to the gym. The key is to take small easy steps. Build your exercise very gradually and six months later you will be in the habit of doing half an hour exercise every day. You will do it automatically, without even thinking about it.

The final tip is to ensure that you never miss twice in a row. Most people quit because they broke the chain, but we all know that not exercising for one day is just a blip on the radar, without real consequences. Just tell yourself that you will not miss twice in a row.

Most people talk about making change and achieving goals. Unfortunately, just willpower and desire won't get you there. The truth is if you want to make a change you need to have a plan for implementation. That is why the workbook with the planning templates works.

Hundreds of studies have shown that implementation intentions are effective for sticking to your goals. They increase the odds that people will stick with habits like studying, going to sleep early, stop smoking and exercise regularly. Governments have used these techniques by asking people exactly when they are going to fill out their tax returns or ask them for the route to the polling station to increase voter turn-out.

HOW TO FOLLOW THROUGH WITH YOUR GOALS

It is simple, people who make a specific plan for when and where they will perform a new habit are more likely to follow through. This is why coaching and mentoring work so well. It is not the desire, willpower or motivation that is lacking, it is the lack of clarity about implementation, when and where which is stopping the action. The simple way to apply this strategy to your habits is to fill out this sentence: I will do [*behavior*] at [*time*] in [*location*]. I will write in my workbook for at least 10 minutes every day at 7 am in my study.

Give your habits a time and a place. Make the time and location so obvious that, after enough repetition, you get an urge to do the right thing at the right time, even if you can't say why. If you want to achieve your goals, you need to plan for exactly when and how you're going to execute them. Simply set a time and a place when you will work on each of your goals.

DREAM AND TAKE CHARGE

You have your dream, know your ideal job, activity or business and the actions you need to take to get there. The clearer that picture the more motivated you will be, but to get results you have to start working on it. Make it a daily habit, set a specific time and specific place to work on making your dream happen. Condition your mind, picture your ideal life, review your goals, do your affirmations. Think about what it will feel like, smell like, look like and how everything will be better than it was before. Focus on what you can do, what you can control, be accountable and take charge. Before you know it, things will start to happen and your life will start to transform.

"You have to dream before your dreams can come true".
~A. P. J. Abdul Kalam

Keep dreaming and doing. Find some time each day to remind yourself of the picture in your mind and if something is not clear work on it. Your mind needs to understand, see that end-point, feel and understand it.

Have some dream time just before you go to bed, remind yourself consciously of your dream job, business or life. Your sub-conscious brain will go to work on creating this as you sleep. Your brain will work overtime while you sleep; it will find ways to make it happen. Everything you think about is processed, and it will start to manifest itself through your actions during your waking hours.

Your picture of the future will gradually become clearer. You will become more excited and share it with others. Visualising will help you become confident and courageous; it will help you to overcome fear. In your dreams you do not fail; you do not hit barriers, you just see success and the sunny side, you do not feel all the struggles, you tend to focus on the end result. That is why it is so energising, so motivating. You need that motivation, that belief and the understanding that you can do it.

Revisit and update your storyboard, re-process the work you have done so far. Revisit your workbook answers, it will create more clarity, and more clarity means more power and more urgency. Think about what you need to do, your actions, to make your dream come true. What new skills, what relationships, what initiatives and what actions will help you get closer. Talk with others, ask them and start doing your first small steps, in your free time, no risks involved.

"You'll seldom experience regret for anything that you've done. It is what you haven't done that will torment you".
~Wayne Dyer

NO EXCUSE!

The message from the above quote is clear, Just do it! Young people have so much enthusiasm. They believe they can change the world. They have new ideas and often make them happen. Somehow when we get older, we lose the belief and passion to make a difference. We become cynical, realistic and start to find excuses. The list of excuses just goes on - not enough time, not enough money, not enough energy or skills, not the right environment, not now, maybe later.

Believe me there is no better time than starting today. I have read amazing examples of people who are becoming full of life during the greatest crisis of our lifetime. The heroes of the COVID-19 time are amazing. There are so many people who feel they can make a difference in many ways. This crisis is a great opportunity, many of us have the time to reflect, make plans and start building our future.

Many are in a situation where they have nothing to lose. So, this might be the right time to start! It is natural to be afraid. Just start with little steps, low risk, one step at the time. It is easy to find excuses, the time to start is today, make a commitment and start now.

"Believing and investing in yourself is the best way to shift your thinking from a paradigm of excuses to one of solutions." ~Farshad Asl

BELIEVE IN YOURSELF, YES, YOU CAN!

Be positive and strong, if you stopped your morning practice, restart! It will help you to think more positively and get more clarity. How do you get there is simple, just start.

- ✓ Start writing things down – use the workbook
- ✓ Start presenting your idea to others, connect
- ✓ Work part-time while building your new reality
- ✓ Approach others, get their input, their help
- ✓ Save money, create a buffer, to allow you to jump
- ✓ Ask for funding or consider crowd funding
- ✓ Get a coach/mentor to advice and guide you
- ✓ Create a business – register your name
- ✓ Find a business partner or team
- ✓ Prepare to take a year off

Remember you do not have to be or become a millionaire, doing something worthwhile, doing something you love to do, and get to your financial goal as identified in the propeller of life is the aim. If you wish to become a millionaire great, but the focus should not be the money, it comes as a result of delivering something valuable, something people or companies want or need, something that will help them.

"Do not let what you cannot do interfere with what you can do".~John Wooden

Don't worry if your plan is still a bit fuzzy; dreams won't happen overnight, once you get more clarity, you will start to see new opportunities. New ideas will come and go, changes will start to happen. It might not go exactly as you planned, technology changes, the world changes, and this will reshape the world as we know it.

Allow yourself to update your plan, evaluate each of the goals, update the storyboard. The most important thing is that you start the process. Once you start, you become positive and enthusiastic. Let me tell you how this worked for us.

Hans' career in 30 seconds.

Netherlands: Farmhand, paper boy, burger flipper, waiter, auction-market hand, factory worker, student, shipyard worker, mechanical engineer, oil company employee, railways employee, installation company employee, student again, windsurf teacher in USA, IT-consultant, software programmer, **New Zealand:** change manager, part-time house builder, general manager, business owner, teacher, student, lecturer, **Middle East:**

student, trainer, sales manager, freelance trainer, coach, author, speaker **Global:** semi-retiree.

Ashirvad's career in 30 seconds.

India: college student, customer service representative, in-house trainer, certification student, change to the insurance industry, assistant manager, area manager, investment and regulatory certifications, study, change to training & consulting industry, associate consultant, project manager, head of practice. **Middle East:** Training consultant, change to corporate, training & organisation development specialist, training lead and coach.

A JOURNEY OF DISCOVERY

What we have in common with others who are full of life is many changes and constant development. There are so many examples like this; I know university teachers who started as a truck driver, an army sergeant, an administrator, an event manager, a farmer, a police officer, a bar owner and some even started teaching after studying to be a teacher. The reverse is equally true. Many teachers end up as consultants, business owners, administrators, farmers and so many other professions.

Life is a journey full of new experiences. Life is supposed to be an exciting journey and adventure. Some like it to be more like a rollercoaster, and others enjoy a slower ride. Many people end up in a job they would never have dreamed off after their study. It is a lot of fun finding out how people started, what they studied and what they are doing now, you'll be surprised!

Hans – my path explained: *I know I need a lot of action, variety and the freedom to do things. I like inspiring and convincing others and making a difference to people. The parts of my job I like are interacting with people, encouraging and inspiring them, creating learning materials and introducing new initiatives. I love the outdoors especially water, travelling and challenging activities. I hate bureaucracy, company politics, and too much routine. So, while working as a professor, I thought about my ideal working environment. I concluded that it would be working to organise leadership development programs on a large sailing boat.*

I found an organisation that did this in the UK (Jubilee Sailing Trust). They sail with groups of 40 people, a mix of able and special needs people and let them work together in a buddy system. To find out what it was all about, I went on a 5-day trip with them one summer. It was amazing; my whole mindset about people with special needs changed. We always see what someone with a physical disability cannot do – like not walking or not hearing or not seeing, and totally miss what they can do. They can be a great accountant, creative person or stock broker etc.

I decided that this was something that should be done in the Middle East. So next, I organised sponsors and took students on a similar trip around the Canary Islands. We had a great time, made a fantastic video and presented the plan to make this happen in the Middle East at an "Education Without Borders Conference". The response was very positive; companies were prepared to fund and government leaders pledged grants. All this was done in my spare time, approved and even encouraged by my employer.

It took a lot of extra time and energy, but it totally changed my motivation, my energy levels, my satisfaction and happiness. I had a great time because I had a purpose. Every day I worked towards my goal and did something towards making it happen.

I got support from all different directions. Eventually, with a verbal promise from the Minister of Education to fund the venture I quit my job. My wife started a full-time job and I started a non-profit organisation called Sail Arabia. Even though I did not get paid, it was one of the best years of my life - I met amazing people, had a wonderfully busy time and learned a lot. I did presentations for Sheikhs, Company CEO's, special needs organisations and Community Leaders. I setup a small board of directors, a business plan on how to get it all funded, budgets and worked hard towards making it happen.

I had a very clear picture in my mind; I knew exactly what the boat would look like, how it would be built and operated. Presenting your ideas to others is easy. People sense your passion, your motivation and enjoy *listening and want to help.*

We received many commitments from large organisations like Banks, Port Operators, Construction Companies. We got commitments from the Dubai Government regarding the building location, all ready to start. Unfortunately, the largest financial crisis, the 2008 credit crisis got in the way, and the project was shelved, companies and governments did not have the money.

I had to give up and start looking for a job which had similar characteristics and quickly ended up as a corporate trainer, something I still do ten years later. Now as a freelance facilitator/trainer/coach I work for myself, travelling, seeing new, interesting people every week, training different topics and thoroughly enjoy my life.

It allowed me to buy a sailing boat – actually two, one in the Caribbean and one in Europe, which I sail during my free time. My next dream is working 4 months a year training and 8 months sailing and slowly, slowly I expect the sailing to take more time and the training to take less time, eventually sailing 10 months a year and train 2 months a year.

No, it did not happen exactly as I wanted, but often this is the case. We plan and create the path and journey while we are walking on it, making decisions about which way to go while travelling. No, I did not become a millionaire, but I found a job I thoroughly *enjoy and I have a great life! What more do I want?*

Ashirvad – my path explained: *I knew I had a passion for travelling and used to be very excited when my dad as a journalist would travel the world. The pictures I saw, and the stories I heard, increased my resolve to become a journalist. At the time I thought this was one profession that would let me see the world! Communication has been my strength ever since school and college days, as I would win many speech, singing, and essay writing competitions. With this resolve, I began my university degree in Mass Media and planned to specialise in Journalism in the final year.*

Before my final year of university, I joined a call center during summer break to make some extra cash. The entire first month was training and that was the first time I was introduced to the profession of a trainer. I resolved that this is something I would like to do in my career and I could still travel training all around the world. Teaching others was always my strength and I used to home tutor as many as 20 kids of all ages since I was 16 years old. My mom was a teacher and I always thought of this as a noble profession.

So, in the final year, I specialised in Advertising, which was the other option in my university degree. As soon I finished studying, I joined a call center with a clear goal of becoming a trainer. My first manager –

Bindiya Dayalani Desai took a keen interest in my career and gave me a development plan to become a trainer. If I hit the targets, she had set for me she would support me in becoming a trainer. Passionate about moving into training, I hit every target that was set for me and cleared the certification to become a seconded trainer within the first 9 months of working. Since then there has been no looking back, I became a communication and process trainer in the Insurance Industry and moved to become a training consultant at the age of 25.

As a Training Consultant, I travelled to many cities in India and went to 6 countries to conduct training programs on Sales, Customer Service, and Leadership. After 4 years of success in this career, I decided to move base to Dubai to get more international experience and fuel my passion for seeing the world. I started working with Hans with a dream of doing well as a training consultant in Dubai. Unfortunately, the company lost many of its key clients. I also realised that there was a strong bias in the region, about an ideal training consultant. Certain age, gender and nationalities were given higher preference.

This prompted me to get back to the corporate world and I joined SIG Combibloc Obeikan as a Training Specialist working under Sriram Rajan, an experienced and award-winning HR Professional. Under his expert guidance and because of the empowerment he gave me, I was able to create and deliver award winning programs and focus on self-development. Within 3 years I completed my MBA, got my Chartered Membership with the CIPD and a coaching qualification from ICF. I started speaking at events in Middle-East and decided to write a book.

I have now been to 16 countries for training, coaching and speaking assignments. My current job in Air Arabia lets me positively impact the lives of thousands of employees across a group of 11 companies spread over 150 destinations. Working with an empowering and inspiring manager – Ronald van der Molen helps me grow and create a positive impact. The staff tickets support my dream of seeing the world and the work itself requires me to travel across various offices around the world.

Transforming your life will often mean hard work, some pain and suffering. But you will be happy to endure this because it enriches your life and brings you closer to your dream. Your colleagues or friends might take the easy road, make fun of you because you do all the extra things, you study, develop, try new things, take new initiatives and take on extra duties. The satisfaction from charting your own course is just so good; you keep going. Your conclusion will be: "I should have done it much earlier".

You'll always regret not having tried to do what you love
You'll never regret having tried and failed.

We have covered exactly what you need to know to start living a full life. The final part of this book will introduce the "Full of Life" model. It will analyse and cover the most common reasons why people do not feel full of life. This analysis will help you to understand where to put more effort and show you what is required for you to finally live a full and fulfilling life.

Develop an appreciation for the present moment. Seize every second of your life and savour it." Wayne Dyer

Full Of Life Living

"After all these years, I am still involved in the process of self-discovery. It's better to explore life and make mistakes than to play it safe. Mistakes are part of the dues one pays for a full life".

~Sophia Loren

FULL OF LIFE LIVING

We trust you started your journey towards living a full and fulfilling life. We hope you are well on your way. If you find it hard and do not quite realise what is missing in your life, and do not understand how you can make your life even better, just keep reading.

This part will introduce the "Full of Life" model. You will understand what "Full of Life" living means and what it feels like. It will help you to analyse where you need to add some extra effort. When you are "Full of Life", you are aware of the following three key elements:

1. **Understand WHO you are**
    your personality and identity

2. **Understand WHAT you want**
    your passion and purpose in life

3. **Understand HOW you get there**
    your plan, process and action plan

In part 2 you discovered **WHO** you are, your likes, dislikes, your strengths, your talents, your weaknesses. You have become aware that you are unique, you know yourself and what makes you tick, your core needs, beliefs and personal values. You created your personal identity statement. You have something unique to offer to the world and are aware of the impact you can make both at work and at home.

In part 3 you discovered **WHAT** you want, what you would love to do, what you feel is worth fighting for, your purpose, your passion, your calling, your mission. You know the legacy you want to leave, what ambition you have and what skills you need to develop to continue to grow and make an impact. You understand the areas of your life you need to focus on, what it takes for you to make a difference. You know what you need to focus on.

In part 4 you planned and explored **HOW** to make it happen, you created a plan, goals, milestones and actions to achieve your mission. You visualised it regularly to make it come alive. Energy and enthusiasm flow through you and positive things are starting to happen. You decided on and committed to action. You have taken the first action step towards your dream and started to roll out the plan.

The "Full of Life" model shows the relationship between these three areas of awareness and helps you to analyse your current position. When you are aware of all three and work towards actualising these – you start living a full and fulfilling life, as per the diagram displayed.

However, if one or more elements are missing, you may not feel fulfilled and make the most of life, despite your best intention to do so.

The model shows a Venn diagram consisting of three circles of awareness. It describes three common mindsets, when awareness of one element is missing or not achieved.

People tend to feel either **Empty Inside** (limited purpose or meaning), **Apprehensive** (playing a role, not authentic) or **Guilty** (no action plan, or not committed).

FULL OF LIFE – THREE CIRCLES MODEL

FULL OF LIFE
Authentic / Engaged / Successful

DREAMER
Guilty
No Commitment
(**How** is missing)

PROFESSIONAL
Empty Inside
No Purpose
(**What** is missing)

Who
are you

How
will you get there

What
do you want

ACHIEVER
Apprehensive
Not Authentic
(**Who** is missing)

To help you relate the model with your current life situation, we have named the three mindsets. As you go through the remainder of this section, reflect and relate your life's circumstances to the '**Professional**', the '**Dreamer**' and the '**Achiever**'.

THE PROFESSIONAL

You know **WHO** and **HOW.** You know who you are, your strengths, weaknesses, psychological make-up, your ambition. You have a plan and know **HOW** to get there. You execute your plan and get paid for your skills and talents. You are competent at what you do, feel you are a professional and tend to feel satisfied because you use your skills to make a living. You tend to feel that something is missing. You do your job, do it well, get paid for it, but it does not give you the satisfaction you desire, you might pose the question: "Is this all that life has to offer?" mainly because you lack a sense of purpose or meaning.

When your **WHAT** is missing it could mean that you are unclear about your wants and needs. You might feel off-balance as you focus all your skills and efforts in only a few areas. Often you miss a real understanding of why you do things. You might have never reflected on your purpose, missing and calling in life.

You need to implement the Propeller tool to check the balance in your life. Have a deep look at the areas in life that are important to you and where you would like to be in each area. This will help you take a balance approach to **WHAT** you want.

You would then need to develop your purpose and meaning in line with your skills, so your work becomes a calling. It might be as simple as becoming aware of the impact you have on other people's lives – awareness of being a good parent or a great friend. Awareness of your impact in building your community will bring a feeling of purpose or meaning in your life. Understanding the mission or vision of the organization you work for will help you see the big picture.

Finding your **WHAT** will help you to be "Full of Life". As a result, you will become more enthusiastic, more innovative and more engaged.

The "Professional" profile fits a large group of people who are feeling neutral and are running on autopilot. Professionals might enjoy and find meaning during their free time, but these good times might be short-lived. If you can find meaning through your life, work or business – it will become a game changer for you. If you are a "Professional" go and re-read part 3 and review the workbook exercises. Build your balance and become aware of your purpose and meaning. Use the tools provided to understand how you can use your unique talents to make a positive impact in this world.

THE ACHIEVER

You understand **WHAT** and **HOW.** You feel balanced in life, know your purpose and meaning, you know what you want to change in the world and the impact you want to have. You have also found the **HOW**, a way to achieve your purpose and make an impact. You have a plan and execute it through a job, activity or opportunity; you are full of enthusiasm.

Unfortunately, since understanding **WHO** you are is missing, you feel apprehensive. You might feel that you must play a role and cannot be yourself to be successful. You often lack authenticity and worry if you are the right person for the job. You might feel fear of being found out. If you miss understanding what your talents and strengths are, you might feel you have to swim against the flow all the time.

Understanding **WHO** you are means finding your true self, your unique you. Reflecting on your personality preference, your values and beliefs with help. This will give you increased self-belief, self-acceptance and self-confidence. Understanding and accepting that you are unique, different from everyone else will give you peace of mind. These new insights will help you to be more authentic. It might even change the contribution you make to others in your life, work or business.

The "Achiever" profile fits people who are enthusiastic, who have a great idea, a great plan but often lack awareness of their talents, skills and abilities. They make things happen, but wonder if they could do more. If you are an "Achiever", you need to have a good look at part 2. Be honest with yourself, become self-aware and assess your personality, talents, beliefs and values. When you understand your unique identity, you will become authentic, and feel good about yourself and your place in the world.

THE DREAMER

You understand **WHO** and **WHAT.** You know your strengths, talents, the things you love to do. You also know **WHAT** you want to do to make the world a better place, the impact you want to have, your purpose. Congratulations you found your dream. Unfortunately, like many other dreamers you rarely actually make it happen because you miss the **HOW**.

As a "Dreamer" you lack a clear plan or the commitment to act, often because of fear. The fear of change, the fear of failure, the fear of hard work or the fear of standing up to your environment. You procrastinate and tend to feel guilty. You know you could have a made a real impact and often end up living with regret.

The "Dreamer" profile fits those who make a living, do their job, but live with regret and blame themselves for not acting and following their dream. You need to go back to part 4 and create an action plan with small first steps. These quick wins will give you the confidence, energy and enthusiasm to succeed.

If you are a "*Dreamer*", you need to find the right formula and understand that it might take some tries and some experimentation to deliver your dream. Just work on that plan, commit and start taking small steps in the right direction – it will make you feel much better, keep working towards your dream, be creative and enjoy your life in the meantime!

FULL OF LIFE

Living a full and fulfilling life requires a clear understanding about **WHO** you are, **WHAT** you want and **HOW** you get there. It is a constantly changing journey of discovery, which brings fulfilment, joy and satisfaction into your life. Your journey of discovery will be a full and purposeful life filled with personal growth, constant new experiences and positive engagements.

When living a full life, you enjoy what you are doing, feel you make a difference, enthusiastically work hard to make a valuable impact. You are a valuable and respected community member, employee or entrepreneur.

As a "Full of Life" Person You Are:

Authentic
(understand and live a life according to who you are),

Engaged
(you believe in what you do, your purpose, meaning),

Successful
(you commit and execute your plan successfully)

You are one of the "lucky" ones. You build a new company, find your niche, deliver results and make things happen. You are the respected volunteer in the community, who everyone knows and sees as a role model and great example.

When you are "Full of Life", you will feel good about yourself, what you do and the impact you make. You can be who you are, which gives you a sense of authenticity and confidence and personal presence which comes from deep inside you.

Being "Full of Life" is a journey rather than a destination; it is a great journey with always changing twists and turns. The three areas **Who** you are, **What** you want and **How** to get there are certainly not static.

When you are young, you discover new skills and talents, new opportunities and new worthwhile purposes. While when you get older, you might focus on passing on some of your skills to a new generation, you pass on your experience; your purpose might shift from doing, to helping others to do.

Working at and staying aware of **WHO** you are, **WHAT** you want, and **HOW** to get there, will enhance your understanding of how to make a difference and impact the world. You might start a new study, create a new business or take on a new job, move to a different part of the world, or finally understand who you are. Just keep working on all three; that is the journey of a lifetime.

"Start where you are, use what you have, do what you can." ~Arthur Ashe

FULL OF LIFE TREE

this

"full-of-life" tree is

for those who want to be different

who have the courage to follow their dreams

where others stand out wanting riches and fame

distracted by competition to be better and have more.

you value just you, your impact, your passion, your life

who you are, what you do and how you get there

do not doubt, be proud and make a difference

be an example, make the world a better place

with others, for others, again, and again

always optimistic

move forward

keep going

be different

heal people

lift-up humanity

you are the difference

between the world as it was

and the better place it will become

Every Day You Are Alive Is A Special Day!

SOME FAMOUS EXAMPLES

The following well-known examples are people who became successful and are often labelled as "lucky". The stories will show how they continue to grow their three circles. When reading these think about their path, what was missing and what they did to become full of life and successful.

RICHARD BRANSON

Richard Branson was born on July 18, 1950, in Surrey, England. His entrepreneurial projects started in the music industry and expanded into other sectors. He founded the Virgin Group which now includes more than 400 companies.

Richard struggled with dyslexia, had a hard time with educational institutions. He dropped out of school at the age of 16 to start a youth-culture magazine called Student. **He found his "HOW."** The publication, run by students, sold $8,000 worth of advertising in its first edition, launched in 1966. Virgin Music followed with a record shop on Oxford Street, London. With the success of the new store, the high school dropout was able to build a recording studio in 1972. Being part of a commune, hippie-scene, he had very good focus what the world should look like. **He found his "WHAT."**

The last circle to fill in was his "WHO" understanding who he was, his strengths, skills, and talents. Struggling with dyslexia does not readily fill you with confidence to convince and manage people. However, when he signed Mike Oldfield, with his single "Tubular Bells", an instant hit, it showed Branson that he had the skills of picking the right people and this was followed by signing other aspiring musical groups including the Sex Pistols, Culture Club, Rolling Stones and Genesis, helping to make Virgin Music one of the top six record companies in the world. Under Branson's leadership, the Virgin

Group eventually reached 35 countries around the world, with nearly 70,000 employees.

The Virgin Group now involves many organisations including airline, trains, logistics, telecommunications, Hyperloop and space travel.

WARREN BUFFET

Known as the "Oracle of Omaha," Warren Buffett is an investment guru and one of the richest and most respected businessmen in the world. Born in Nebraska in 1930, Warren Buffett demonstrated keen business abilities at a young age. As a son of a stockbroker, he demonstrated a knack for financial and business matters early in his childhood. He was quickly aware of **"WHO"** he was, understanding his strengths, abilities and talents

The **"HOW"** was also clear for Buffet. He formed Buffett Partnership Ltd. in 1956 in his hometown of Omaha, and by 1965 he had assumed control of Berkshire Hathaway. Overseeing the growth of a conglomerate with holdings in the media, insurance, energy, food and beverage industries.

Warren often visited his father's stock-brokerage shop as a child and chalked in the stock prices on the blackboard in the office. At 11 years old he made his first investment, buying three shares of Cities Service Preferred at $38 per share. The stock quickly dropped to only $27, but Buffett held on tenaciously until they reached $40. He sold his shares at a small profit but regretted the decision when Cities Service shot up to nearly $200 a share. He later cited this experience as an early lesson in patience in investing. This was the development of his **"WHAT"**

He developed all three circles after that by identifying under-valued companies like Berkshire Hathaway and quickly became a millionaire. He focused on the development of Berkshire Hathaway and expanded the company by buying assets in media (The Washington Post), insurance (GEICO) and oil (Exxon).

Buffet is passionate, successful, happy and still driven to make the world a better place. In June 2006, he announced that he would be giving his entire fortune away to charity, committing 85 percent of it to the Bill and Melinda Gates Foundation. This donation became the largest act of charitable giving in the United States' history. In 2012 a prostate cancer diagnoses did little to slow him down. Well in his eighty's he still ranks near the top of the Forbes world billionaires list and still goes to work every day!

J. K. ROWLING

Joanne Rowling was born on 31st July 1965. Joanne grew up surrounded by books as her mum and dad loved reading – she says, "I lived for books ... I was your basic common-or-garden bookworm, complete with freckles and National Health spectacles." From an early age, Joanne wanted to be a writer. She wrote her first book at the age of six – a story about a rabbit called Rabbit. When she was eleven, she wrote a novel about seven cursed diamonds and the people who owned them. There was no doubt about her **"WHO"** and **"WHAT"**

After Wyedean Comprehensive School she went on to study French and Classics at the University of Exeter. Her Classics studies would come in very handy later when she was thinking up all the spells in Harry Potter, many of which are based on Latin!

J.K. Rowling first had the idea for Harry Potter while delayed on a train travelling from Manchester to London King's Cross in 1990. Over the next five years, she created the seven-book series. She wrote mostly in longhand and amassed a mountain of notes, many of which were on scraps of paper.

She arrived in Edinburgh in 1993 with three chapters of Harry Potter and the Philosopher's Stone in her suitcase. By now she had a baby daughter, Jessica, but continued to write during every spare moment she could find. When Joanne had finished the manuscript, she sent the first three chapters to several literary agents, one of whom wrote back asking to see the rest of it. She says that it was 'the best letter I had ever received in my life'. Finally finding her **"HOW"**

After finishing the first book and while training as a teacher, Harry Potter was accepted for publication by Bloomsbury. Harry Potter and the Philosopher's Stone quickly became a bestseller on publication in 1997. As the book was translated into other languages, Harry Potter started spreading around the globe – and J.K. Rowling was soon receiving thousands of letters from fans.

She is extremely successful. The Harry Potter books have since broken many records. In 2007 Harry Potter and the Deathly Hallows became the fastest-selling book ever, selling 2.65 million in the first 24 hours in the UK. The Harry Potter series is now published in 80 languages, and over 500 million copies were sold across the world. In 2015 J.K. Rowling's 2008 Harvard commencement speech was published under the title 'Very Good Lives: The Fringe Benefits of Failure and the Importance of Imagination.'

J.K. Rowling received many awards and honours, including an OBE for services to children's literature, France's Légion d'Honneur, and the Hans Christian Andersen Award.

BE EXTRA-ORDINARY

Now I understand, I hear you say, but they are extraordinary, or they were very lucky, at the right place at the right time. I hope you agree that they all started as ordinary and developed a clear path in their mind to become extraordinary something that was achieved through hard work, struggles and pain.

They developed all three circles – **WHO, WHAT** and **HOW** and after their initial success, they continue to develop their three circles further. All three became successful and famous without looking for it. We can't all be famous, and we don't need to be either, but we can all feel good about ourselves and live an amazing and full life!

It is possible to be happy, successful and full of life without being famous. Who do you admire? Who is on your radar locally? Just think for a moment and write down five names of people you feel are standing out from the crowd, in your organisation, church, sports-club and social circle. Who would you shortlist for an award or commendation?

What do these people have in common? They are very convincing; they believe in what they do. They know **Who** they are, **What** they want and **How** to make it happen. As a result, they became authentic, engaged and successful. This can be as a volunteer in your social group, as an employee in a business or as part of the family. They are the people we respect and admire. They make a difference through their contribution and the impact they have.

Angela's Story– continued

It is now more than a year ago that Angela re-defined herself started to work in a positive way towards her goals. She wants to become a university lecturer or trainer in her home country, the Philippines. Making the world a better place by helping people to be more sustainable in their lives and buildings. To do this, she needs to be the expert in the field, train and teach.

She changed jobs, and is now working at the Dubai Expo 2020 site. She started a Masters in Sustainability Development. She is educating people at work by giving regular training presentations about sustainability.

In her personal life things changed as well; she recently visited her sick mum in the Philippines. The court case for her daughter came to an end. They won the overall and appeals cases and received a positive settlement, which helps her daughter to re-start her life and allow her to follow her dream to go to Canada.

Angela recently won two sustainability awards as part of her job and established herself as an expert in her field. She looks so proud of the awards photos!

As part of her social life, she found the love of her life and is in a stable relationship. Still early days, it is great to see the two of them sitting hand-in-hand by the fire during the weekly runs and at a recent camping trip.

Most things are changing and developing in the right direction. Angela keeps working hard, finding a balance in her life. She tries hard to only focus on what she can control and to let go of the rest. This is part of her step by step process.

A new purpose and more balance brought anxiety issues under control. Her "happy pills" are no longer required. There is still a lifetime of things which can be done. She has a clear dream and working on that dream gives her a deep sense of satisfaction and a feeling of peace in her life. Her inner scorecard is intact – giving and caring for those close to her, even if this is not always appreciated. It gives her internal satisfaction.

For now, Angela enjoys every day, has a reason to get out of bed and feels good about herself, the people around her and what she does – she is very grateful.

She is living her version of a full life...

People who dare to be authentic, who understand their purpose, know how to make the world a better place and who act and follow a plan - feel good about themselves.

In some cases, they love their "work" so much that they want do it well past their retirement age. They define their job more than their job defines them. They show who they are; they show their unique self and their purpose every day.

When you are brave enough to set your own course, you start to live from the inside-out. You will feel highly motivated, doing something toward achieving your goals. You no longer measure and compete against others. You don't work in a scarcity environment, you know there is enough for all, you become happy and satisfied – not because you make millions, but because you create your own path.

The process does not stop when you have developed awareness about what was missing for you and subsequently developed that particular area. All the examples given show people who started the journey and who are continuously developing themselves further. They develop each of the three circles, redefining and recreating their purpose, staying curious and developing new skills and working towards new innovating opportunities.

ACT, JUST DO IT

We still see so many people who agree, who really understand and still end up doing nothing. They like the message and say "it was a good read", but I just can't move myself to start. If this is you, then let us help you with an action plan. An action plan which is guaranteed to work for you. It will make you happier, more successful and get you on your way to living a five-star life. The very first step to do is go to the website (http://www.fulloflifebooks.com) join the community, download the workbook, join the online course or commit to one-on-one or group coaching and mentoring program and start your journey of a lifetime. You will find different options and events which will help to make you accountable and shape your life.

Full Of Life Organisations

"High Performance does not like a lot of unnecessary processes and rules, If you trust employees with your mission and with hundreds of important daily choices, you can also trust them to handle their vacation schedule, their paid time off, and the tools they need to get the job done."

~Cliff Oxford

A FULL OF LIFE ORGANISATIONAL CULTURE

Given our background in organisational culture transformations, learning and development, organisational development and change management, we thought we give you a little information about how Full of Life principles would apply in organisations.

If you are in a leadership position, or can influence strategy then please read this chapter to understand how you can build engagement in your organisation through adopting our self-engagement strategy and become a "Full of Life" organisation.

Recently an article in the Guardian described that people in their teens and seventies are happier and feel a better sense of self-worth. This was based on seven years of U.K. national statistics. The research paper concluded that people tend to feel it is easy to be "Full of Life" outside of their working life.

During your working life, you probably work 40-60 hours a week. This means that the majority of your conscious time awake is spent at work. The question of how we can be "Full of Life" - at work" is therefore very relevant. There is a clear business case for self-engagement, because 'full of life' employees are more productive, resilient, effective and deliver better results.

People are the organisation; it is all about the people claims Tom Peters, the author of "In Search Of Excellence". We all heard companies proclaim that "our people are our most important assets", although many companies do not look after these assets.

Most organisations drive people to productivity through external forces. Although research clearly shows that forcing people to give their best is not working. Driving people using a stick or a carrot to do their best does not work. Especially in the current environment where we rely on employees to use their creativity and imagination to be innovative.

Most organisations still drive employees and use tools like key performance indicators, threatening performance appraisals, incentive programs, and bullying managers. We all know deep down that people give their best only when they want to and when they are motivated from within so why continue to only push people to deliver results.

As culture change consultants we have been involved with many organisational initiatives to initiate company culture improvements. During these interventions, it is very common for employees to view the purpose of the organisation as "making money" and shareholders as the most important stakeholders.

We are amazed how companies show very similar characteristics as the people within. Some organisations are just "Full of Life", motivated from within to achieve their purpose willing to adapt, learn and continually grow and develop, while others are just doing what they are doing and failing to deliver all their potential. The same principles we see for individuals apply to organisations, business units, departments or teams.

Organisational culture is one of the few competitive edges' companies have in the current fast-changing environment, where everyone has access to the same information, the same skills and the same knowledge. Companies benchmark against each other and share the same army of consultants, poach talent and knowledgeable employees from their competitors. Knowledge itself is becoming a commodity, but how we become authentic, engage and work together is still very hard to copy.

"Full of Life" companies are companies where every employee understands the companies' **Who** are we. **What** do we want and **How** do we get there.

"Full of Life" companies help employees to understand the companies' identity, values and behaviour rules.

"Full of Life" companies help employees understand the companies' purpose and meaning to society.

"Full of Life" companies help employees understand the companies' strategy, action plan and progress.

"Full of Life" companies help employees to use their strengths and talents as part of their daily tasks.

"Full of Life" companies help employees to become "Full of Life" and self-engage.

Engagement is a hot topic in many organisations. For years organisations seek to engage their employees by organizing engagement events. However, the long-term impact of these events is questionable. Yes, it temporarily takes away any demotivation, but true engagement needs to come from the inside-out. Organisations cannot engage employees they can only give clarity about the organisation's who, what and how and allow the individuals to align their who, what and how with the organisation. The organisation's leadership, executives, managers and supervisors need to support employees to make this happen.

FULL OF LIFE MANAGERS

Most companies have all the ingredients but miss communicating clearly. The employees, the team, the department or business unit are not aware of the key elements **Who**, **What** and **How**.

The leadership fails to provide clarity, managers often do not understand that these key areas are drivers of success and tend to focus only on what is measured and drive the people to achieve. This externally driven motivation just does not engage employees. To attain internally driven employee motivation each manager needs to explain and repeat the companies who, what and how message. They need to know and care for their employees, help them to understand the organisations vision, mission and values, assist and encourage each employee to a position where they can use their natural talents and personal strengths and grow, thus ensuring "Full of Life" employees.

Most managers fail to inspire people and give them the direction they need to make decisions. Most employees believe the company just needs more profits and shareholders receive the benefits, that is why only 13% of employees are engaged.

Companies need to communicate their **How** through a clear strategy, process, action plans and progress updates. They need to communicate **Who** through role modelling and enforcing the organisations values, which binds employees together and helps them understand who they are. They need to communicate **What** through a clear company vision, purpose, and community impact. This is what will improve engagement scores.

"Full of Life" organisations communicate **Who**, **What** and **How** to each employee and deliver on their potential. It all starts with an enlightened CEO, brave enough to care about employees first.

NAHDI – A Saudi Company

I was asked to deliver six workshop sessions at Nahdi in Saudi Arabia. Nahdi has its headquarters in Jeddah and is a leading Saudi retail pharmacy chain. It manages and operates a nationwide network in 125 cities and villages across the Kingdom. Nahdi beliefs in operating "community pharmacies", providing products, services, and community education initiatives focused on health awareness and prevention. This approach makes Nahdi one of the most prevalent and the fastest growing companies in the region.

I was asked to deliver a workshop on performance management preparing employees for the roll-out of a new version of the performance management component. The systems had gone through some iterations, and they were trying to ensure to make it a more objective and fair system.

Arriving at the head office, the first thing that struck me was the low-key head office — an unimposing building in the suburbs of Jeddah. I was greeted by the Senior Department Manager of the Culture and Talent Development Department. I did not expect the casual jeans and shirt and felt a little out of place with my suit and tie while everyone else was in casual clothes.

I passed the awards cabinets on the ground floor – showing evidence of a large range of awards, one caught my eye from "Great Place To Work", Number 1 company in Saudi Arabia. Other items included recognition awards from customer and supplier organisations. I started to become more curious. On the lift doors and next to it were posters encouraging employees to use the stairs, care for your health.

I setup for the workshop in one of the Nahdi Academy training rooms. A very colourful environment with colourful chairs and large writings on the walls, stating inspirational company purpose, vision, mission and values. They call their customers "guests" and want to be the most trusted and loved pharmacy-led retailer making a difference in the life of their guests. Nahdi provides hope and impact by adding heartbeats to each of their guests' lives.

The CEO opened and closed each workshop session, something that I do not witness very often. You know when this happens that they are involved. He told a small story which was not about performance – but was all about instructing managers to care for their employees, helping them find the right work area and job where they can excel.

The CEO talked about making a difference. How he helped others to make tough career decisions. Advising a valued employee to move away from the department he was leading was not easy for both. But eleven years later, after they met at an event, the ex-employee showed his appreciation for the advice received, which helped him to become the CFO of a large organisation.

The CEO acknowledged to his people that this is their job – to make a positive difference in people's lives. As a manager it is your job to care about your employees, even if that means short term losses for your department or the company – it will help everyone in the long term.

That was the message, and it is so seldom seen that it makes you sit up and take note. The interesting fact is when talking to employees within Nahdi, they told me that it is not just talk, they assured me that this attitude is genuine. *What you see is what you get* was their unanimous assertion.

Each of the workshop sessions had the same message, but different stories, all from his own life. I believe that the organisation is differentiating itself in this region through its leadership and enlightened organisational philosophy. I am sure the company with evolve further, and people will be willing and engaged to give their best.

Talking to the culture and talent department, it is clear, that they follow a very deliberate strategy to make this happen. Initially, it was driven by individual managers, some projects and events. A structure with multiple layers was built around it ensuring the whole organisation understands and develops consistently in line with the philosophy.

Creating an environment that makes it easy for staff to love their job makes already a big difference, the next step is to try and find ways to make employees accountable for taking the initiative and freedom to find their ideal job. To get them to do what they love, find their niche and focus on their strengths.

FULL OF LIFE ORGANISATIONS

Magic happens when organisations become full of life. Their full of life employees, use their strengths, ability and determination to their best, to deliver the organisation's vision and mission. They belief in themselves and in their organisation.

Employees are internally motivated, fully engaged and enjoy their work. They enjoy giving their best and are very productive as a result. Organisations need to guide and support these employees rather than control them.

FREEDOM WITHIN A FRAMEWORK

The least the organisation can do is to understand each employee, understand each job/role and aim to match the two in a dynamic environment. Ensuring that everyone understands how they can deliver, and achieve the purpose of the organisation, business unit or department. Motivation comes from wanting to use our gifts, deliver results and make a difference. We see this with the birth and development of many tech companies like Apple, Facebook and Microsoft. Enthusiasm did wonderful things in the garage of Steve Jobs, Bill Gates and the dorm of Mark Zuckerberg.

- Google has long encouraged its employees to devote 20 percent of their time to side projects, which is one reason why it remains one of the most innovative companies in the world. For companies that invest in side-project initiatives, the outcomes can be incredible: Gmail, Google Maps, Twitter, Slack, and Groupon all started as side projects.

- Informa, a training and conferencing organisation gives trainers a lot of space to develop training courses which make a difference. Trainers deliver workshops related to their passion. 'Women in leadership', 'Coaching for performance', 'Emotional Intelligence' and many others. Each trainer operates as a freelancer. Eventual commercial success is in both the employee and the company's interest.

Empowerment That Works

I have facilitated hundreds, maybe even a thousand workshops about strategy, purpose and how to get staff to become more engaged. One thing which works is simple and works every time.

The workshop reviews the vision, mission, values and purpose of the organisation, followed by an evaluation of strengths and weaknesses. After this we brainstorm as a group what can be done to deliver the strategy, to make things better.

Simply discuss what needs to be fixed that is broken, what new initiatives should be taken and what new ideas could be implemented to reduce expense, increase efficiency or improve sales or services.

When genuinely asked, by the top of the organisation, with a commitment to implement the best ideas the results are amazing. With the expectation for each person to deliver a presentation about their initiative to the leadership, magic will happen.

Employees who are genuinely encouraged and not

held back by their line managers, come up with great ideas. They are so engaged to do well and together with their teams they will amaze you. Especially when they understand that this is a unique opportunity to deliver and make a difference.

The things I have seen that people come up with are simple solutions to the key problems they see. Simple does not mean small. Some examples of projects implemented are:

1. *A new chain of hotels, using a new model.*
2. *A new marketing system which sells last-minute empty seats, which would have been lost.*
3. *A cost savings initiative which delivers savings of more than 30 million US$ in a year.*

Each of these initiatives, big or small were driven and implemented by the originator and his or her team. They feel responsible and accountable. Full engagement is what happens to deliver their project. In most situations, it changes the overall organisation culture from the inside out. People become enthusiastic, use their talents and gifts to make the organisation a better place.

We must give people the freedom to deliver, to use their creativity and use all their skills and talents to deliver better quality, better results, reduce waste, improve sustainability and above all increase engagement and ownership.

Engagement and ownership require freedom, without freedom, empowerment and ownership will not happen. When you let the staff drive new initiatives, talent will float to the top automatically – it is probably the easiest way to engagement.

EMPLOYEE SELF-ENGAGEMENT

Organisations that take employee engagement seriously follow the below approach.

- Run a survey: Internally if cost is an issue and externally if you are looking for a benchmark
- Run a workshop: A workshop is run with the management team, showing the results and agreeing on the top areas to improve.
- Create an Action Plan: Various department level workshops are run to create an action plan to improve engagement based on employee feedback and the top areas agreed by management.
- Communication: The survey, its findings, the top areas and action plan are all communicated to employees so they see the impact of the employee engagement survey and action plan.

This approach is quite effective as long as employees are honest in their feedback and the actions are really implemented.

Having written this book, we propose an additional step in employee engagement. We call this employee self-engagement. Just as an organisation is responsible to understand what is causing a lack of engagement, each employee is equally responsible to understand how engaged he/she is at work. A full of life employee is engaged when they understand WHO they are, WHAT they want and HOW to get there. The current approach to employee engagement assumes that all the employees are full of life and only certain external factors are causing dis-engagement.

We propose that each employee takes 100% responsibility for his or her engagement by living a full or fulfilled life. Each manager take responsibility to provide the support for self-engagement of his or her team and each leader takes responsibility for his or her department or organisation. We have listed some ideas for self-engaged employees to build a full of life culture in an organisation.

THE COMPANY RETREAT

As part of your annual company retreat. Give multi-functional teams a few days to come up with an idea, work on it, and present a finished product to the entire company. The creativity and the camaraderie build among teams will be amazing - make it a collaborative instead of a competitive experience and let employees choose which idea to work on. People are most engaged when they get to work on things that interest them.

THE IMPROVEMENT PROJECT

Ask employee teams to come up with key projects to improve the organisation in some way. New innovative ideas, new branding, new products, new services, any actual problem the company is struggling with. Make sure the teams will present to the senior management and video record these presentations. Often side projects are ideas created by employees and worked on by teams without leaders. Assign business leaders as mentors to provide guidance, so you get ideas which are aligned with the business. Everyone plays their best when they know the rules of the game and have a coach to show them how to win.

THEIR VIEW – THEY VOTE

Teams often vote that side projects are one of the best things the company does each year. They will tell you they love getting to know colleagues from other departments and learn about what they do and how they do it. Everyone finds common ground and feels closer as a company after side projects. Teams should be intentionally cross-functional because you end up with ideas that never would have come about in a typical workday environment, like a completely new and automated way to connect with our customers. Some of the ideas are game-changers for your products, your services, and your teams - directly impacting the bottom line.

THE ULTIMATE: DO WHAT YOU LOVE TO DO

We know from a large body of research on organisational behaviour that most people want some form of choice and voice in what they do at work, and that this can spark greater commitment and improve performance.

Human-relations thinkers made this connection nearly a century ago, and since then management experts have advanced the argument. Robert Burgelman and Joseph Bower have shown a relationship between the autonomy of both individuals and units, and the growth of innovative ideas and ventures within companies. Kenneth Thomas and others have emphasised the impact that freedom can have on empowerment and motivation. "Freedom" means trusting employees to think and act independently on behalf of the organisation. It may also include allowing them to find fulfilment and express themselves.

With the explosive growth of the internet and social media, freedom of the outside world is banging at the corporate door, demanding to come inside. Yet most leaders are still afraid to open it because they continue to view freedom as a threat to order. Instead of pouring resources into exploring and guiding employee freedom experiments they pour resources into regulating and controlling employee behaviour, which makes organisations feel stifling and restrictive for many, especially younger employees.

The real issue is the persistent use of a simplistic, outdated management model in which leaders dream up a strategy, devise a corporate structure to support it, and install systems to enforce it and ensure employees toe the line. Letting employees have a say in what they do and allowing them to do what they are good at, will deliver amazing results. Some examples of this approach are: Semco Brazil and Netflix

SEMCO BRAZIL

Riccardo Semler was introduced to me through 'Maverick' a best-selling business book I had to read as part of my MBA in 1996. Riccardo Semler is best known for his radical implementation of democratic management. His management style is characterised by reducing or eliminating many of the standard management tools, and giving employees a lot of autonomy and freedom. By doing this he took Semco Partners, through explosive growth, from $4 million revenue in 1982 to $200+ million, Key to his success formula is treating its 800 employees like responsible adults. Most of them, including factory workers, set their own working hours. And they vote on many important corporate decisions. More than 150 of "management level" people set their own salaries and bonuses. Ricardo Semler received a great deal of recognition for this. He is now a well know speaker, writer and takes his management philosophy throughout the world. His focus on employee self-engagement and workplaces dominated by self-directed teams instead of managers has earned him many awards and world-wide recognition. Management associations, labour unions, and the press have repeatedly chosen Semco the best company in Brazil to work for. The top five managers, work their because they want to make a difference, including the former human resources director of Ford Brazil, a 15-year veteran Chrysler executive, and a man who left his job as president of much larger company to come to Semco.

NETFLIX

Maybe you know Netflix because of its success as a global media company. In management circles Netflix is known for its hands-off approach to management. Netflix leaders treat employees like responsible adults, they assume people do their best work when they are not monitored and don't have to ask for approval. Netflix describes its culture as a blend of "freedom and responsibility." - Employees are encouraged to use their own judgment within the set and communicated strategic priorities. One of its strategies is to minimise rules and value flexibility over efficiency.

As a result, Netflix has many employee-based initiatives, like new films and TV content, innovative social media campaigns and much more. Netflix also lets employees make their own choices about vacation time, maternity leave, and travel expenses, rather than looking to HR to impose limits. Once employees grasp the company's needs, they are trusted to have its best interests at heart and to behave accordingly. It is rare that people abuse that trust. This blend of freedom and responsibility has obviously paid off at Netflix with Netflix services being available in almost every country in the world and well over 100 million subscribers. The company attributes these successes to its empowered, committed, innovative workforce.

STAND UP, RISE AND TAKE CHARGE

These and many other examples show the need for self-engaged employees that create self-engaged cultures. Leaders play a key role in introducing this concept to employees and then consciously building a culture that supports it. Full of life organisations require enlightened leadership, the courage to try and deliver an open, transparent and trusting environment.

Designing and delivering a self-engaged full of life organisation is a journey and not a destination. It is just as much an adventure and step by step process as finding your path individually. It requires courage and leadership. The results are amazing and more than worthwhile.

Final Words

"Share your knowledge.
It is a way to achieve immortality."

~Dalai Lama

TAKE CHARGE, REVAMP YOUR LIFE AND OTHERS'

We realise that all these words and stories about becoming aware of self, purpose, ambition and living a full life or creating a full of life organisation can be a little intimidating. We want to encourage you to experiment, to try new things. See the beauty of life in everything you do, take steps towards feeling good about yourself and making the most of what you do.

You are always in control of what you focus on, what you think, your attitude and your feelings. Stay pro-active, set your course and start your journey.

We trust that what we have shared will give you a solid foundation to be able to live a full life, using and developing your talents and strengths with a clear purpose and action plan. That way you will feel good about your contribution and the impact you have in this world. Living a full life is all about feeling proud of what you have done and being an example and role model for others to follow. We hope that this book has inspired you to take charge of your life. We would love to hear from you the impact that this book in your life.

SHARE YOUR STORY

As you know, part of living a full life comes from helping and supporting others. When you practice what is suggested in this book, you will be an example for others on how to live a full life. Your next step is all about supporting others to change their lives and help them to achieve the same as what you did.

Coach and mentor

Coaching and mentoring others and passing on your knowledge will not just benefit them, but also benefit yourself. You don't just become happier helping others find their passion, but you also become more committed yourself to continue the process. Go and help others, tell your story and make an even bigger impact.

Join the Full of Life Community on LinkedIn and Facebook. On the fulloflifebooks.com website, you find other resources, and options to share your story with others. Put your name down as a coach, share your experiences and make someone else's life better.

Share this book

Share this book with your family, friends and people at work. The book is also available in e-book, print and audiobook format based on reader preference.

One last thing

If you enjoyed this book, found it useful we would be very grateful if you'd post a short review on Amazon or the store you bought it from. Your support does make a difference, and we read all the reviews personally so we can get your feedback and make this book even better. If you'd like to leave a review, then all you need to do is click the review link on this book's page on Amazon.

Thanks again for your support!

References, Sources And Additional Information

Part 1: Reboot yourself

Books:

Mind power into the 21st century *by John Kehoe*

The Miracle Morning *by Hal Elrod* -

Brain Food *by Lisa Mosconi*

Change Your Brain, Change Your Life *by Daniel G. Amen*

The Power of Positive Thinking *by Norman Vincent Peale*

Learned Optimism: How to Change Your Mind and Your Life *by Martin E.P. Seligman*

The Happiness Advantage *by Shawn Achor*

Websites:

https://fulloflifebooks.com

https://www.miraclemorning.com/

https://jamesclear.com/atomic-habits

https://www.ted.com/talks/simon_sinek_how_great_leaders_inspire_action

https://thewest.com.au/news/australia/new-spirit-leads-to-happy-day-ng-ya-371734

TedX by Sarah Knight - https://www.youtube.com/watch?v=GwRzjFQa_Og

Part 2: Who are you?

Books:

Personality: What Makes You the Way You Are *by Daniel Nettle*

Understanding Yourself and Others *by Linda V. Berens.*

The 16 Personality Types *by Linda Berens and Dario Nardi*

Blueprint: How DNA Makes Us Who We Are *by Robert Plomin*

On Becoming a Person *by Carl Rogers*

Websites:

https://fulloflifebooks.com

https://www.simplypsychology.org

https://www.ted.com/talks/brian_little_who_are_you_really_the_puzzle_of_personality

https://www.ted.com/talks/susan_cain_the_power_of_introverts

Part 3: What do you want?

Books:

Find Your Why *by Simon Sinek, David Mead et al.*

Finding Your Own North Star *by Martha Beck*

The Passion Paradox *by Brad Stulberg and Steve Magness*

What Color Is Your Parachute? *by Richard N. Bolles*

Unwrapping Your Passion *by Karen Putz , Janet Attwood, et al.*

The Subtle Art of Not Giving a F*ck *by Mark Manson*

Websites:

https://www.ted.com/talks/shawn_achor_the_happy_secret_to_better_work

https://www.workaway.info/

https://www.idealist.org

https://www.catchafire.org/

https://movingworlds.org

http://rahamoharrak.com/

https://opinionator.blogs.nytimes.com/2012/06/30/the-busy-trap/

Part 4: How do you get there?

Books:

Daring Greatly *by Brené Brown*

Painless Project Management *by Pamela McGhee and Peter McAliney*

Goals! How To Get Everything You Want - Faster Than You Ever Thought Possible